SONGS ONLY YOU KNOW

SONGS ONLY YOU KNOW

SEAN MADIGAN HOEN

SOHO

Published by
Soho Press, Inc.
853 Broadway
New York, NY 10003

Library of Congress Cataloging-in-Publication Data

Hoen, Sean Madigan, 1977–
Songs only you know : a memoir / Sean Madigan Hoen.
p. cm
ISBN 978-1-61695-336-2
EISBN 978-1-61695-337-9
1. Hoen, Sean Madigan, 1977–
2. Rock musicians—United States—Biography.
I. Title.
ML420.H53A3 2014
782.42166092—dc23
[B]
2013045379

Interior design by Janine Agro, Soho Press, Inc.

Printed in the United States of America

10 9 8 7 6 5 4 3 2 1

For my mom, and my sister… and my father, too.

My intention was to tell this story as truthfully as I could, to someone else, people I didn't know, in a language they would understand. These characters and places and events are still very real to me and this is how I remember them. Some names were changed at the request of those characterized herein; one or two were changed at the author's discretion. Aspects of my bands' histories have been compressed, while certain musical performances feature composited elements, in hopes of better representing the spirit of the music. My mother's power of memory and clarity of observation helped make this a more accurate book, though we've agreed to disagree about the spelling of a certain dog's name. I went with the one I preferred then and still do.

One thing I wanted to include but didn't, a very inconsequential detail, this saying I heard on a long drive through one of those flatland states that sooner or later begin to feel endless: *You've gotta get to it, in order to get through it.* Something like that . . .

PART
1

1

The aluminum bat leaned against the garage wall, next to a rake and a hoe and four bicycles with flat tires and rusty chains . . . I didn't think it over, just grabbed the thing by its handle and kept walking, out the back door and down the driveway, cutting onto the sidewalk, all the while possessed by a harsh internal music. Tonight's was midtempo and repetitive, a minor key blaring silently and in time with each footfall. Just about anywhere, anytime, there'd be a song in mind, and I never tired of moving notes, shifting the rhythms, sliding one chord into the next. I'd do this at work, at family dinners, while listening to my girlfriend Lauren on the phone—no one suspected the storm of guitars happening in my thoughts. As a kid sitting in church pews I'd written my earliest songs, reinventing the solemn melodies of the Catholic mass as dramatic rock epics of mayhem and destruction. They'd always sounded best in the low ranges, and the one I was hearing tonight was no exception. I saw the bass tones waving out to drench whatever was before me: houses and parked cars, the roadside mailboxes lining the street. Twelve-something A.M. The kind of boiler-hot Michigan night we got once or so a year.

After a couple blocks, as if surrendering to the trance, I veered curbward and cocked my elbow and swung the bat just hard enough to ruin a postbox, the hatch of which fell open as the sound of crumpling aluminum snapped through the streets. I stood there feeling it—metal-on-metal impact jolting through my arms. The streets led in every direction. I had no idea how far I intended to go.

This was August of 1996.

I was eighteen and things had been looking up since I'd started my first band a year earlier, a mean-sounding three-piece I believed had the stuff to take us around the country, maybe farther. My hair was buzzed to the scalp. With each step, my steel-toed shoes clapped the sidewalk. I'd left the house shirtless, thinking the darkness might cool things down, but I was sweating before I'd turned out of the driveway. Though I considered myself a shade too pale, a few pounds too skinny, just then I was unashamed. No one was around to see.

My pace doubled as I scanned the street, keeping an eye out for the headlights of my sister Caitlin's Ford Escort. Six hours earlier, our dad had made off with her beloved two-door, driving straight from the parking lot of Brighton Center for Recovery to who the hell knew where.

The moon, probably. Over the rainbow.

I turned onto Ridgewood Drive, a central road that wound through the neighborhood—subdivision, they called it around there. Friday night, yet the streets were so still, so quiet, my footsteps echoed off garage doors. It wasn't hard to imagine the place deserted, the homes vacated, jutting nails where pictures once hung, wall-to-wall carpet imprinted by the legs of long-gone furniture. My friends back in Dearborn called my new hood a McMansion village. The kind of place glimpsed from any midwestern freeway, a sprawl of prefabricated colonies just outside whatever major city you're approaching. Façade towns of vinyl siding and numbskull architecture not meant to survive too far into the future. Other than certain windows lit from inside, every house looked the same to me, especially up top where their rooftops met the sky.

The bat was feeling lighter by the second.

I gave it a shake, passed it from one hand to the other. And then the song inside changed, a tonal variation corresponding to the moment, quiet at first, like someone faded the volume knob only to begin inching it slowly toward mind-searing decibels.

Back at our house, Mom and Caitlin had gone to bed nervous, mounting the stairs as though, before they reached the top, they might hear the Escort pulling into the driveway. Still, like any other night, they'd yanked their blonde hair into ponytails and scrubbed the day from their faces. If I knew them at all, there'd be some prayers going on. They hadn't said much, other than "I don't believe this." They hadn't quite learned to speak the words "crack cocaine," and neither had I. To say it was to acknowledge the arrival of an alien terror, something not meant for people like us, decent, true-blooded Catholics.

All of us but me, anyway.

Though I'd long ago coerced my mom into naming our black-bearded terrier Ozzy, Mr. Osbourne himself had once seemed the devil incarnate. As a kid I'd stashed his albums in the cleverest places, knowing even then the grief it would cause my sweet mother to find her twelve-year-old son's copy of *Sabbath Bloody Sabbath*, its jacket decorated by a demon-inclusive orgy presided over by the number 666. Now Ozzy was seven, and heavy metal was old news, a studded-leather cartoon. I was on to Black Flag, and Mom was facing a truer menace.

We'd landed in Ridgewood Hills two years earlier by means of my dad muscling up the ranks of Ford Motor and saving stock options along the way. We'd gone from used Pintos to Taurus station wagons, bargain-brand everything to the usual supplies you find at the mall. Dad said we'd moved because Detroit was a lost cause—a maniac on Greenfield Avenue had flashed a knife at my mom just before our place went on the market. Truly, the motive had been to widen the distance between him and the drug netherworld. Mom hoped a move twenty minutes west would do the trick, to this town whose name I rarely spoke.

The sidewalks had no crabgrass. The cars were new, tucked into garages. Sodded lawns and rock gardens, motion-sensor lights tripping on when the wind blew. The lie I told most often was that I still lived in Dearborn, the city I'd been raised in, fifteen minutes from the Ambassador Bridge and flanked by Detroit to the north and east. There my family had known simple days. Dearborn had giant parks and record stores and doughnut shops, backstreets on which my friends and I biked from one neighborhood to the next, down to the Rouge Steel plant where blue flames rose toward the sky. They called Detroit the Motor City, but Dearborn was where the Ford Rangers were made from iron ore shipped by the boatload up the Rouge River.

I knew jack about cars, but I'd been ashamed to leave, had driven back each morning to finish high school in the land of Ford. In a matter of five hours, my alarm was set to wake me for my latest job as a groundskeeper at a golf course set on the concrete banks of the Rouge—a toxic passage rumored about Dearborn to turn your tongue black if you drank from it. My parents made the same commute: Dad to Ford Motor and Mom to Dearborn's public schools, working as a speech therapist. Caitlin had switched districts without a gripe, reporting so little about her enormous new school and her ability to disappear there. I had two years on her, but my sister's book smarts and extra-credit volunteer work made it so that she'd be graduating a half year behind me. She fixed lattes at a coffee shop in the new town, earning more than I did, once you counted her tips. Had she known what I was up to tonight, she'd have followed me out in her nightie, whispering commands in her small voice. She'd be tugging at the bat with that scared, angry look she reserved only for me, or my father.

I TOOK A SWING, chopping in rhythm with my tune in the making, certain it would dissolve before I'd ever pluck it on my guitar. In the distance, a sprinkler system began clacking away, giving me a beat to work with—the *rat-tat* of it. Caitlin and I had learned about our dad's problem three weeks earlier, the very day he left for Brighton Treatment Center. One night he's chiding me for having slacked on college in order keep my band going; the next, he's a confessed addict. Twenty-one days in detox was supposed to do the trick, and I'd honestly thought it would, had not believed we were in a major situation until he hijacked Caitlin's Escort and shot to hell the chances of anything ever being the same.

An aluminum bat and rows of postboxes stretching for miles.

As his son, I felt the urge to respond dramatically, though I had little in mind beyond walking and swiping at the air. To conjure something that might scare him straight if the headlights of my sister's car came rushing down the street. I'd step into the glare.

And what then?

The music inside me was on the fade out, another song lost to the ether.

As if it might propel me forward, I tried to picture my father dragging from a crack pipe but summoned instead the guy I'd known: an early-rising warhorse of a man. A wearer of creaseless

suits who was also gifted with locker-room charisma and exper-
tise with a hammer. I knew his firm handshake, his soft spot for
underdogs, beautiful-loser types who had no chance of winning
but just might snap their necks trying. Base pleasures engaged
him intensely, contemplation was regarded with suspicion. His
eyes were faintly blue, revealing so little of his mood, whatever
shape it might take at any given moment. He was an earnest
hugger and world-class jokester one minute; seconds later, my
use of the saltshaker might send him into a fury. Whenever he
rattled the pages of the *Detroit Free Press* and called my name, I
could never guess what was coming, but until earlier that day I'd
more or less believed every word he'd told me.

Now imagine the pipe inserted between his lips, the flame
lifting toward the poison . . .

I cut the bat hard, following through with the swing. And
this was true, what Dad said about certain muscle memories, that
they always come right back to you: riding a bike, swinging for
the fence. I hadn't held a bat in years. Pulling it close, I saw my
best friend's name scrawled in black marker across the aluminum
barrel: WILL. Damn thing had found its way into our boxes during
the move, an artifact of something distant and other: summer-
morning baseball games, the weedy diamonds at Ford Woods
Park. Will and I kicking the dirt, wadding chaw into our gums.

I planted my feet to give another mailbox a half-assed
smack, lost heart before the swing. Ridgewood Hills was the last
subdivision before miles of farmland to the west and in the distance the cars traveling the highway sounded oceanic. Pressed
against my cheek, the bat was cool metal. WILL: faded black
ink scrawled wild style over the barrel's sweet spot. The bat
belonged to a time when jotting your name on your belongings
was running the risk of wussiness, but Will had his reasons for
personalizing the thirty-two-inch Easton. It had gone missing

early one season, and he'd stood there scowling beneath the brim of his mesh-and-foam hat, thwacking his glove against his thigh. Will had a stutter. Back then, it was at its worst when he was anxious or pissed or girls were around.

"Fucking bat" was all he'd managed as the park cleared.

"Don't worry," I'd said. "We'll find it."

Tall, dapper, brown-mopped Will was the closest thing I had to a brother. We'd long ago developed a shared-thought channel inaccessible to others. Even with me, though, he'd maneuver around words that gave him trouble, skirting questions and situations, which may or may not have rewired his brain to interpret reality from slanted angles. "How's life out there in Candyland?" he liked to say of my new residence. "About ready to do a little burn job one night after everyone has said their prayers? Are you ready for gasoline?" We didn't talk about life. The truth was in the pauses after a joke, then the hiss of our laughter. He'd been five years old when I met him. Like many friends in the old neighborhood, he'd acknowledged my dad as a force to behold—the stout, agile mentor who'd tossed the ball with us, who'd made a show of pressing me above his head with a strength their fathers did not possess.

A CAR MOTORED DOWN a nearby stretch. I pulled the bat to my thigh until the stillness returned. I'd been walking ten, fifteen minutes. No sense arose to indicate my dad was out there anywhere, but piece by piece the fable of Will's Easton was coming back to me. Strange as it seems, I never once think of that August night without reliving the tale of my best friend's bat. How, the game after it vanished, I'd been on the mound, chucking fastballs. Dad had spent a thousand nights coaching me through the windup, the snap of the elbow, and I could pitch the ball straight up the middle—hard as I could, straight as I could. A few innings in, a portly marmot-faced kid named Moe had stepped to the plate, his team groaning *Moe, Moe* as he wielded the bat. From the mound, I'd seen it: the silver Easton, gleaming and new. I waved Will over from third.

"There's the rat," he said, chaw in his teeth.

"I'm gonna put a curse on him," I said.

We'd been—what?—eleven, twelve years old? Already bored with ball games, coming into our own as a duo forged in blood oaths, the heaviest metal, the ghastliest horror flicks. Pentagrams and electric guitars, phantasms that defied Sunday mornings in church. Cassettes my dad had smashed. Thrillers that gave Caitlin the heebie-jeebies.

Will shuffled back to third, and I wound up to chuck one straight at Moe's breastplate. A fastball. By some miracle of instinct he fumbled away from the pitch, cursing and tossing Will's bat to the dirt. From the outfield someone let loose a war cry that silenced the earth, until Moe's coach said, "Shake it off."

Only at a distance of years can I admit I was a kid of pulled punches. A daredevil prankster—stealthy yet without true guts. I'd feared just about everything and was angry about being afraid, all of which changed me into a tyrant if ever a viable, deserving victim presented itself. I held steady as Moe pulled his helmet tight, returning to the plate. And a feeling came over me like my limbs were senseless and my teeth had grown giant. The windup, the pitch. Moe ducking as the ball streaked over his head, saying, "What the goddamn shit?" How coyly I'd given my pitching arm the noodle shake. And, yes, I'd felt for Moe, baffled and squinting. I'd thought about giving him one straight up the middle, but I needed Will to know I'd see it through.

A curse was a curse.

I wound and pitched again. A sinker that jerked him into a spastic dance.

"You hit me, and I stick this bat up your ass." It sounded

almost complimentary, the way Moe had turned his head as he said it.

"It's not your bat," I told him.

That's when Moe knew what it was about.

A FEW BLOCKS AHEAD on Ridgewood Drive, a large wooden sign graced the subdivision's entrance. Gold letters painted on stained-green wood: RIDGEWOOD HILLS . . .

Hills that had been dozed and sodded and assigned street addresses.

I got the idea to batter that sign into splinters, jagged shards of green wood my dad might view as he made his way home, once his drug run finally ended.

How many swings to tear it down?

Twenty, thirty.

Will would see the green scars on his Easton when I returned it after all these years. He'd tell the story of Moe and the curse, how there'd been one last pitch, right into Moe's buttocks. After the game, Moe shook our hands, saying, "Swear, I just found it. I didn't know."

I'd crunched Moe's palm respectfully, no hard feelings.

And like that, the curse was lifted.

• • •

Just before the subdivision entrance, I came to a three-way corner where Ridgewood Drive met with a final side street. Up ahead I could see the turnoff from the country highway and a murky shape I knew to be the wooden sign. A streetlamp glowed. That close to the neighborhood's edge, you could sense the unlit countryside sprawling all the way to Ann Arbor. You'd have thought I was in the wilds, the way that darkness felt like some great mind above, whispering knowledge I couldn't understand. A hundred or so yards ahead, a pair of headlights dilated at the entryway, beaming up the street.

I thought it might be him.

I began crossing the intersection as the lights rushed forward. The engine whined at an anxious frequency, pushing too hard for that time of night, on that kind of street. But whether or not this speed demon decided to turn, the right-of-way was mine; I drew the bat close and slowed my stride.

The vehicle steered wide to turn up the cross street. Twin rays swept the pavement, and I saw what was what: a cherry-red minivan, accelerating on the turn, its chrome grille charging straight for my bony ass. Walking defiantly—a half step more—I hoped for the sound of squealing brakes. Until my instincts rebelled, lunging my body headfirst the instant the headlights flooded entirely over me.

The bat left my hand as I tucked into the dive. Aluminum clanged, tires ground. The clunk of my bones. I felt the pavement scrape over my back, and then I was reeled onto my feet again, jogging forward to keep balance.

That flightlike thrill as adrenaline rushes through . . .

I'd never felt so purely the nearness of my own death. Truly, though, I'll never be certain just how close I came to being run down or if I was taunting the moment, provoking it to be become something it was not. The minivan—now unmistakably a Ford Aerostar—sputtered on without apology, which at that instant seemed the most psychotically rude thing I could imagine.

"Motherfucker." I raised a fist.

The screams I'd been perfecting with my band had leathered my vocal cords, providing me the dubious ability to summon bestial howls at the cue of a snare drum. I could go from a mucousy, guttural roar to a high, nasty pitch I'd feel right in the center of my face. My next words ran the scale, echoed through the streets: "Watch where you're fucking going!"

The van's tires squeaked out one harsh, staccato yip. Its rear end fishtailed. Reverse lights flared as the vehicle revved backward, giving me time to snatch the bat from a patch of damp grass. Then the van braked hard, lurching before going still. What I heard most was the snapping of my pulse while the driver's-side window peeled down revealing a man a few years younger than my dad. Crew cut, curly up top. Red T-shirt. From the look in his eyes it appeared there'd been a tough day at the office, the factory, the eighteenth hole. He was quite possibly shitfaced.

"Stay outta my goddamn street," he said.

I cocked the bat to make certain he saw it, and the guy smiled. He didn't look the tough-dad type. My old man could have taken him, but this mindfucker had one of those normal-joe faces that at certain telltale moments will reveal its ulterior sicko—and here it was: a hateful grin widening by the second.

I'd gone out miming a search for trouble, and so it was delivered, along with implications on what it would mean for me to back down. Gripping the bat I counted *one-two* repeatedly, something I'd done before lighting Dumpsters afire or skateboarding down the shingles of Will's roof. *One-two, one-two.* Sooner or later, *three* usually came, and I'd be mindless, tossing the match or rocketing toward the crash.

"Screw you, man."

"Little prick," he said.

The minivan's interior lights snapped on as he opened the door. One leg stepped to the pavement while the other remained bent, rooted inside the van. An arm extended. He had something to show me: a handgun. Not pointed at my heart. Not ordering my hands to the air or anything of the sort but harmlessly dangling from his fingertips as if it were a piece of evidence he'd plucked from a lover's underwear drawer. His wrist was limp. The gun hung black against his red shirt. If he'd turned the barrel on me, there's a chance I'd have stood like that until he fired.

I flashed him my wildest eyes, channeling Manson—any number of maniacs I'd seen pictures of. That's how I gave up. Glaring was as brave as I could be.

"Now," he said, face half lit by the interior bulbs, "stay outta the fucking street."

He yanked shut the door and peeled out.

The minivan ascended the slightest incline toward an unknown area of the neighborhood. If only Will had been there, seeing it through to some different end: his bat confiscated as evidence while I was cuffed and hauled to the clink or scraped from the pavement. A lawsuit. A funeral.

Instead—here was another story I'd never tell honestly.

I sprinted after the taillights, keeping off the sidewalk, scrambling through unfamiliar front yards. A few blocks up I found the minivan parked in the driveway of a house just like ours, only the walkway to the front porch was lined with shin-high halogen path lamps. Crouched behind a shrub across the street, I raised my head to watch the lamps sequentially go dark and come aglow again as a figure passed each one.

"Ay!" I yelled, swiveling to tear ass home. "I know where you live."

MOM WAS PACING THE hallway when I slipped through the back door. Ozzy grazed her legs, clacking his nails along the floorboards. All the rooms were dark as I made for the front window to monitor the street for headlights. Bits of asphalt were cratered into my back and I felt the burn of a skinned elbow. Somehow

I'd worked myself into a frenzy that had canceled all thoughts of my dad.

"Are you waiting for him?" Mom said.

The blue robe she'd worn for years was tied at her waist. As a child, I'd nestled in its dangling sleeves when she'd read novels or watched *Dallas*. Her blonde hair was pulled taut, revealing fully her huge eyes shining wetly against her soft, freckled skin. A small mouth, like mine. If she'd so much as smoked a joint in the seventies, if she'd ever cursed or knowingly wounded a living thing, I was aware of it. Nor had I sensed any limit to her kindness, which asked very little of me in return; what she wanted most was for my sister and me to live lives unburdened by heavy pain. One of my friends in the old neighborhood called her "Ma," and another had claimed she looked like an owl, a pretty owl-woman. Tired as she was, her face was strong, a beautiful sight.

"You should go upstairs," I said.

It had been years since I'd told her much about my life, yet in her presence I'd feel our moods altering each other without a word. An emotional telepathy I shared only with her. She took a breath, getting a read on me.

"What's with the bat?" she said.

The Easton was turned down at my side, my palm balanced on the butt of the handle. Any other night she'd have pleaded with me to return the bat to where it belonged. She'd have asked questions that shamed me into admitting the right thing to do. Just then she might have been hoping Dad would sulk through the back door; if he had, she might not have said a word to restrain me. In her bedroom upstairs Caitlin would be volted awake by sounds of me demolishing the kitchen table and backing him into a corner. Mom might close her eyes, praying that enough would be enough.

"I'm gonna wait for him," I said.

"Get some sleep," she said. "Letting this control us won't do any good."

Outside the windows, the street was empty. The gunman must have been peeling off his shirt, sliding into the sheets next to his sleeping wife. Down the hallway, his kids dreamed openmouthed in the air-conditioned twilight. As I lay awake in a bed my father had built by hand, I wondered if the man kept his firearm near as he slept, if it had even been loaded. Possibly he'd relive the scene with each coming day as his minivan rolled through that same quiet intersection. He'd remember why he carried a pistol. Staring at the ceiling, waiting for sleep, he might figure he'd done the right thing.

Through my bedroom's open window the highway was a distant white noise. Caitlin lay just beyond the wall—resting soundly, I hoped. She'd always be the one I worried most about, tucked away as she often was, and just out of reach.

There was still a chance Dad would drift home to spend the night on the couch. The worst would be over. Tomorrow morning we'd piece everything together. Or does a person sleep at all once he's toked from that pipe? The worst pipe packed with the worst drug. Does he actually come back? I reached for the box fan on my windowsill to crank it on high, and through the whirring of the blades the music returned, deep chords ringing slow and heavy. Will's Easton lay beside me on the mattress, and already I knew what I'd tell him about the man and the showdown and how, when he'd ask me to repeat the story again and again, I'd describe the flash of the gun.

2

Caitlin's four-cylinder Escort was a dinky, white, egglike sedan she'd been driving the past eleven months, since she'd turned sixteen. Stacked in the glove box was an unlikely assortment of cassettes. Mozart, Carole King, the Smashing Pumpkins, mixtapes I'd made showcasing punk rock's somber moments: the Replacements' "Go," "Long Division" by Fugazi. A rosary dangled from the rearview and fortune-cookie scripts were held with a paper clip beneath the emergency brake; all of which, I hoped, would remind my dad of Caitlin as he pulled into a dealer's driveway or alleyway or whatever it was.

Come morning, though, I was thinking most about a cassette I'd left in the Escort's tape deck: my band's first demo, our song titles—"Blamesday" and five others—printed on the shell. My family had been expected at Brighton Treatment Center the previous afternoon for Dad's exit evaluation, and I'd been running late enough that Mom and Caitlin had left without me in the station wagon. Though Caitlin trusted no one with her car, she'd made the mistake of leaving behind her keys, which

I'd snatched, intending to analyze the band's new recording on a different stereo. I'd blared the tape the entire twenty-five-minute drive into rural Michigan, where Dad awaited us in a farmhouse-turned-rehab. They might have heard me coming if not for those puny Escort speakers just sort of rattling as I maxed the volume.

The band was onto some genuinely ugly sounds, our mission being to corrupt all traces of harmony. When notes felt too "right," we augmented with wrongness. Lyrics were pulled unexamined from some part of myself that I couldn't otherwise locate: A rite of passage, bought and sold / See how we've grown to fill our cage. More than tough or hard, we wanted to sound painful. Crazy. We wanted to take it all the way, whatever that meant, and had just enough skill to set ourselves on course.

Our twenty-minute demo tape—now at my dad's fingertips, awaiting his turn of the dial—held the proof.

He suspected my guitar and secret life of cultish gatherings to be the cause of my lackluster grades, so I hid all evidence of the music for both our sakes. Things between us had begun turning a few years earlier, when I gave up my baseball mitt for an imitation Stratocaster I'd funded by delivering the Dearborn Press and Guide. He'd threatened to snap the instrument in two. The sound of it, even unplugged, goaded him. We'd have fared better had I, even failingly, striven for honor and experience through fierce, competitive sport. Teamwork. High fives that become hugs. We'd shared such moments when I was eleven. Now I understood he'd prefer to cancel large parts of who I'd become with age. Recently he'd uttered the words "Fuck you" to me for the first time and meant it so completely that I'd lowered my head to silently agree. Music—my drive toward it—upset a brute fear in him because songs reached me in ways he never could. Who'd guess that in the seventies he'd grown his hair and attempted the classical guitar? He'd owned the first four Zeppelin albums. Now Dad called Robert Plant a "whiner," Mick Jagger a "fruitcake." I dreaded what he'd make of my band's down-tuned noise, punk and hardcore and Mahavishnu jazz, impulsively fused. My asylum wails rising from the Escort stereo. I could only hope he wouldn't listen carefully enough to decipher whose screams they were.

THIS FOCUS CHANGED THE instant I came downstairs to find Mom in her robe, sitting with a cup of coffee at the kitchen table. She hadn't opened the newspaper or switched on WQRS, Detroit's sole classical station. No matter how often I passed through this room—countrified wallpaper and unscarred countertops— it reminded me of something assembled by Allen wrench and wood glue. Caitlin remained in her bedroom, though I doubted either of them had slept. The lights were off. The sun was rising on Saturday morning.

"Are you okay?" Mom said.

"You heard from him?" I asked, and her eyes said she hadn't.

In the day's early light the creases on her forehead and the sunspots on her sternum were plain to see. Her capillaries erupted when she was flustered, leaving her cheeks a blotchy pink. "How could he do that?" she said. "Right after we met with those doctors and everything."

Brighton's clinicians had counseled my mom, sister, and me separately, encouraging us to "talk openly" before order-ing us to reconvene in the rehab's central office. That's when Dad had entered, husky and guilty eyed, wearing jeans and a T-shirt, his ash-blond hair disheveled like he'd just risen from a two-week flu.

The whole scene already looked black and white in my mind.

"Those morons don't know what they're doing," I told my

mom. When Dad wasn't around, I liked to act as though I had an edge on things. "What a joke."

"They're specialists," she said. "They've seen this before."

The experts—I felt suckered. No sooner had Dad taken his seat than the head doctor began quoting shorthand transcripts of what we'd said, interpreting our testimonies aloud, his curt restatement of our words rendering them truer than when we'd spoken. *Your wife feels you're emotionally unavailable; your daughter doesn't trust you* . . . Were these trained professionals? The woman interviewing me asked if I loved my father. For an answer I'd told her about my band, how we planned to ravage the country one city at a time.

"Did you sleep?" Mom said. I gave her a one-armed hug, not wanting to admit I had. "This is all so unreal," she said. "Isn't it?"

I refilled her coffee and took a seat beside her.

"It's my fault," I admitted, which felt true. Dad had asked me for the Escort's keys once the four of us stood unobserved in the rehab parking lot. He'd worked up a plot about his support group's plans for a going-away party, affecting a penitent tone—"They've been good to me here"—while looking my mother and sister in their teary eyes with an earnestness that made me believe. Caitlin protested, but I hadn't thought twice. My father had never missed a mortgage payment. Whatever he'd promised—vacations or corporal punishments—he'd always come through, so let him reassure us of his manic love when we needed him most. I'd handed over my sister's key ring, dangling pink rabbit foot and all, the minute he'd reached out his hand.

"You dad's very sick." Mom took the tone people use when categorizing addiction as disease, the drug fiend as unwitting victim. I could tell, suddenly, that she'd spent one too many nights trying to wrap her mind around this problem and how crushed she was to know that I'd now joined her, both of us staring ahead into the terrifyingly unknowable near future. What happens tomorrow? An hour from now? She kneaded her temples. "But, you know, people get through this kind of thing. We have to stick together."

She touched my arm.

Moments later, Caitlin entered the kitchen with her blonde hair raked into a headband and a dry, practical expression. In the ragamuffin style of 1996, she wore baggy jeans and a thrift-store T-shirt, a dark, almost-mulberry shade of lipstick. Five foot six. Slightly round in the cheeks. Her eyebrows were darker than mine, lending a gravitas to her scowl.

"So, where's he taking my car?" she said, as though the vehicle were at risk of contamination. "What kind of places?"

My sister tried to talk tough, but she was a softy through and through, more so than any of us. Beyond the family, she was timid, the quietest in any room. At home only she had the nerve to snarl back at my dad, deflecting his anger so quickly it stunted him. A funny thing: to watch them go around. Caitlin turning his phrases inside out with a boldness I'd never manage. This morning her lady-finger wick had been lit, sizzling. She was ready to detonate, if only he'd show his face.

"I've gotta go to work," she said. "He ever think of that?"

Mom suggested taking Dad's Ford Contour and Caitlin shook her head, showing signs of a long, hard cry that was about to break. Yet, as if in protest, she remained stoically against missing a day's work, the weekend tip jar. It was her way of rallying to get us all up and moving. Mom took the cue and chauffeured my sister to the coffee shop in the station wagon, Ozzy riding along.

Alone at the kitchen table I drummed my fingers on a place mat. There was a song to be mined from any crisis, if you had the knack. Close your eyes, and the chords silently arrive, the

closest approximation of what you feel then and there. Everything else was numb. The only evidence on me of last night's
trouble was a skinned elbow and grass stains on the blue jeans
I'd slept in.

I decided to call in sick to work—a relieving idea because I
was, literally, the shitheel of the golf-course maintenance crew.
My uniform was caked with green dung and stored, at Caitlin's
request, in the garage. Management had sussed me out as someone who'd never actually swung a club, and therefore I spent
entire days scooping Canada-geese droppings from the fairways,
breaking only to comb disrupted sand traps. Twice, I'd been
struck by an errant drive; another had whistled past my ear.

Not today.

I got the manager on the line to tell him there was "family
business."

"You ain't the only one" was what he had to say about that.

WHEN MOM RETURNED, WE sat with another round of coffee.
One of those times you dread turning on the television or busy-
ing yourself with errands because who knows what panic might
be triggered. *Tell your family about your triggers* was how Brighton's staff had put it. What were ours? Better to remain still.

"We'll just take it easy," Mom said.

She sat beneath a framed watercolor of our old Dearborn
house, powder blue, each of our names written in calligraphy
above a bedroom window. Ozzy was a black lump on the porch.

"That stuff," I said. "One hit and you're addicted."

I was only beginning to comprehend that the ordeal might
be more than a fluke, what my dad called freak things: a baseball knocked from the sky by a soaring pigeon; my uncle zapped
by lightning on his prom night; a cougar escaped from the
Detroit Zoo. One in a million. As for crack, I'd seen programs

in school warning of its warp-speed annihilation, the way its fumes turned people hollow faced and destitute in what seemed a matter of days.

"What if they come here looking for him?" I said. "Dealers?" Friends of mine had been hunted around town for owing their pot suppliers; how the crack world did its business, I imagined, was a whole other bag. Fear shot straight through me. "We're talking about killers. The scum of the earth."

"No one is coming here."

Mom hadn't changed out of her robe. Saturday's business— groceries, weeding her garden, dusting the banister—could wait. Her grief was visible in her lowering face, her small twitching chin. She'd once had a way of neutralizing my childhood worries, consoling me with smiles. Before moving to Ridgewood Hills I'd never seen her unravel, even when she'd been my fifth-grade English teacher, standing before a classroom in which I'd worked stridently to be chief clown. Until recently, she'd explained Dad's absences as business trips to Mexican Ford plants and last-minute sporting excursions, but I'd heard her shouting from their bedroom, into the phone, her voice darkening over the months. Then came a night he'd called after work claiming to be headed to a Red Wings preseason game. Mom had rifled through the *Free Press*, thrashing pages as she read that the Ice Capades were the only thing happening that week at Joe Louis Arena.

Dad's compulsions—marijuana in the basement and his haywire temper—Mom had known about their entire marriage. The hard drugs she'd kept secret for a couple of years, attending Al-Anon and couples' therapy, offering goodness the chance to intervene before she yanked the alarm. How to reconcile the sense that, as mind-shattering as all this was, it provided an instant dimension for things I'd already known? Trouble

I'd sensed on some level beneath thought and language, in my crackling nerves and an inalienable, primal fear I'd mistake for a weakness of character. However deeply buried, the truth had its influence, altering me, screaming from the bottommost source of all things.

"Maybe I should have told you sooner," she said, swirling her coffee.

We liked ours the same, heavy with milk, easy on our stomachs.

"No," I said, "it's okay."

I understood the urge to protect someone from troubles they didn't need. I'd never tell her about the man with the gun or the time I'd been jumped at a gas station. It would be years before I'd reveal the name of my band—long after we'd called it quits—or the locations of the dank Detroit basements and clubs where I first stood before an audience. And I can't honestly say I'm not grateful for those teenage days I lived unaware of my father's disgrace, when the only problems on earth seemed to be mine.

DAD CALLED FROM A pay phone late that night, more than twenty-four hours after he'd disappeared. Like every call that day, I picked it up anticipating his voice and the diatribe I'd lay on him. "Lemme talk to your mother," he said, implying *now* with his bone-tired rasp—all it took to force me into laying the phone on the kitchen counter.

I looked up, into the attached living room.

Mom sat in a chair, her eyes already on me, and I gave her a slow nod.

Caitlin bolted up from the couch. She'd been watching television in her nightie, ready to bare claws at any sign of our dad. When Mom grabbed the phone and said, "Where are you?" Caitlin crowded her, pleading, "What's he doing with my car?"

"Tim," said my mom.

It was never good when she used his name.

Caitlin grabbed for the receiver. "Tell him to get back here," she said, "right now," but I restrained her. The television was full volume. Ozzy paced below us, whining through his nostrils. "Let me go," said my sister. "You big jerk."

Caitlin didn't have guitars or secret concerts going for her, no co-conspiring madcap like Will on her side. She went alone to work soup kitchens and sponsored impoverished children she'd seen on television. She'd drifted school to school, friend to friend. Tae Kwon Do to kickboxing, ice-skating to softball. I'd seen her twirling across the ice as cold rushed over her tights, or standing dazed in the outfield with a mitt too large for her hand, always with the same look on her face—no idea why she was where she was—freezing if ever the ball did travel her way.

"Lemme talk to him," she said, a tone like she intended to deal the blow that would end all. "I don't care what he's smoking."

Mom let this go on without even a scowl or wave of her hand. She may have wanted my dad to hear the other end of things. When I finally reached for the phone, she let me take it from her, which seemed an acknowledgment that I'd stepped onto an adult plane. Also a chance to speak with impunity. I knew nitrous oxide and psilocybin mushrooms. Blotter acid, green windowpane gel caps; a concoction called Martian juice, indigenous to Dearborn. I'd smoked opium in a tree and another time in Ford Woods. I would have told you I was a streetwise guru of narcotic thrill.

"All right," I said, as if I'd guided a hundred bad trips. "I'll come get you."

Through the receiver my dad's voice was a mess of huffs and half speak. "I'm fine," slurring into, "don't worry," then an explosive wheeze that seemed to confess he'd finally and totally destroyed himself. A hoarse tone as he drawled my name, dragged it out in a sad wheeze. Valium was part of his comedown program, he'd confessed to the doctors, and I was thinking of this cold fact as he said, "I love you . . . god, I'm so sorry," heaving these words out to me from deep in some crack hell. I was imagining his face in a kind of detail I'd never forget, the horrible look in his eyes as he let out a sharp moan and went silent. He'd been reduced to absolutely nothing but pain, the most horrible sounds I'd ever heard.

"Where are you?" I yelled, at a volume I'd never before aimed toward him.

"I'm so sorry," he said again. He mumbled, "Nah, nah, nah."

Mom was there when I looked up. Focused on me, kneading her fingers, otherwise perfectly still, speeding through every possible strategy to end this right now while having no idea what happens next. Caitlin's white-hot panic, looming in my peripheral vision as I grasped for my next words. Everything happening seemed like some hypothetical episode being acted out—whatever I *imagined* people doing while accosting their father midbinge. It was too new to be real. Just three weeks earlier he'd confessed to Caitlin and me in that very kitchen, his sleeves rolled and tie undone, saying, "I have a drug problem." I'd asked what kind. He'd said, "Cocaine," and my mom said, "Crack, Tim. It's crack," until he'd banged the table while Caitlin stared through me, knowing better than anyone that we were entering a nightmare.

We were still there.

"Tell me the cross streets," I said into the phone, flailing a hand.

Caitlin pressed her cheek against mine, forehead grinding against my temple, trying to get an ear on things.

"Don't let him trick us again," she said, but I was getting somewhere with my old man. I'd grown deft at predicting the swing of his moods, had learned to jive my way through the worst of them; tonight I sensed the rare opening: his weakness, pure shell shock.

"Give me the streets, man."

I strong-armed Caitlin from the phone, and she began crying in her soundless, embarrassed way. I'd already begun nursing a delusion that she could be spared, kept oblivious to the ghastly possibilities that were becoming clear to me: pictures I'd seen of dead basketball stars in the eighties. The gaunt fiends who scrounged for crack money outside Detroit concerts. Crack whores, crack motels.

"Don't let him hang up," Caitlin said as Mom stood watching, knowing this commotion was the truest thing my dad could experience. Hoping, like any sane person, that it might bring him home.

"Tell your mom and sister I love them," Dad said.

I wasn't about to cut him loose.

"The fucking cross streets."

He sighed and cursed himself before naming a junction that sounded possibly familiar, way out in metro Detroit's surrounding countryside. North Territorial and Seven Mile, about as far from the drug zone as you could get. "There's a gas station," he said. "I'll be in the parking lot."

"Twenty minutes."

I hung up, and Caitlin snatched the receiver from its cradle, saying, "Let me talk to him," weeping into the dial tone with everything she had.

YEARS BEFORE, ON A family vacation, I'd heated a Petoskey stone on a grill and carried it in a baseball mitt to Lake Michigan's shore, where I suggested Caitlin add it to her rock collection. The vilest of many schemes I'd used to torment her when we were kids. By the time she'd plucked it from the sand, the stone was still hot enough to send her slowly to her knees, staring at me with those blue death stars—sadly perplexed that anyone alive could be so maliciously idiotic. This was now the look in her eyes, her face contorting into a wounded expression as I insisted on going alone to find our father and bring him home.

"Why you?" she said. "It's my car, you know."

We'd attended a humble Catholic grade school, a place of clip-on ties and plaid skirts and chewed, outdated textbooks. Gym class was in a bingo hall. At recess I'd held court with guys in my grade, breezing about Metallica or Kati Karl's visible bra strap, while far across the yard I'd see Caitlin wandering along the aluminum fence that enclosed the premises. Things came easily to me then, friends, bonding over arcade games and horror flicks, playing it cool when it came to my whimpering fear of girls. Caitlin ached with shyness, drifting off, making herself unknown. One year her only friend was a bashful, small-boned girl named Priya Johnson, the sole black kid in her class.

Wearing a plaid jumper, whispering to Priya while dragging her fingertips along the schoolyard's rusted fence—I wanted badly to believe my sister would always be that way. That girl. Out of earshot yet within a safe, visible distance.

"This is bullshit," Caitlin said, letting fly a rare obscenity.

"Your brother will go," Mom said. "You stay and keep me company."

My sister wilted onto the countertop.

Her blonde locks spilled out, lush and streaked with auburn. While I'd been towheaded and sallow enough that childhood antagonists had crank-called our house whispering, *Albino freak*, Caitlin's skin was a faint bronze and would remain so throughout the fall. She was pretty, in her unpolished way. A likable, blue-eyed confusion. A suicide attempt the year before, enough pills in her tiny stomach to collapse a boar. Over what? The same unnameable gloom that fueled my musical obsessions? It was impossible to say, there in the thick of it, as I laced my boots and left to meet my dad.

• • •

Pulling out of the driveway in Mom's Taurus, I rolled down the windows and punched another of my band's cassettes into the deck. Demo tapes: an audio calling card for greater things. We'd dubbed fifty or so, and the plan was to play our first gig that autumn, after which we'd hit the road. It defied conventions of punk authenticity to be caught listening to your own tunes, an ego move expected of pursed-lipped rock stars posing for glamour shots while wearing their own band's T-shirt. Once I had the wagon cruising steady, I shouted along with the sound of my own voice, shrugging to the groove, tapping the gas pedal to the beat of the kick drum.

With the right tunes, I'd plowed through what I'd believed were hard times: the gray days after Lauren, my girlfriend of three years, introduced me to self-pity by knotting tongues with the school quarterback, or Dad knuckling my forehead about the dunce-level marks and behavioral citations on my report cards. I daydreamed songs, entire albums spinning on repeat. I didn't necessarily need a stereo, but the stock Dolby NR deck in the Taurus intensified the bass. The overtones swirled as the air rushed through the opened windows. The roads were empty. I reached out to palm the wind.

Listening to the band's music, our mistakes were what I

liked best. A drumstick thwacked a rim. My guitar sizzled over a bum note before sliding into place. This was the kind of group I'd longed to be a part of. So many nights I'd spent composing "Musicians Wanted" flyers, listing the names of admired bands—Deadguy, the Dazzling Killmen, Universal Order of Armageddon—along with my parents' phone number. It had taken a year of huddling with Will at the fringes of increasingly far-out gigs before I grew bold enough to tack my xeroxed queries on the walls of local record shops. The first and only response had been from a drummer who went by his last name, Repa.

I'm not messing around, he'd said on the answering machine. *Are you?*

Mom replayed the message, chuckling as Repa's meaty voice infiltrated the kitchen. Days later I'd pulled up his driveway to see him emerge from the garage wearing a black shirt, black boots, and black jeans. He had a strong jaw, a large face with Cro-Magnon angles and dark, anxious eyes. First thing Repa had asked was if I went to many shows. *Shows.* You didn't call them *concerts.* Hardcore punk shows—though punk, as the saying went, was dead. Come to the funeral.

"Some," I'd said, yanking my amplifier from my truck.

"Me, too," Repa said. "But the best shows happen when I'm alone in my room."

Blaring headphones, eyes closed, envisioning yourself performing to a crowd of filthy hundreds—I'd understood exactly what he meant.

"That's the real truth," he said. "Nobody else around."

Imagine what my dad would think of Repa, the finest musician I knew, yowling satanically as he attacked his vintage Pearl drums. Or Ethan, our bassist, four years older, a veteran of the scene who towered above with a brown pompadour and bargain bin clothes and a fawn-eyed stare that was intent on getting however crazy we were gonna get. *Queer as steers,* Dad might have said, one of his corny gibes. *Boneheads, shitheads.* Yes, we were three freaks, playing for hours and toasting with coffee mugs at a diner, naming ourselves Thoughts of Ionesco after a French playwright I'd been told was absurd, yet whom none of us had read.

Officially a band.

"Brutal" was the word we used to describe our songs, and it was a benchmark, too. "More brutaler," Repa might say, when the chords required a less-melodious touch. We'd spent a year rehearsing in Repa's basement, during which I tried every lick I knew, pulling out twisted free-jazz chords I'd stolen from Dad's old records—leftovers from those rarely mentioned days after he'd dropped out of the Air Force Academy and grown sideburns.

If he'd listened to our cassette, had he been able to hear it?

His unintentional influence.

THERE WAS NO GAS station at the corner of North Territorial and Seven Mile. The two roads, in fact, didn't intersect. The surroundings were nearly rural out that way. Beyond the headlights, the streets were dark, and I passed few cars, checking their make as they blurred by. I drove until I found the nearest Amoco, closed for the evening and unlit at the mouth of the highway. Aside from the chain-locked pumps and garbage bins, there was nothing to see. Not even a streetlamp glowed above the lot. I waited by the pay phone, picking it up to check for the dial tone. And there was one, so perhaps I'd found the place. Only minutes before Dad might have held his ear to that same piece of black plastic; it was possible I'd just missed him, that he might return any moment. The night was hot as ever. I had a full bladder. I unzipped and let it go on the concrete, watching the stream puddle alongside the tires of the station wagon. No one else was around.

But I waited there awhile, just long enough to know for sure.

• • •

Two days later a priest called to tell us that my dad had made his way to a church rectory. This time my mom went to meet him. Apparently my parents had been in counseling with the priest, a diocese-appointed expert on addiction who oversaw a quaint Catholic parish in the downriver town of Wyandotte. Mom had once dragged me to mass there; now I understood why.

It was late afternoon.

I'd returned from the 6:00 A.M. to 3:00 P.M. shit shift in time to catch the gist of things and make a routine call to Lauren that, like most of our recent speed-talks, divulged nothing personal, only the perfunctorily good news that my band had practice later that night.

"Cool," she said. "I want to hear it." Then she asked, "What's wrong? You sound like a different person?"

I got off the line as quickly as I could. Caitlin appeared, sleuthlike, in the kitchen, wincing at my shit-covered slacks, minding my business because she didn't want to be alone. "You stink," she said, and I edged nearer to her until she shrieked. "They should give you a special suit or something. It's wrong to go around like that!"

I scraped a brown-green fleck from my pant leg and brought it to my lips.

"Sicko," she said.

This was an improvement. She'd been skimping on meals

and depriving herself of television. While she'd resigned to driving Dad's car, she was spooked by the emblems contained within: his coffee mug, his baseball hat. Everything now a clue to some larger mystery. She wanted to know what we were supposed to tell people.

"Nothing," I said.

"What are you gonna tell Lauren?" she said, high pitched, fretting this particular idea more obviously than she'd prefer to let on, nevertheless sharpening an angle I'd hoped to avoid altogether. "What's Lauren gonna think?"

Because whatever kind and pure memories I had of my girlfriend were quickly being moved to the outskirts, along with those of my sister herself and my family and everything I'd known—let the music come rushing in. Anyway, Lauren was leaving in a week to live in a Michigan State University dormitory, where she'd introduce her genuinely huge smile and curious hazel eyes to a world of young, hungry strangers. Maybe the best moments of my life so far were spent reclining in her hand-me-down Crown Victoria as we played the Beatles and the Misfits until we lost track, holding each other tight; but they were easily shoved aside by brooding irrationally, vindictively, over how she'd betrayed me with a quarterback named Joe, how she trusted in a Christian god and enjoyed Dave Matthews Band and therefore couldn't possibly know who I was.

"This," I told Caitlin, "is family business."

She glared, her eyes totally clear. I couldn't really look into them, but knew they were pleading for something more than I was prepared to give: that she and I would finally crack ourselves open and let our feelings bleed out all over the floor; or maybe just that we'd have an actual conversation about any of this, even the smallest piece of what was happening.

"So what does that make me, then," she said, "if my dad is a drug fiend?"

"Same thing it makes me."

MOM CAME THROUGH THE back door with such forward momentum I thought she'd arrived alone. Seconds later, my dad staggered in. The sight of him intimidated me, despite his bloodless color and the trembling of his limbs the moment he glimpsed Caitlin, who stared him dead in the eye until he could no longer bear it. His hair was matted, his skin glazed with sweat. He ducked his chin to his neck as he began to cry with animal force, more spasm than sorrow, as though it were his only bodily expression left to wring dry.

I went in for a quick hug, trying out a new, manly grasp. His scent, the salty odor of nights we'd spent tossing baseballs or riding bikes. Could this be the same man, whom I'd never before seen shed tears, now weeping against my shoulder? It made me feel I was the sole person on earth whose forgiveness might cure him. I slapped him on the back, meaning to say, *Go ahead and cry until you're done*, but with a heavy breath he choked off his sobs and released me, opening his arms to Caitlin, who drew away.

"Hi, crackhead. What did you do with my car?" She wrapped her arms around herself. While it appeared to require a grave effort, she kept her eyes trained on him.

"Cait," he said.

Then he said "I love you" to my sister—to all of us.

"Don't 'I love you' me," Caitlin said. "Stupid. Real stupid."

At that my parents went upstairs, where Dad would spend the evening shivering in bed and sweating through the linen. But to remember this—the Ridgewood Hills house and the sound of footsteps above, the refrigerator humming and the sun going down beyond the windows—is to remember the four of us together. Because he was home, and because we still had a chance.

More than that, it's to remember Caitlin beside me, scowling with that same old what-the-fuck on her face. A scene I'd give anything to return to, because at the time I could only stand scratching my arms, hoping to insist by my lack of expression that none of this scared me.

As she had been—that's how I'd wanted her to stay, twirling her hair, journaling on her bedroom floor, until this mess was filed in the family joke book along with those once-calamitous but now-amusing tales of me urinating on mom's sewing kit or ass flashing a neighbor. Dad would be up the next morning, suited for Ford Motor and off to the office before I awoke. Caitlin would douse her Escort with air freshener and soon forget all that had happened, and I could still snatch the cassette from the car and make it to Repa's in time for rehearsal. There was a new song we'd been cooking up, our most brutal yet. We'd been calling it "the sludgy one," and I had lyrics in mind as I hugged my sister and escaped through the back door.

3

The three of us, inside a conversion van.

Seatbelts that didn't give or retract, one size fits all, no tightening the slack, just these frayed, knotted up straps, decapitation-ready. Gray-blue interior that camouflaged the many years of DNA stained deep into every reachable fiber. The window roller handles had been ripped from the passenger doors, but we'd saved one and used it like a skeleton key to crank the panes up and down, preferably down, to mask the van's unique odor, something mature and organic that'd been there since Ethan won the thing at a police auction several months earlier. In tow were sacks of canned food and boxes of our newly pressed twelve-inch album. Cassettes overflowed from a paper shopping bag, fed one by one into a Hitachi boom box we'd duct taped to the dashboard. Cigarettes. Buck knives. A road atlas. We had bedrolls and an imitation Colt .45, as well as Will's Easton, which we'd elected to call the peacemaker. Who knew what might happen out here, blazing the land. It was June 1997, and after nearly a year of Rust Belt road trips, the band was a week into its first national venture, gigs booked from Chicago to Houston to Gainesville, then up the Eastern Seaboard. "On tour," we liked to say.

Hardly a person outside of Michigan had heard our name.

The mission was to play for dear life, taking each city by surprise and leaving copies of our record in the hands of the converted. I was nineteen, finally making a go at something, with a backpack and a paycheck's worth of cash to spread over the weeks. It gave me the feeling my existence was at stake, or that, by committing to the journey, I might reinvent who I was. Through the windshield, I caught my first real glimpse of the country, the plains and billboards and wooden crosses in cornfields, all of it stretching on and on, farther than the movies had imagined. Our equipment was packed tight beneath a plywood loft that slept one. Ethan had done the carpentry and slapped decals on the back door: I HEART COPS. NO LOT LIZARDS. KILL WHITEY.

Repa had christened our chariot: the Orgasmatron.

An '85 Chevy G20 conversion van, corroded silver with a red pinstripe.

"A love machine," said Repa. "She's gonna take us all the way."

I'd been handling the driving and had begun putting Michigan and everyone there out of my mind the minute we'd crossed the state line. Our next was stop was Cincinnati, too close to the Great Lakes for me.

Back home, my family and I had lived one long, sleepless year, but things had been quiet ever since my dad returned from a second rehab that March. He'd spent the winter at a state-of-the-art facility in Atlanta, during which time he'd undergone quadruple-bypass surgery at the nearby Piedmont Hospital. His heart, his mind—everything strangled. After three months down there, he'd quit treatment without the doctors' approval, and I alone had escorted him home on an eleven-hour drive up Interstate

75. He and I, in a rented sedan. In the days since, we'd all been holding our breath, praying in our own ways that he was sober.

My mom, I trusted, was keeping watch over things while I was away. That she believed our family could be healed made me believe. Only Caitlin had grown skeptical, leery not just of my father but of dangers everywhere, especially to the planet. She worried about the proliferation of bottled water, the plastic waste burrowing into the earth's crust. As summer neared she'd begun fretting over the chemicals in fertilizer as much as she fretted over the whites of our father's eyes, which were often shot through with red. September was coming fast, though, and Caitlin had enrolled to attend Michigan State University, which comforted me only in the sense that she'd be joining Lauren, now a sophomore, who knew that vast Big Ten campus and had become something of a confidante to my sister, someone who'd remind her of home.

Let me be gone for seasons and seasons—I wasn't homesick.

Whatever my troubles, they were assuaged by the open road and the fact that the band was sounding crueler by the night. The van seemed to require a fierce concentration to keep it on the move; the brakes shuddered and the wheel was loose in the steering column. I likened it to flying a plane: easy does it, coasting through the turns, avoiding turbulence at all cost.

"You're a smooth daddy," Repa said. "Real cautious."

He wasn't encouraged to drive the van. We'd seen him in action in his Buick Century, chomping the wheel with his teeth and air drumming. He sat in back, black clad, on a bench seat, sporting a drastic buzz cut. For breakfast each morning, he guzzled unheated clam chowder from aluminum cans. "My soups," he called them. "The perfect meal."

No matter what city we pulled through, Repa put other drummers to shame, but the ado fellow musicians made over his talent didn't affect him. He'd already disowned the punk rock cosmos. You'd think it was because we never knew if we'd be getting paid, on what floor we'd unroll our sleeping bags, or what abysmal sound system, if any, we'd play through—Repa's antiscene vitriol had little to do with any of that. It was the lingo he despised, the tongue-pierced punkers making out in the bathrooms. The three-chord guff of the bands we played with; the tattoos and white-boy dreadlocks; the schlock politics. "I'm burning my records when I get home," he said. "Everything but the biker rock and true metal."

Since the tour's first show, Repa had wandered the streets of whatever town searching for local drunks to enlist as audience members. "This guy's with me. VIP." What acumen he had with these folks, mumbling to them in sublingual tongues while sharing bottles of King Cobra and Wild Irish Rose. "I love you, man," he'd say, arm around a trench-coated beggar. "Only honest son of a bitch in this place." And it happened that some nights these men were our truest fans.

Throughout our Cincinnati gig, a guest-listed wino stood at the stage's edge, raising a nicotined thumb and yelling for Hendrix. His was the only clapping evident between songs, and beneath the lights he appeared agelessly decrepit, a sunburned scab posed before a mostly empty barroom. Onstage, Repa whacked his cymbals with a joy that assured me he was performing for the drunkard alone. It made me jealous—this outsider infiltrating our vibes. We were in the middle of a long piece, working up a crescendo when I strutted toward the derelict, bending notes and stooping to wrap my lips around his putrid thumbs-up. A good long suck, right down to the knuckle. A rindy, bitter taste.

Immediately, I feared the worst—staph infection, hepatitis.

The man smiled, holding aloft his yellow thumb as if awaiting a second wetting. I stepped back to the mic just in time
to scream the final chorus. At last, the few punks at the bar
applauded, and Repa, the one I'd hoped to impress, let loose
one of his backbeat howls.

The club's staff had made a stink about Repa and me being
underaged. They'd threatened to boot us. Now they were probably wishing they had. We'd brought no big tippers to the bar,
little more than an unpaying wino and some heavy wear on
the eardrums. Once we'd finished, the man helped us carry our
gear from the club, hoping we'd slide him a buck, which we
did. As we boarded the van and waved good-bye, he once again
raised his thumb. "Thanks for the lick," he said. Which put a
smile across Repa's face that just about made up for the fact
we'd not been paid a cent. The next gig was Houston, a fifteen-
hour drive.

IN THE EARLY MORNING, we crossed the Arkansas-Texas border
with a thousand miles worth of insects smeared on the windshield. The bugs had grown larger and stranger the farther south
we drove, splattering the glass like condiments on a dinner tray.
Their deaths marked the nighttime hours, until the sun rose
over the highway. The needle was steady at seventy miles per
hour; any faster, and our old van rattled epileptically.

Ethan could sleep through anything. Unconscious in the
passenger seat, he wore, as he would the entire journey, a pair
of black athletic shorts that nearly revealed his scrotum, which
he itched unknowingly. His latest tattoo, a band of stick figures
sprinting the circumference of his calf, was oiled and glistening.
Occasionally, he smacked his lips and sighed.

From the backseat, Repa grumbled the make of each passing
semitruck. *Peterbilt. Volvo. Peterbilt.* If the music didn't work

out, he intended to become a trucker. Behind the wheel, I was shirtless and shoeless, carved with featherweight muscle from a regiment of pretour calisthenics. With every traveled mile I sensed a mythology in the making, a history I imagined musicologists discussing years later. Sweat from our performances encrusted my jeans. Texas in June—so hot I felt made of hydrogen, a combustible element inside the Orgasmatron.

The only orgasms taking place were private toss offs, when one of us drew all-night security duty while parked in bad hoods. St. Louis, Akron, Little Rock. A lack of romance was no concern. We talked little of girls. There was the unspoken assumption that Repa was a virgin, and Ethan was the busted-hearted type who made you believe he'd lived the blues. I'd been making trips to Lauren's East Lansing dormitory every few weeks, never certain where we stood, but she indulged the dark, narrow ideas I had about art. "Whoa," she'd say, when I'd describe the band's music, though I'd yet to play it for her, for the same reasons I kept it from my family: I worried she wouldn't understand. I didn't want her to understand. Or deep down I knew she had the power to undermine my anger—my only source of artistic currency—simply because she'd love me anyway and in spite of. My mom adored Lauren as much as Caitlin did, counting among her many graces the connection she allowed to my otherwise withdrawn life. On the road, I tried to put aside memories of Lauren's whorls of light brown hair, how she'd once cuddled beside me when the sad songs played.

By early afternoon, we were deep into the Lone Star State, ahead of schedule for Houston. A major metropolis—it gave us hope the evening's crowd might arrive en masse.

My left arm hung sunburned from the driver's-side window. My bare foot held the pedal steady. Texas was an expanse of petrified dirt and yellow plains. Repa grunted, ashing his Camel into an empty soup can, while Ethan awoke to pull a dime bag from his steel-toed shoe.

Then came the signs: WACO, TEXAS. 6 MILES.

We cheered.

Visions of a lunatic barricading hostages in a blazing compound. Branch Davidians. Christ figures rising above the plains.

"Koresh," Repa said. "Where's the holy man?"

"It was the government," said Ethan. "Koresh was a patsy."

We'd not seen a car for miles until entering Waco proper. Then came a siren, cherries whirling in the driver's-side mirror.

"No," Ethan said, stuffing the drugs into his shoe. "The fuzz."

Law enforcement seemed to radar our band. Our inaugural gig, at a Ypsilanti punk house called the Sugar Shack, had been busted during our fourth song by cops who griped that they'd heard us a mile away. A month later, authorities were summoned to an Ann Arbor club when our audience conspired against a pack of neo-skinheads who'd thrown the *sieg heil* one time too many. From the stage, I'd watched the bodies swirl as Repa parted the crowd wielding a claw hammer he used for nailing two-by-fours onto the stage, antislippage for his thundering bass drum. The sight of him gave pause to the fascists and anyone else who'd moments before seen him bashing cymbals.

"The hell is this?" I said, with an eye on the mirror, edging the van toward the highway shoulder. "We aren't speeding."

"It's those damn stickers," Repa said.

"Remember," said Ethan, a veteran road dog. "Tell 'em we're Christian rock."

Seconds later, a suntanned Texas Ranger ordered me onto the asphalt. His face was a network of ruts. Cowboy hat and a silver badge—the whole deal. There was little doubt he'd toss us in the clink for a dime bag. The tour, over like that.

It was to my dad's credit that I knew how to address my superiors, to look them squarely in the eye and nod diligently. The sturdier the handshake, the better, and at times like this I snapped into form.

"Couldn't have been doing more than seventy, sir. Had the cruise set."

The Orgasmatron was 170,000 miles old and without a single working amenity: no air, no stereo—no cruise control.

"Might wanna get that speedometer checked," said the copper.

My hair was a greasy, uncivilized feature. Caitlin had given me a butcherous trim that left me looking like a mental patient with a penchant for ripping clumps from his scalp. I tucked the blond strands behind my ears as the ranger sized me up. Barefoot on the side of the highway—that's when you feel the glory of the Texan sun.

"You on some kind of mission?" the cop said. "What's in the van?"

"We're a band."

"From way up in Michigan," he said.

The pavement was molten, a floor of coals. I shifted from foot to foot, rolling from heel to toe.

"We're modern jazz." I said this with utter conviction.

"Better watch your speed on my highway. I could ticket you for driving shoeless, if I wanted."

I liked the grip of the pedal on my bare sole, curling my toes around the edges.

"Better wear shoes on my highway."

"Yes, sir."

He nodded me back to the van. So long, without so much as a handshake. Then he sat in his cruiser as I started the engine and pulled carefully onto the empty road. But once the

Orgasmatron was moving again, taking a good mile to regain highway speed, I let my bandmates know the score.

"I beat him," I said, "with my mind."

YOU LEARN A THING or two about a brother, cruising thousands of miles together in a steel box. Snoring together in parking lots, breathing one another's tang, sharing gallons of warm OJ and filling the emptied containers with communal urine, pulling over only for the show or when the tank runs low. As the country blurred, we told the same stories, embellishing until they became fabulous lies. I could recite the best of Ethan's childhood misadventures and Repa's demoniac rants as if they were my own. When, to accentuate a point, someone stamped the Orgasmatron's floor, clouds of gray dust billowed up into the sunlight.

I'd never before felt a part of something the way I did that band—a sense of belonging, being irreplaceable. My bandmates saw me at my most inspired, screaming every pain I had access to, though I'd told them next to nothing of where I'd come from. They seemed to prefer it this way. They were unaware of Lauren; they'd never seen Ridgewood Hills or met my mom. They'd never heard my sister's name. I told them I hardly knew my father, which had come to feel almost true.

Days before I left on tour, my dad had listened to our album. I'd accidentally left a stack of the records in the garage, one of which he'd snuck to the basement to give it a spin on his old United Audio 1229Q. How long he'd endured our sound I'll never know, yet I still flinch to imagine his displeasure. Dad's time in rehab, however, had weakened his powers of criticism. When I next saw him, he'd politely handed me the platter, saying, "I could hardly believe it was human beings."

So much had happened since that night a summer earlier

when he'd gone missing with Caitlin's Escort. The only bit I told Repa and Ethan was that I'd had a gun pulled on me. I juiced up the scene to make it sound like there'd been a hair-raising showdown. The truth was that after Dad returned from the Wyandotte rectory, we'd thought he'd been cured. But he'd vanished again and again throughout the fall. Mom took calls from relatives who'd heard from him, and I found lipstick-smudged cigarette butts in the ashtray of his car. Mom confiscated his credit cards. Caitlin suspected he'd swiped money from her purse.

Our father . . .

Suddenly his eyes were dead circuits, an unknown catastrophe going on behind them. The past October he'd arrived at a wedding manic happy and tweaking, sweating through his dress shirt. Pale. Clammy. Mom and I whisked him to a nearby movie theater, where we'd bought tickets to whatever was playing. Dad sat between us, lit by the flickering of an action film, kneading his arms in a Technicolor comedown. At least Caitlin hadn't been there. By late November Mom had checked him into the Atlanta Recovery Center, a facility known for curing the tough cases. Unlike Brighton, the Atlanta asylum kept patients for an indefinite time, as long as it took. After a few weeks, Dad's left arm went numb, and he'd fainted, winding up in a cardiac unit and calling to tell us he'd be undergoing quadruple-bypass surgery three days before Christmas.

And when these memories began to haunt me, I'd crank the volume on the boom box, making my attempt to get personal with the road, the rolling plains and wind turbines. Wild dogs on southern backstreets. Ghost towns. The van so small beneath the sky. I'd analyze our songs, how to better fret the chords the next time we took the stage. When in need of a real distraction, I'd ask Repa to recount a dream from which he'd woken up bellowing one night, about a giant house of flesh, with steel handles bolted to its supple exterior. "I was making love to it. I hope I dream it again," he'd say, and I'd see it rippling above him, a faceless mound of sex, as we laughed, on and on, making our way to the next show.

WITH THE ORGASMATRON PARKED outside a small Houston club in an old cantina, Repa and I opened the back doors and unloaded our crates of albums. We'd do this upon arriving at each destination. In Houston, Repa unboxed a single twelve-inch, groaning with the realization our vinyl platters had been warped by the southern heat. "This frickin' sun," he said. "They're going limp on us."

With a few hours to kill before sound check, we began sliding the misshapen discs from their jackets, attempting to bend them back to form. We'd recorded our nine-song album in a flurry of first takes over a single afternoon, and it felt like the sole accomplishment of my life, the most honest thing. Yet when I was in another mind, the pride I felt was erased by my shame over our songs, the mad sadness I knew no other way of expressing—it made me protective of our records, one hundred of which were pressed on limited-edition orange vinyl.

"If we sit on them," I said, holding a deformed twelve-inch to the sunlight. "Maybe then."

The parking lot was crabgrass and cracked asphalt, on the outskirts of something.

"Warden used the cheap stuff," Repa said. "Horseshit vinyl."

"What did you expect?" said Ethan.

Mike Warden was an irascible character with a knack for flying his ambitions to the edge of triumph, only to giggle when they went ablaze shortly thereafter. Weeks earlier, he'd released our album on his label, Conquer the World Records, established 1992. Though he'd barely turned twenty-five, Warden's punk fanaticism and jackass business practices were already scene legend, made notorious by bands and fanzines who'd accused him of death threats, of fudging numbers and ordering unauthorized reprints. A Florida hardcore act had recorded a twelve-inch bearing the title *Warden Can Suck It.* He was dimpled and curly haired, a media mogul, Detroit-style. His infamy trailed us everywhere. Promoters refused to book us due to our CTW affiliation, but Warden's earnest insanity endeared him to me from the start. He was genuinely deranged and made no attempt to hide it—a blunt honesty I longed to be near. Ethan called him Conquer the Colgate because he'd once caught Warden masturbating with toothpaste inside an RV full of touring musicians.

"Total piss." Repa grunted.

He had no respect for Warden, any of this.

One by one he smacked the warped LPs against the Houston blacktop. Even in the Southern heat Repa wore black denim and motorcycle boots. Ethan sat on the Orgasmatron's fender, using a Sharpie to black out the CTW logo on the salvaged albums. I set one aside for myself, the most warped I could find.

"Think anyone shows up tonight?" I said.

"Hell no," Repa said, driving home a point: Warden had booked this gig.

I'd had a private desire to see the CTW logo on a record I'd made, knowing Warden would distribute them to lands we'd never reach on our own. He talked about Europe, saying, "We've gotta get you overseas. The Germans will love it." So what if the vinyl melted? There was still Germany, and a thousand more promises Warden had made—one being that Houston would be a big gig, a scene awaiting our arrival.

"Anything Warden," Ethan said. "I told you it's a mistake."

"Get Colgate on the horn," Repa said. "Tell him we want a hotel tonight."

The deal we'd struck with Warden was that we'd be paid in albums, ten percent of each pressing. CDs, too, but who cared? Before leaving town, I'd gone to fetch our copies from his lair, where he'd answered the door cloaked in a blanket and holding a flashlight. He lived in Detroit's bowels, in a house that had once been a hub for subcultural activity. A family of ferrets had also resided there for a time, along with several vegan anarchists, one of whom gave free tattoos in the attic. All but Warden had since deserted, but not without first smashing the front windows and looting the joint.

"You better sell a lot of records," Warden said, by way of inviting me inside.

Having maxed his credit paying for our albums, he hadn't been able to cover the bills. His electricity had been disconnected. I'd followed him to the kitchen, led by the beam of his flashlight. There were empty pizza boxes and a mangled cage where the ferrets had slept. A warm stench radiated from decomposing fruit on the countertop. Warden moved at the stove to light a burner with a match, pressing his face near the flame. "At least there's still gas," he said.

"Christ, man." I'd yanked up my T-shirt to mask my nostrils. "That smell."

He turned toward his refrigerator. "Look at this," he'd said, opening it and slapping a sack of vegetables to the floor. Then he got an arm around the back of the contraption and, with the door hanging open, wrestled it from the wall. Contents spilled forth—condiments and rotted tofu, green bread and Styrofoam containers. After hauling it halfway across the room, Warden attacked the fridge's interior, for a moment gracefully, with the style of a martial artist. Then he lapsed into troglodyte barbarity, swinging his arms like clubs.

"I'll get rid of the smell," he said, reaching to open the back door.

Leveling his spine against it, Warden attempted to shove the monstrosity through the crumbling wooden doorframe. When he gave up, the fridge was lodged in the doorway: half in, half out, going nowhere.

"I guess you want your records now," he'd said. On his way to the attic he snatched his flashlight, wiping his nose as the stove's burner hissed blue—and not much later, our albums were in my arms.

COME SHOWTIME WE PLAYED to the barmaid, the promoter, and the headlining band—San Diegans, who all the while bounced a racquetball across the dance floor. Our songs echoed back at us from the far wall of the room, but we played fiercely through it, whatever was there.

Once we let loose, it didn't matter how many people were watching, whether we were in Houston or Bad Axe, Michigan. Repa closed his eyes. Ethan played facing his amp, convulsing with the low end. We did what we'd come to do, which was to forget where we'd come from. I dropped to my knees and howled any which way but into the microphone, keeping true to the lyrics nonetheless. One line went *Sing the recovery lie / I've got the cord tied / To thin the bleeding / Old flame clean me tonight*, and another song screamed *The lie is in the wind / So breathe it to me* until my vision began to tunnel and my lungs crumpled together.

And then one of the San Diegans caught the racquetball on a bounce and held it.

As they neared the stage, the bartender turned her stare our way, and the soundman returned his unlit cigarette to his ear in order to—why the hell not—see this moment unfurling. Ethan walloped his strings with a fist, and Repa dragged out the last song longer than anyone could bear. With nothing left to scream, I let the volume smack my head in any direction. My hands went numb, but I heard my fingers making sense of the guitar, until the three of us locked eyes and stopped perfectly in time.

"Yes!" shouted the promoter. "Badass."

He clapped loud and fast, as if to arouse some invisible audience to applaud the thrashing we'd given ourselves. All others present had yet to relax their wincing faces, thankful only that it was over. The promoter must have felt guilty about all this, because afterward he led us to his parents' house, where we were each assigned our own room, to lie naked on fresh sheets as our clothes spun in the wash. A tremendous southern estate, though you'd never have suspected it from the guy's tattooed neck and the silver-dollar-sized earrings punched into his lobes. He even offered to gas up our van the following morning. All he wanted in return was a record.

"So I can say you crashed with me, way back before anyone knew who you were."

4

Copper bedposts. A ceiling fan. Track lighting, but no clock. It took a moment to remember what state I was in and why I was lying naked in a queen-size bed. I watched the sun illuminate the drawn shades until from somewhere in the house came the digital explosions of a video game.

Signs of life in Houston.

Outside the bedroom door, my laundry sat folded in a tidy pile. Stepping through the home, I began to dread all things family—I remembered I had one. It must have been the framed pictures in the hallways: the promoter arm in arm with suntanned people looking too much like him to be anything but siblings, smiling with a sort of conspiratorial mischief Caitlin and I hadn't shared since we were children. That's how I missed her, in flashes of guilt. I'd mailed a postcard to Will but had yet to call home since the band left Michigan.

"Help yourself," the promoter said, about the phone, hardly bothering to turn from the video screen.

A few rings. Then Caitlin answered with a midmorning rasp. "You're not causing trouble," she said, "are you?"

My sister was not above irony. For my November birthday, she'd given me a mauve sweater with an oversize golf ball embroidered across the chest, a canny nod toward my previous status as a hateful, underpaid scooper of fairway goose shit. As I'd opened it, she'd laughed herself to the floor—a rare burst of glee amid the family sorrows she'd been taking so hard. The cable-knit atrocity must have cost twenty bucks, and she'd wrung every penny out of the joke, gesturing for me to try it on. This was her humor—rarely spoken. When it came to words, Caitlin was heat seeking, impossibly literal.

"Doing anything stupid?" she said.

"I'm fine."

"You better be careful, brother," she said, passing the phone to Mom, who explained that things back home were basically copacetic. Caitlin was working extra hours pouring coffee, saving her tips, preparing to live in the Michigan State dorms. Dad, three months out of rehab with four new valves in his heart, was making it to Ford Motor every day, rising to his usual 5:00 A.M. alarm.

"He's upset, though," Mom said. "Ford gave him a bad performance review for the first time."

Each morning, before heading to work in Dearborn's schools, Mom had been attending mass. Now that summer vacation was here, she might have been putting in extra hours at the pews. I watched Repa pecking though the estate's record collection, shaking his head with each flip of the album jackets. I heard a shower running—Ethan making the most of the home's plumbing. Our host thwacked the controls of a pixelated go-kart that sped across his giant television.

"Be careful out there," Mom said. "Don't make me worry."

"We're good."

"Where are you?"

"Texas."

"Is it hot?"

"Yeah," I said. "Real hot." And when I said, "I love you," I said it low enough that Repa, pulling an album he approved of from the stack and checking for scratches, couldn't hear me above the promoter, who shouted, "Outta my way!" again and again in a fit of virtual road rage.

IT WENT LIKE THAT: van sleep in truck stops to posh suburban bedding. The excitement of never knowing what came next. Anarchist communes; outdoor riverside stages; crowds too narcotized to stand; crowds of drug-free youth dancing violently with giant X's marked across their fists. Houston to Austin, through Fort Worth, and northward to Denton, where we pulled up to a ranch-style house with a lawn of dirt. On the porch, a gaggle of black-haired kids sat with beers between their feet. According to our itinerary, we'd located the place—the evening's gig.

"This it?" I said. "Who's the promoter?"

Ethan consulted our rumpled spreadsheet of dates and addresses and contacts. "Spider," he told me. "That's what it says."

The trees lining the street were infested with gray sacks, nests of some kind, sagging from the branches. Repa walked to a tree and pulled out his lighter, reaching for the lowest of the cocoons.

"You don't wanna do that." A shirtless Texan in a black mesh hat stepped out of the house, wagging a finger, a black widow tattooed on his breast. "Hell, nah."

This was the place, all right.

The porch dwellers flashed us the stink eye, parting apathetically as we carried our equipment into the house. The usual rub: locals sizing us up as we rolled in our speaker cabinets. None of us were punk rock protocol. Me, barefoot with my home-cut locks. Ethan in cock-printed shorts and a five-dollar Caesar he'd commissioned from an Ohio barber. Repa was sallow and jowled, a dark horse ready for any apocalypse that might rain down.

An audience usually made its decision within the first thirty seconds of our first song. They'd either wince and head for the door or begin stamping their feet, bobbing their heads. Whatever. We played as if the sunrise depended on it.

"Paying the dues" was how Ethan put it.

Despite its ghastly trees, Denton was on our side. By the time of the show, forty or so belligerents had crowded into the living room, some stripping naked as we tuned our instruments. The walls were painted an unthinkable red-pink. Spider had removed the furniture, if there'd been any, and Repa arranged his drums so that he'd play with his back to everyone. At the first smash of Repa's cymbals, the front row bonded in a flesh-toned rendition of the running man dance, jogging in place as their genitals wagged to the beat.

We burned through a song, then another. Someone leaped from a windowsill and was passed over raised hands, hydrating the room with a beer mist. When the neighbors complained, Spider ordered the show into an empty bedroom, and our noise resumed, half the audience watching through the doorway, the heat reaching toward the thousands. Packed somewhere in a shoe box is a picture of me, midscream, framed against that bedroom wall. I barely recognize myself in the magenta-faced young man, eyes bloodshot, a glistening artery protruding from his neck. Yet, seeing the photo, I can almost feel again what it was like to be free of everything, screaming for my life.

We played every song we knew. By the end, only a few stood before us, naked and sweating, pleading for another.

"One more," Repa said.

"We already played 'em all."

"Then make it up."

We improvised a five-chord pattern, six-eight time. A leg breaker—never to be recreated, scalded once and for all into the plaster of that Denton bedroom. If only for a moment, we'd taken the reins of a sound we'd been chasing. Repa, I could tell by his rolled-back eyes, was finally satisfied. So was I. Say nothing of the crowds, the records sold or not sold, we would return to Michigan triumphant, carrying something that could not be taken back.

Repa kept the rhythm slamming, even as Ethan and I sat cross-legged at the foot of our switched-off amps; when he'd finished, he walked out of the house to a smattering of applause. Spider passed his mesh hat through the house, pestering the crowd to cough up a buck for the entertainment.

"What's the name of your band, again?" he said. "That's right. Yeah, yeah. Y'all was crazy. How about a beer?"

Repa took night duty in the van. While the party continued, Ethan and I spread our sleeping bags across the bedroom floor we'd sweated upon just hours before. Not much later, we were lying in the shadows of our amplifiers. From the room's doorway, Spider touched the brim of his cap to bid us good night. "I saw a wolf spider in here earlier," he said. "Gotta keep an eye on them. They'll spin a web in your mouth as you sleep and pinch your nostrils till you suffocate."

It was after our best performances, just before sleep, when the tones of home began calling loudest. I'd rest my head on a strange floor and hear Caitlin weeping, hear phrases spoken in my mother's gentle, worried voice. The force I employed to avoid thinking deeply about my family might have been used instead to propel me toward a life of profound usefulness had I only been able to transfer the ungraspable powers of denial. Everything I did was shaped by a desire to escape the truth: that we—myself and the people I loved most—were on a horror ride. But once Ethan began to snore, I'd close my eyes and soon enough begin reliving the time six months earlier when I'd slept on a cot the night before my dad's quadruple bypass.

The feeling of being holed up in a courtesy room for out-of-town families at Piedmont Hospital, North Atlanta. Mom and Caitlin lying feet away, sharing a bed. December 22, snowless in Georgia. The room was decorated to look like a hotel, wallpapered and outfitted with a television, none of which altered our awareness of the institution's fluorescence looming just beyond the door.

And beyond that?

On the cot, I'd had nightmares of being onstage, my hands mittenlike on a guitar I couldn't remember how to play. Caitlin had thrashed in the sheets, stealing most of the bedspread as Mom made not a sound, and by the time we'd entered the cardiac unit the next morning, my dad was already wired to machines. "Good," he'd said, unwrapping the Christmas gift I'd brought him, a Beatles CD anthology of outtakes and false starts. "I need some music."

Some trips exhaust you long after they've ended. Mom couldn't smile, and I'd seen the signs of fury and forgiveness cycling through her. A crusty, magenta third-eye boil had risen from her forehead and would remain there for weeks. Caitlin was gaining weight and losing it again in a span of days. I'd been having spells of breathlessness that I believed were caused by throat nodules, wounds owing to my pterodactyl vocal style.

We'd all stared down at my dad lying there in a green paper gown, weak in the face, supine on a gurney.

They were about to carve his chest open and graft arteries onto his heart, a fact that brought my attention to the glugging beat of my own.

"Thanks for being here," Dad said, gripping my hand as a nurse shaved his chest to prep him for the incision. Dark blood leaked from a razored mole. He twitched his jaw, searching for a funny line that would settle our nerves.

Barely 8:00 A.M.

He'd stared at me with an awful sobriety in his eyes, which were faintly blue, very much like Caitlin's. He was bargaining with unknown forces, cutting deals and making vows, and I'd felt an old pride resurge, faith in a superpowered father capable of small miracles. "You're a good son, in case I haven't told you lately," he said while the nurse wiped his blood and shaved hairs with a sanitary napkin, slapping on adhesive EKG electrodes.

Caitlin's bleached hair, a darker blonde at the roots, was a slept-upon mess, tumbling over my dad as she bent toward him and whispered. A moment before, she'd told my father, "I hope when you're better, you'll learn your lesson." But she began crying as he held her, saying, "Cait, Cait, Cait."

She and I wandered to the cafeteria, letting our parents say whatever they needed to. When Mom reappeared, Caitlin followed her to the hospital chapel. I walked to a bus stop to scribble in a notebook until the hours blurred and dusk fell on Atlanta, by which point my dad was conscious enough to relay the news.

"The doctor said it's good for about twelve years."

He'd been stoned, blissed out from the best of the pharmaceutical best. His torso was bandaged, and he'd barely had the strength to lift his head and peer down at his reassembled chest.

The next day was Christmas Eve: Caitlin sleeping against my shoulder on a quiet flight home. Dad left behind in the hospital, pumped full of morphine and back to square one in the rehabilitative process, with brand-new music but no means of tuning in.

"IT WAS PERFECT." REPA toed my ribs with his boot. "Slept like a baby."

Through the bedroom windows, the sun lit his Cro-Magnon face. I'd never been happier to see him. Once the heat inside the van became too much, he'd walked Denton's streets to swipe his debit card and enter a twenty-four-hour ATM vestibule, where he'd sprawled in its AC until a patron startled him awake. "Good as new," he said. "But you should have seen that lady's face."

For me it had been a baked, grimy slumber. My hair was damp as I rose, scratching at clusters of small red welts across my back and ribs.

"How's it look?"

"Real sick," Repa said. "Like scabies."

Ethan groaned, half asleep, scratching himself with both paws. He, too, had been gored. Bite marks about his neck and face—attacked in the night by the Texan beasts of summer.

"Hell," said Repa, meaning: *Enough, already, of this dirtass scene.*

We rolled our amplifiers through an assemblage of sleeping punkers in the living room to load the Orgasmatron beneath the cocoons hanging in the tree branches. The sun was up, and my thoughts were emptied of everything but a gladness to be leaving one place for the next—the best I'd felt in a while. Before we made for the highway, Repa pulled a drumstick from the van, giving one of the nests a good smack, and then we were off, having earned just enough money for coffee and gas to the next city.

By THE TIME WE hit Philadelphia, we were road crazed. The three of us sprinted down Lancaster Avenue, chasing a gimp dog until we'd cornered the animal inside a fenced lot. We hugged one another as the mutt hobbled after pieces of jerky we tossed it. I'd lost track of what day it was and how long we'd been gone, but it felt at once like a day and a decade. We'd knocked over Atlanta and done the same with Tampa and Gainesville and so on. Now we felt Detroit's gray magnet pulling us homeward. The dog was as magnificent as anything I'd seen.

"We should take it with us," Repa said.

"Champ," Ethan said, cooing at the mutt. "He's a champ."

When it came time to play, we drank throughout the show and then some more. Over the weeks, I'd felt my tolerance rising to where a full-on drunk took more beers than I could keep track of. Repa's Philadelphian plus-one was a vagrant in a Hawaiian shirt named Leroy. He passed bottles with us after the show, impersonating celebrities as Repa fed him quarters. We stood outside the club, a half block away.

"I love you," Repa said. "Do Dangerfield."

"I love you, too." Leroy laughed. "But what I really love is some crack."

I was in the early phase of a blackout, where just enough blood to the head can give you back to the world for moment.

"Gimme a buck," Leroy said, and I grabbed him by the collar. I hadn't known I had this in me or where it came from. Lit with booze, I felt serenely violent, smelling Leroy's breath as he hooked his fingers around my arms. A bottle fell to our feet. I whispered to him—some foul, unspecific thing about what I thought of his kind. The look in Leroy's eyes: *No, not this again.*

He growled, dribbling onto my wrists, until Ethan charged me with a shoulder, railroading me to the van and urging me into the backseat.

"Hell's wrong with you?" Repa said. "He was a nice guy."

Ethan peeled the Orgasmatron's tires.

Leroy had vanished into the evening, up in smoke.

Philadelphia's night traffic moved swiftly. A few blocks up Lancaster, I realized I'd jarred something loose: the sensation pooled in my chest, rose up my throat and welled my eyes. At a stoplight, just before the tears came, I slid open the van's passenger door and leaped for the street, where I ran through the avenue, crying and laughing. Ethan paced me in the van, slowing traffic. Cars honked. I put it on for them, dashing up a grass embankment and somersaulting down as Ethan grumbled from the window. Repa was chirping, *Get 'em, get 'em*, and I knew he was calling to me and not about me.

"Get 'em."

At the next stoplight I crawled into the van, having freaked away the tears. Then we were moving again, and not a moment of this felt out of step with the fits we threw onstage. I was drunk enough that I might have confessed, told them my story from beginning to end so that they'd know exactly who I was and why I was beside them, but I was years away from that kind of language.

Repa composed himself, snapping open a beer.

"You get it all out?" Ethan asked as Repa said, "Aw, you know there's lots more where that comes from."

And we were off—to the next thing—without having bothered to get paid.

As THE ROAD SHORTENED between Detroit and our traveling show, the van became a quiet vessel. We'd changed, all of us, and weren't certain how things would be once we returned to our old lives. We'd tired of our cassettes and opted for the sound of the engine. Everything I'd sought to outrun was rushing forward to meet me. Driving north out of Knoxville, we took I-75, the highway I'd traveled with my dad three months before I headed for Detroit by way of Atlanta. Mom had sprung for me to fly down and chaperone him to Michigan in a rental car.

I'd always remember what he said, the moment I met him in the rehab lobby, a suitcase, literally, in his hand.

"I didn't get their stamp of approval. But I learned what I need to know."

Headed north, we played the Beatles CD I'd given him. He'd asked about the chords, the way the songs were put together, and I'd answered as though I knew: there's verses and a repeating chorus and these things called harmonies that most people tended to enjoy. At some point I would realize we'd never actually had conversations, exchanges of words and ideas that truly advanced our mutual understanding. We spoke clipped phrases punctuated with "I guess," buying time between words by clearing our throats, sighing. I'd lost any handle on how to be with him because my role was changing, empowered by his shame rather than anything to do with honor. I'd tried imagining I was in training for the band's tour, which at that time had been merely dates on a spreadsheet. I wanted to be ready for the all-night drives, the long hauls. It was midnight in Kentucky when Dad told me to pull over.

"Let's get a room," he said.

"I'll drive it in one shot. Save money."

"Your old man's tired."

A mute television flashed over us as we shared a motel bed. When Dad rolled onto his back to occupy the better part of the mattress, I'd curled near the edge, worrying that one wrong move might shake loose the vein work that had been done inside his chest. Taking I-75 north the next day, we let the CD spin on repeat as Dad did his best to tell me about his new friends: doctors and truck drivers and gay men, all with the same incurable disease. "Good people. Trying to do the right thing."

The music played: three botched takes of "I'm So Tired," a Lennon-less run-through of "I Me Mine."

"I guess even they screwed up sometimes," Dad said.

At the drive-throughs, he ordered diet sodas, chicken instead of hamburger. Chewing my fries, the smell of grease and the salt on my fingers, I'd felt guilty enough that I didn't enjoy a bite. Dad snatched several from the bag, chomping before he could think any more about it, saying, "Just one. . . just one ain't gonna kill me."

THE ORGASMATRON PASSED THE same Ohio landmarks, scenery my dad and I had glimpsed a season earlier. I wondered what I'd tell him about the tour, and whether, during my time away, he and my mom were back to holding hands the way they once did. I thought of Caitlin leaving for college, and of Lauren, that I might visit her dorm room once I'd caught up on sleep. I hadn't outrun anything, but even the past felt changed, somehow reduced in size by the new experiences I'd added to it.

We crossed the Michigan state line at the hour of the crows, so tired we'd begun to hallucinate. Ethan swore he saw a wolf pack scatter across the road, and Repa was out of clam chowder—the empty tins rattled beneath the seats. A strip of sunburned flesh had turned to scales on my forehead. As daylight rose, we unloaded our gear into Repa's basement.

"All she wrote," Repa said, fingering a scraggy new mustache as Ethan counted our loot, saying, "We're two hundred bucks ahead."

Enough to get us started on the next mission—which was soon to come, I hoped.

As I drove to Ridgewood Hills, my car's steering wheel was unfamiliar. And so was the sight of myself, bearded and rat-skinny, in the bathroom mirror. The softness of my own bed and the look on Caitlin's face when she woke me later that day to explain that Dad had moved in with his parents, that he'd relapsed while I was away, and that our house was going on the market—I was, after all, returning to a new life.

5

Summer of '97 was a seller's market, and the house went in no time. My parents listed it at a bargain price, and by early August it belonged to a family of four I'd never met. As for Ridgewood Hills, I'd never been so eager to ditch a place. After three years of lying about where I lived, I'd once again be able to honestly claim Dearborn—its doughnut shops and dollar movies, the Rouge River's toxic shimmer—as my home. One of Mom's brothers tipped her off about an affordable place on Dearborn's west side, which she'd snapped up from an elderly lady who was on her way to a nursing home. "Must've been meant to be," Mom said. "I can fix it up."

She gave me the address, and I drove past one afternoon. A simple brick two-bedroom, painted white, tucked in the corner of Telegraph Road and Michigan Avenue. At the edge of the lawn stood a small oak, its late-summer leaves green and fat. In the backyard was just enough space for gardening, a quiet passion Mom referred to as "*my* music." Head east a few miles on Michigan Avenue, and you'd be at Will's; three minutes farther and you'd reach the Detroit city limits. Blocks away was a record store where I could see myself working. The band had just rented a practice space a short drive north on Telegraph, before Seven Mile Road.

I was a twitch embarrassed to be nineteen and living at home, but, seeing the house, I figured I might as well crash there until the band went international. Many musicians holed up in their mom's basement, saving for vintage equipment while biding their fameless days. A recording advance, publishing rights, and residuals: I would have told you I didn't have that fantasy, but I did. Not of music videos and stadiums, but of a sustainable living.

Caitlin had been silently protesting our parents' divorce. She'd never revered our hometown the way I had and took a dreary interest in Mom's new place. She'd begun skipping shifts at the coffee shop. One day she lopped her hair into a punky, boyish mop I thought looked just great. Mom worried it was a cry for help. Though Caitlin would be leaving for Michigan State in a matter of weeks, Mom offered her the second bedroom; she wanted her to have a place to come home to. Bedrooms, a sense of home—these things mattered terribly to my sister. I'd get the basement, which suited me perfectly.

Back in Ridgewood Hills I began packing straightaway, discarding anything that wouldn't serve as a muse or ruse for my musical identity. I shed years of clutter—Day-Glo T-shirts, baseball caps, and yearbooks—destroying evidence of who I'd been, while harboring a secret vision that my life's debris might one day fascinate a cult of music aficionados. Here was the chance to do away with incriminations: baseball cards, my baptism candle and hockey trophies. All that would be left to identify me would be my records.

What I'd salvaged from my bedroom could easily be hauled

away in my latest 'mobile, a turd-brown '87 minivan with a smashed back window. The only things Mom insisted on keeping were family photo albums, a few of which she'd yet to locate.

"Where are those albums?" she said. "Find those albums."

She wanted nothing to do with our old furniture; my dad could keep it. He'd been staying not far from Ridgewood Hills in the basement of a condo his parents had moved into after leaving the Dearborn Heights home they'd owned since the 1960s. My parents had lived their teenage years directly across from each other, on a street called Evangeline. Dad long ago caught his first glimpse of my mom beyond the newly paved road. Mom's folks were still there, in a cavernous four-bedroom that now faced a family of Arabs who'd repainted Dad's old house and done away with the ever-present American flag.

As children, Caitlin and I had stared out the windows of my dad's old home, pining for the alternate universe—about thirty yards, door-to-door—across Evangeline. The flags on porches and trimmed shrubbery, the geometric baby-boom architecture, gave the impression that the neighborhood would never change. It had seemed perfectly logical then that my parents had lived within spitting distance, and we'd referred to the two sides of Evangeline Street respectively: Dad's side and Mom's side.

On holidays, tradition was that Dad's side came first, where inside the front door we met the fragrance of baking ham and dozens of relatives. Dad's eight siblings and their spouses. Our cousins—multiplying so quickly they became hard to remember. In the living room were crucifixes and needlepoint tapestries. Above the mantel were graduation photos of all nine children, the last few smiling. My dad, the third oldest, stared intensely out from the past in a black-and-white portrait, artificially pigmented so that his eyes were sky blue, his hair a pastel yellow.

We'd be there a couple of hours on Christmas and Easter. Grandma might take to the piano for a seasonal number, while Grandpa watched *The Lawrence Welk Show*, a drink in his hand, until the time came to carve the meat. Sometimes he'd hum along to Grandma's playing, reminding us he'd been a crooner—the Frank Sinatra of Buffalo, as my dad told it. Based on Dad's accounts, my grandfather had been a number of things: A minor-league baseball pitcher. A jujitsu expert, who could paralyze a grown man with a swift Vulcan-like grip of the collarbone. He'd owned gas stations and doughnut shops, was a man of renown at the local Knights of Columbus Hall.

One thing everyone agreed on was that Grandpa had been orphaned, abandoned early in the century by Irish immigrants. My last name was an adopted syllable belonging to a stern German woman who'd taken him in and put him to work.

"A street kid," Dad would say. "Your grandpa was in Irish gangs," though I never got close enough to the bald liver-spotted man in the La-Z-Boy to test these legends. Dad often said that Grandpa had given it to him worse than I'd ever know, reminding me of it each time he took a belt to my bare ass. Seeing Grandpa clicking the remote and grinding cigarettes— how quickly his face changed from grin to scowl when someone obstructed his view of the set—I could believe it.

No place demanded better manners. Dad used to rake a harsh comb over my scalp as we proceeded up the driveway. "Please" and "thank you" would not suffice. His command was not to "give one-word answers" to questions posed. He'd once offered an ice-cream reward in return for my carrying on a sufficiently coherent conversation with my grandfather, but the old man's presence canceled every trace of my personality. I went blank. I could not—did not want to—be found.

Caitlin averted scrutiny with a girlish coquetry as we both

endured the time on Dad's side, anxious to cross the street. We knew it pained my dad to see us rush the door of Mom's parents, bursting in as though we'd earned our freedom. No matter the occasion, Mom's parents had presents waiting: candy and AA-battery-powered gadgetry, plastic oddities they'd read about in the paper. We called Mom's dad Papa. We called her mother Lady Grandma, for her faux-silk scarves and White Shoulders perfume. Always, she'd offer up her famously charred cookies. Mom's youngest brother, Steve, snuck whoopee cushions and handshake buzzers into my pockets; as I got older, he slipped me recordings of his rock albums. AC/DC and Ozzy Osbourne.

Between Mom and Dad's families there'd been, at most, a wave from their opposing porches and a routine greeting called over the curbs. Two decades of visiting both homes, yet I'd never once seen my mom's parents cross the street to drop in on Dad's side, or vice versa. Separate worlds, we understood, divided by Evangeline Street when it was paved in the early sixties.

MOM HAD COME CLEAN to her parents about Dad's problem and her impending divorce. She'd visited them to confess the general details, but did she use the word "crack"? The class A mother of all narcotics. Or did she simply say "drugs"?

I'd hoped we'd return to Dearborn without anyone suspecting a thing. Telling Lauren of my parents' separation, I'd described the arrangement as a sort of vacation and gave her no opportunity to console me. "Do you feel okay?" she'd asked, eighty miles away in her dormitory. "Is Caitlin all right?" I imagined her adventuring deep into college nights while exploring the ceremonies of coed living. Smoking joints in the moonlight. Keg parties. So little chance our relationship would survive, but neither of us had the heart to wield that sword on our own without definitive reason.

"It will be good for everyone to get out of here," I said.

Lauren didn't know about the drugs, though she would. Our cover was blown, and starting with Mom's parents, the world was going to learn about Dad's crack and our busted home.

ONCE I'D FINISHED PACKING my bedroom, Mom assigned me the task of boxing up our basement's clutter. I swatted Christmas wreaths and tinsel into bags and shoved old sporting equipment into boxes. The only items of interest were the photo albums and scrapbooks, my parents' high school annuals. And though I was certain of having once flipped through the yellowing Polaroids and news clippings, they now revealed things altogether different: Dad's proud, chiseled face. Mom in a pink jumper, a flower in her hair. I stood there examining their young, unknowing eyes and felt something I never had before: pity for my parents' younger selves and this future they'd never have bargained for.

Caitlin and I knew the vague outlines of their pasts. Mom had told us about the afternoon Dad pulled up next to her outside the high school to ask if she'd like a ride. He'd driven to school in the van his father's doughnut shop used for deliveries. The day he'd rolled down the driver's-side window was the first time he'd spoken to my mom, though they'd been neighbors for years. His light blond hair was close cropped and parted fastidiously in the antihippie style of 1967, his neck thick from shoulder lifts in the weight room. He'd played in a state championship football game at Tiger Stadium that fall, losing by a touchdown to a team from Detroit, but would soon be on his way to the Air Force Academy, full-ride scholarship.

My mom, a year younger, was small in the waist and had

grown her blonde board-ironed hair to her shoulders. Bashfully pretty—you could tell from her sideways glance at the cameras, smiling at the surprise of the flash. She'd loved books, the Moody Blues, and worked for the school newspaper. She'd seen the Beatles at Olympia Stadium in '65, and her prized possession was a dictionary she'd won in a writing contest. Dad had been a forgivable troublemaker, a former altar boy at the Catholic church both families attended.

"Do you like him?" one of Mom's brothers asked the day my dad dropped her off.

"He's okay."

"But he has those big muscles."

And every time she told the story, she said, "You know, I'd never noticed before he mentioned it."

Nineteen sixty-eight: they went on a few dates, diners and drive-in movies. They saw each other until my dad left for basic training, en route to the Academy's Colorado Springs campus, where he wrote her letters from his military-style dorm. Mom's parents urged her to sharpen her typing skills, maybe land a secretarial job at Ford World Headquarters. She also claimed that her parents had been tougher on her than we'd ever believe; though who'd imagine Papa or Lady Grandma raising their voices, their gentle hands?

When Mom was accepted to a university two hours west of Detroit, her parents balked. Having barely ventured beyond the Michigan state line, she took out a loan, on a hunch that there might be life beyond typing memos. Western Michigan University was as extravagant as she could manage. "A rinky-dink school" she called it, telling of her life there, a flicker of time in the mill town of Kalamazoo.

I'd pieced together my father's years at the Academy through scenes he recalled as we tossed baseballs or stopped for a moment on a rink, our skates dusted with ice shavings, when we were alone and I was his apprentice. Little of what he told about those days had much to do with the Academy itself. Dad talked about singing R & B hits in the back of the bus with the black cadets, about rabble-rousing and all manner of hijinks. The time he tore his scrotum on a daredevil ski jump in the nearby Rockies, barreling over a boulder the size of a house. These yarns unraveled as he was teaching me how to throw a fastball or to dig the blades of my skates into the ice.

"I wasn't fast, but I was quick," he'd say. "You gotta learn to use your leverage."

On the rink, he'd demonstrate a slow-motion body check, bending low to dig his shoulder into my ribs.

"It's not always how big you are. It's how you use what you've got."

I was lean—scrawny. Eventually I grew two inches taller than him; built like my mom's brothers, he'd say. But when it came to running the fifty-yard dash, stealing bases, or freewheeling on the ice, I was as fast as anyone. I'd inherited none of his girth or killer instinct, but I could motor my legs so fiercely that no one could catch me.

I TOOK DOWN MY first fifth of whiskey a few nights before we left Ridgewood Hills for good. The house was mostly packed. All that was left standing were our beds, surrounded by boxes, the cardboard flaps taped shut and labeled. Will and I had nipped the bottle—Jack Daniels, that fabled rock and roll elixir—on our way to a show downtown. Will had keen musical tastes but was impressed that my band's low end rivaled his favorite records and did so on a budget. Which urged me to impress upon him that I was, truly, as unhinged as the art. On our way home from the gig, I decided to guzzle the fifth, let him witness the result.

"You crazy Mick," Will said, after I'd taken the first dramatic pull.

I'd grown fangs and was frothing at the gums before I'd knocked back half of the bottle. I could no longer taste the whiskey's burn or gauge its powers sip by sip. We cruised Detroit in Will's truck, blasting tapes he'd made of pop 45s slowed down to 33 rpms—Eddie Money death sludge—as I howled at the vacant buildings. Soon enough, Will called it a night, insisting on chauffeuring me to Ridgewood Hills. I agreed, mostly because I wasn't ready to be alone. As we pulled off the highway, I asked to be dropped near my grand-parents' condo, where my dad may or may not be asleep in the basement.

"Gotta walk it off, man."

Will didn't argue. He pulled to the shoulder on a quiet stretch of road, a half mile or so from the condo.

"You cool?" he said.

The nights were dark out that way. The electric fuzz of the city could not be found in the sky above. That breezy silence I'd never gotten used to.

"Walk it off" was all I managed, butting my knuckles into his.

"Take it sleazy."

It must have been 2:00 A.M. as I'd stumbled out of his truck. After a few paces, I began wheezing. Each inhalation took place inside my head, a hot pant with each footfall, in between which I muttered lyrics. The world quaked in front of me; I might have been viewing it from inside a gas mask. The liquor was working its way through me as the condo's porch lights came into view a few paces up the road. There were several attached homes that all looked the same, but I knew the one.

After I'd banged the screen door a few times, my grand-mother appeared, a small, able-bodied, gray-haired woman, fidgety in the porch light, without her mascara. She squinted until she realized who I was. She asked if I'd been drinking.

"Uh-huh."

But she showed me to the staircase, and in the basement I found Dad asleep on a mattress in a semifinished storage room. A frosted sheet of plastic came aglow in the ceiling as I snapped the light switch. The walls had long ago been papered, but the closetlike space held little more than a dresser and an alarm clock. Where he'd hung his suits and ties was anyone's guess.

I had no plan; only then did I realize it. I'd been lured there by something. Fear. And a drunken urge to look it in the face.

Dad sprang from the bed, anticipating an intruder, but I ordered him to sit down. My license to rage—every worrisome thought melted away so that there was nothing but raw impulse. He must have seen in my eyes the type of hell I was capable of making. He was shirtless, the surgical scars like dribbled wax on his chest. From his neck a silver cross dangled on a chain. Though he wore only his underwear, he made no effort to cover himself. He sat squinting, pulling at his jaw.

"What's wrong?" he said. "What's happening?"

I'd been spending time with a certain poem by a drunken madman, in which the wordsmith claimed there wasn't a man on earth he feared being alone with, as long as both of them were chained to opposing corners of a cell. Believing his black thoughts could paralyze the most heinous men, he'd probe their minds with verse, drive them inward until they chewed their wrists to escape his crazy sermon. There in the basement—it went something like that.

I set loose a horrendous spiel I'd never remember entirely, saying god-awful things—most of them lies—simply because I could. Each time Dad attempted to stand, I commanded him back to the bed. He covered his ears and pounded the mattress.

I told him Mom was drinking every night, that I'd been smoking rocks, just to show him how easy it would be to man up and quit, cold turkey.

"What?" he said.

"You know," I yelled. "You know what I mean."

"Keep it down," he said. "Your grandpa's asleep up there."

As I remember it, I felt not a tinge of anger. It was something more, a desire to goad him into a fight that would shatter all boundaries. My grandfather, we knew, was living his final days, and I threatened to walk upstairs and bust the old man's legs.

Dad shot up, raising a fist. I cocked mine and squared my shoulders, until he threw himself back to the mattress. It was the first power I'd ever exerted over him, brutally and with vague knowledge of his unreciprocated love for his half-alive father.

"Fuck, fucking, fuck," he said. "I'm sorry for everything."

It wasn't long before I'd burned through whatever lunacy was keeping me upright. The room twirled, and I crouched to keep my balance, finally toppling onto the carpet and crying in a way I hadn't since I was a kid. The last thing I remember saying was, "You've always thought I was a pussy"; his voice quickly softened, and he began speaking quietly about a time I'd been blindsided by an opponent twice my size on a hockey rink.

I'd recently done everything I could to erase any evidence I'd ever played the game, had tossed away every photo of myself in a jersey, stick in hand.

"I thought you'd be out cold," Dad said. "But you got right back up."

It'd been a first-rate cheap shot, meant to paralyze. The impact of the flying elbow knocked the helmet off my skull, sent my body propelloring before it smashed against the ice.

A semifinal game. The bleachers full, the crowd groaning as I came to.

"You got up," Dad said, "and scored the winning goal."

This was true. Though I'd never been much good for anything other than skating with a frantic speed, the puck had come to the blade of my stick, and I'd made a sprint, eluding defensemen before faking out the goalie, wristing the puck into the upper-left corner. The crowd cheered, banging the Plexiglas. A blast of manic inspiration I'd had no idea I was capable of.

"That's how I think of you," Dad said.

For a moment, the floor ceased spinning. Dad reached out a hand. His sallow face and sleep-matted hair and scarred body came fully into view as he pulled me close. And I let myself fall into him. And this I hadn't forgotten, because the sensation came flooding back to me: the strength of his arms, holding me as a child, the safest feeling I'd known because it'd been true, then, when love required only the most fundamental expression. My cheek pressed against his bare shoulder, the freckled, familiar skin, and I rested like that for as long as I could stand it, until from his deathbed my grandfather howled through the house, "What in hell's going on down there."

STEERING CLEAR OF HIM for the next few days, I hoped what had happened would be eclipsed by the anxieties of moving. Dad came by to do yard work without asking for assistance or coming inside, while Caitlin spared several family keepsakes from the Dumpster. We'd pulled apart our house into two separate loads, yet there always seemed to be something we'd missed. I was giving the basement a final once-over when I came across the last of the pictures, a small vinyl album containing shots of my mom with a dimpled, curly-haired young man of Mediterranean pigment. They wore winter hats and smiled, holding gloved hands. She looked about my age, a little older. When I found her in the kitchen wrapping dishes with newspaper, I flashed the photos.

"Jeez," she said. "Where did you find those?"

"Who's this guy?"

"I dated after your dad broke off the engagement. We were engaged on and off for three years. He never knew what he wanted. But when I'd see other people it drove him nuts."

This was news. The lore I recalled was that Dad popped the question in a parked car, outside a Howard Johnson's Restaurant on Telegraph Road. Wearing the ring, Mom had joined him for a steak dinner, and this was the tale of innocent, inauspicious beginnings Caitlin and I thought of as we passed the restaurant countless times over the years.

I gave the photo a second look, despising the young man: such an amiable-looking fellow with easy-going eyes and that hairpiece of tight, fusilli curls. You knew he'd achieved the good life somewhere; he had the face for it. And there was my mom, gleaming blondly beside him, pretty as ever. I was just coming to understand that for every one of life's turns, there are a thousand unknown alternatives left behind. Here was one of my mother's, encased in a laminated sleeve.

"Maybe I could have been this guy's kid," I said. "Looks like he has a perm?"

"Oh, throw those out." She continued swiping empty cabinets with a feather duster. "What else did you find down there?"

"Dad's guitar." His six-string Alvarez with a fist-sized hole near the bridge, indicating what frustration the instrument had given him. I'd played my first chords on it, a relic that dated back to a brief phase when Dad wore a denim jacket and ordered jazz LPs, many of which I'd slipped into my own crates.

"He hasn't touched that thing in twenty years." Mom was in a spell, cat-climbing the countertops and dusting crumbs as I stood below, ready to catch her. "I gave him that guitar, you know?"

These people who'd strummed guitars and collected albums were versions of my parents I couldn't yet reconcile. Caitlin had always taken special delight in the post-Academy photos of our old man shirtless beneath his denim jacket, with lamb-chop sideburns. We'd laughed at the muscled ruffian in flared jeans, wrenching on a VW Beetle as my mom, tan legged, hair parted Joni-style, leaned against the fender. To me, they'd looked pretty happening, smiling, the two of them.

"Our parents were burnouts" was Caitlin's take. She'd been upstairs all this time, refusing to let anyone help her disassemble her bedroom yet not moving an inch to begin doing so herself.

TRUSTING NO ONE WITH my guitars and records, I set them aside on the front lawn. Despite the sunny afternoon, the neighborhood was silent. Garage doors were closed and the blinds drawn, every lawn trimmed in accordance with some virtue of sameness I'd never forgive. Nobody came to see us off. Mom directed our boxes into a moving truck, making sure nothing got mixed up. With nowhere to be, Caitlin sat in her Escort waiting for us to lead her away, while my dad was elsewhere, not about to stand watching as we left without him.

The divorce wasn't yet official, but there was still a sense that the arrangement was a bluff. Caitlin refused to watch as her bedposts were carried from the house. It wasn't that she'd loved living there; it was the haste of our departure. For me, my mother's voice and polite directives to the men stacking our boxes made things easy.

"You take your guitar," she said, sitting on the porch,

humoring me with a nod toward my cracked and duct taped road case. "That's a good idea."

Earlier that week, one of her brothers had called to tell me I was a man of honor for sticking by my mother during these difficult times.

"You take care of her," he'd said.

But I knew it wasn't me carrying the weight, taking care.

When the truck's door was rolled down and latched, I looked up at the house, swearing I'd never see it again—and I never would. Dad had found a condo not far from there. Over the next few days, his brothers would help him haul away our couches and tables. Mom would buy new rugs and curtains. She'd paint the new place blue, if she wanted, her favorite color, the calmest shade she could imagine.

"Guess that's it," she said. "You never liked it here anyway."

The truck left our driveway, headed for Dearborn. I packed my guitar into my minivan, coaxing Ozzy into the front seat as I selected the perfect song for the twenty-minute ride, a punk rock barn burner about making a run for it, going out of this world and never coming back. I turned up the dial as I blazed the highway, speeding past Mom in her station wagon and Caitlin in her Escort, then past the moving truck, and everything else.

6

Repa wagged his head, swung his fist like a hammer.

"Never," he said. "No way. I can't live with it."

We stood in an alley behind an impoverished strip mall. On the opposite side of the building was a Chinese carryout with greasy windows and a few brand-X businesses. Our new practice room was one flight up in a warehouse above a Big Lots discount store. In the trunk of Ethan's Toyota Corolla were two hundred black T-shirts on which the band's logo was printed above the image of a man with a gun to his head. Ethan held one up, spreading it wide for our inspection. If not for his efforts, there'd have been no shirts or decals, no accessories whatsoever, only song.

"It's a shit vibe." Repa turned to me. "You know it."

Tuesday-night rehearsal had been the usual three-hour storm of dirty noise, a half-conscious run through our set—then again and again. Four times was routine, though we'd become so enraptured it was difficult to tell whether we improved anything one set to the next. Our touring had left us in tip-top form, and we always played best with no audience but one another. Local gigs, however, were becoming lucrative—as much as two hundred dollars per show—and our rehearsal space was the fruit of an increasing band fund. Between songs, the three of us had split a case of beer and a handle of Popov, more than usual for a weeknight. We were feeling the effects now that we'd ventured into the autumn evening.

"Can you imagine," Repa said, "the kind of chickenshit who'd wear a thing like that?"

"I got a deal on these." Ethan teetered, an easy kill when it came to booze. His brown eyes took wild courses, as if glimpsing a number of worlds at once. "Only cost two bucks apiece," he said.

Early October. The orange-black hue of the season, the moon visible through the shedding trees. I sensed a good mixture coursing through me—a deep, fuzzy buzz that might last awhile—and wanted the night to end somewhere other than my new basement digs. It would come on like that, the purr of some drunken muse, asking: *What else is there, where else is there to be?* That's when I'd pine for Lauren. It didn't help that we'd met in autumn, four years earlier, tangling on a bed of flannel shirts in Ford Field. It had been my first time; hers, too. A time that could seem so distant, but I remembered the smell of her then: a lotionlike sweetness. Once or twice I'd picked up that scent in movie theaters or concert halls, had trailed it until it disappeared. I thought I might never find it again, yet the fall breeze revived the possibility.

Repa snatched a T-shirt, spreading it wide, dancing with it across the gravel lot, while I pictured Lauren's dorm room, out there in the land of student riots and parties gone Babylon—Michigan State University, a mere hour's drive. I knew there'd be a pumpkin on her windowsill and paper ghouls dangling from the ceiling. At this hour she'd be asleep in sweatpants torn at the knees and some faded T-shirt, the kind of thing only a slumbering young woman could wear with any grace.

"Oh, baby. Yes!" Repa's argument veered toward the abstract. He kissed the silk-screened face, tongued the gun. "Do me. Do me where there's pain." Trotting now, clicking his heels, inspiring Ethan to break into song. They laughed; they traded verse. There could be hours of this. Neither of them noticed me inching away. By the time they'd realized I'd left, the shirts would be folded and stowed, awaiting future scrutiny.

As I cranked the starter of my minivan, driving eighty miles of highway to Lauren's East Lansing campus seemed a valiant idea, a challenge to my wits. I knew the DUI preemptives: slapping my jaw, palming an eye when the lines in the road doubled. Set the cruise at sixty-five; keep the blood sugar up; more beer, candy, nicotine. Windows down. Never, ever use the heater. Just outside the city the highway would open up, stretching empty and dark through the Michigan farmlands. It was a straight shot on Interstate 96, the junction just a few miles away. A quick westward turn off Telegraph Road, before I gave myself time to think it over.

GRAND RIVER AVENUE WAS empty as my minivan rattled into town. East Lansing's bars had closed, the fraternity mansions dark but for porch lights. Night crawlers outside the 7-Eleven and no one else around. I'd arrived this way a few nights the year before, when Lauren had been a freshman, cold-calling her from an all-night diner's pay phone and waking hours later in her bunk. My hit-and-run experience of the collegiate dream.

We claimed we were taking a break, or broken up. But it only took one of us mustering the late-night nerve to call, and once we found each other there'd be an exciting instant when our old passions proved their endurance. She was another world, a place where I sought shelter when my soul was on the fringe. I never knew it until I arrived.

I pulled up to the same old diner and punched the buttons of a pay phone carved with initials and plastered with stickers. The line rang, a jangling moment that forced me to consider my alternative if Lauren didn't pick up: sleep in the minivan, in some lot far beyond the campus's parking-ticket entrapment.

"Hello?"

"I'm on Grand River. Can I come over?"

"You know where to go," Lauren said. "I'll let you in."

• • •

Sun blasted through the dormitory windows, alerting me to the worst headache and a sucked-dry feeling—in a matter of minutes I was scheduled to begin the morning shift at Repeat the Beat Records, where I'd been employed the past couple months. I climbed out of Lauren's bed to reach for her cordless. "Calling in drunk" was how Repa described this type of postbinge operation, when you awake half cockeyed, feeling thrashed enough that your voice conveys an indisputable illness.

"I'm sick, man. Don't think I can make it."

The record shop's manager, a progressive rock connoisseur with a poodled mullet, wasn't yet onto me.

"You sound like hell," he said.

Lauren had left for class. Her hair raking my face as she climbed over my aching limbs was the only memory I had of her having been there at all. The only other evidence was a water bottle nestled in my crotch, a note stuck to it: DRINK. It said so much about why I loved her, though I was no longer in love.

My hair had grown long, chin length, and smelled of stale spirits. I lay down ass-flat on the floor to allow my intestines percolation time. A feeling like rug burn worked itself up my throat. For a while I stared at the ceiling, upon which fluorescent decals were arranged in the shape of a constellation. When this cosmos became too much to consider, I turned to Lauren's walls, decorated with art assignments and poems and a photo of me that I couldn't remember being taken.

And there, perched on her windowsill, was the pumpkin—a sallow, yellowing gourd, really.

Caitlin was nearby, in a dorm I'd never seen. Worse than the bruised tenderness of my eyeballs was the guilt of realizing she hadn't crossed my mind the night before. I'd been putting stock in the idea that here, in this state-college wonderland, Caitlin would have her shot at good living. Surely Mom was also banking on this. Caitlin would be the long-distance proof that our family was carrying on. Her academic awards would outshine my van tours. She'd return to Dearborn blonde and fit, tan from spring-break travels, carrying scholarly medallions that would divert attentions from my expanding gut and mangy hair and the mounting, never-mentioned evidence that I was becoming a drunk. For Caitlin: a career in humanities or veterinary science; something useful and peaceable and immune to future calamities.

I'D BEEN ON CAMPUS a couple days when there was a knock at Lauren's door. She wasn't due back for hours, and I inched down the volume of her stereo, hoping the slow fade would fool whoever was outside into believing the music had been carried off by wind.

Three more knocks.

I'd been indulging in a faux breakdown, the type of catatonic rest I believed any hardworking musician deserved. The greats had holed up in Chelsea Hotel. My reprieve was Marshall-Adams dormitory, where Lauren kissed me hard before leaving for biology, the two of us carrying on as though we each hadn't seen a world of new things we had no way of sharing. Though she must have known the days had temporarily broken me, because she held me tight as we lay watching VHS tapes. In her arms I'd been able to sleep for hours on end, never once thinking anyone might discover me.

From the hallway, I heard my sister call my name.

I walked over and slid the deadbolt.

Standing in the doorway, Caitlin was a wreck. Her eyes had the drear of someone who'd stared too long at the sun. Her blonde hair was tangled and streaked with red dye. She wore a sweatshirt and blue jeans.

"Will you talk to me?" she said. "Lauren told me you were here."

Beneath a shaft of light, standing in the institution-green hallway, my sister came suddenly and fully into focus—clearer than ever before. Funny how, glimpsing someone I'd known my entire life, I saw afresh the sunspots fading into the angles of her nose, the graceful bend of her wrist as she pressed the butt of her palm to her forehead. The first etchings of crow's-feet as she clenched her eyes. Cafeteria food had added weight to her face, rounding her soft cheeks.

"Don't cry," I said. "It's okay."

I followed her outside, where we set out beneath the towering grids of dormitory windows. So many people, stacked atop one another—groping and studying and dabbling in expendable lifestyles. Music was blaring, bad stuff. I'd never have admitted it, but places like that terrified me. After we'd walked far enough that I became lost, Caitlin said, "Can I have your keys? Just go for a drive?"

"I'll drive you," I said, knowing she wouldn't be able to massage my minivan's temperamental ignition. "Where you wanna go?"

We didn't look each other in the eye, a kind of avoidance we'd perfected in churches while shaking the hands of strangers—*Peace be with you . . . And also with you*—before proclaiming the mystery of faith and accepting Christ's Body on our tongues.

"I can't stop thinking about driving a car into a wall," Caitlin said, "so that no one would know I meant to do it."

I gripped her wrist, yanked her until we were standing still. Then she snatched back her arm and avoided me by examining a silver watch Lauren had given her as a birthday present, precious to her, I could tell, like some anti-evil talisman. The sidewalks were littered with scraps of leaves. I felt the thick, prickling lethargy of having sat motionless for one day too many. Chatter sounded in every direction as students reeled by with backpacks. I'd endure it each time I was there, a longing for whatever I was missing out on: the collegiate verve, the mid-American coming of age. Then I'd think of the band and be satisfied that I was where I belonged.

"Don't talk like that," I said. "It screws with your mind."

Caitlin huddled into me, crying slowly. Like my mom, a two-pronged vein rose in her forehead when she was upset. She could seem so childlike, not in her gestures or words but in how completely her face gave away her feelings. This, I knew, was something she regretted about herself.

"I just want to leave," she said.

I held her tightly. Small crowds passed us thoughtlessly—we were typical, indistinct, a couple who'd had a spat or flunked our chemistry exams.

"How long have you been here?" Caitlin said. "Why didn't you tell me you were coming?"

There was no excuse. Over two days, I'd accomplished little more than the alphabetization of Lauren's CD collection, recordings from a couple years earlier that already rang nostalgic—aside from a copy of my band's CD, which I'd confiscated on sight. One more attempt to cleave my life in two: music and all else. I'd also read from her diary, the better half of it about me, and none of those bits were entirely flattering. Between classes, Lauren smuggled me fish sticks from the cafeteria, asking what my problem were as I scarfed the items, wounded by her secret theories about my life. *Distant* is what she'd written. *Unreachable*.

"I was going to call you," I told Caitlin, though I'd already compartmentalized this visit to East Lansing as a private misadventure, a semiclandestine bender.

Visiting my sister should be an official event, a rose-in-hand occasion.

"I hate it here," she said. "These people are nasty."

"What about your roommate?"

"She and her friends stare at me when I walk in. She lets these guys sleep in our room. I came home the other night, and some ass was in my bed. She sucks. She has pictures of herself in swimsuits all over the place."

"Man," I said. "That's sick."

Caitlin said, "I want to die sometimes."

"Hey, now." I gave her a gentle shake.

Having indulged so often in dark fantasy, I felt a glib ownership of her idea, as though I'd braved the trenches of depression and had gleaned profound insight. "It's gonna be fine," I said. "Smart people get that way sometimes."

Caitlin tugged at her sweatshirt sleeves, pulling the ends over her hands, staring off with a look that said, *No, I wasn't hearing a damn word.*

After that we walked aimlessly, saying nothing.

Months earlier, while driving home from the Atlanta rehab, my dad had told me about an acoustic chamber he'd stood inside while studying automotive sound cancellation—his attempt to establish a bond, seeking common ground through auditory science. The chamber, he'd said, was a room-sized vacuum where audio waves were rendered inaudible by the balanced vibrations of carefully tuned, opposing frequencies. Sound pitted against sound, equaling silence; a void where even the most deafening decibels existed unheard, quiet as air, yet occurring nonetheless like mute explosions. This was the silence between Caitlin and me: both of us waiting for some unknowable frequency to lower in pitch, so that whatever was there would begin to wail and prove it existed.

We reached her dorm, where she stood at the door, asking if I'd come by again.

"I'll come back real soon. You just have to take it easy."

"Can't I just take your car?"

Tears had glossed the skin beneath her eyes, and in them was a look as though another night in the hormonal wilderness of Michigan State University would be unbearable. Whatever she meant to tell me, I wasn't ready to understand.

"Goddamnit," I said.

I hugged her, holding on a little longer than usual. Up close, I noticed the puncture in her earlobe where an earring was supposed to be.

"I love you," I said. "Don't let these fucks get to you."

"But they're everywhere," she said.

"Is there anything I can do?"

"Trim that nasty-ass hair before you come back."

"Yeah, yeah. Yeah, maybe."

"Or else I'll do it." Finally, she smiled. "Nice and neat."

Reaching for my bangs, pretending to snip them clean with her fingers.

LATER THAT EVENING, GRAND River Avenue filled with students protesting a campus-wide ban on the football-season tailgate parties for which the school was infamous. Through Lauren's window, we heard the commotion stirring through the courtyard. I'd decided it was my last night there.

"Want to check it out?" she said.

"They're rioting over tailgating? Aren't student riots supposed to be about wars?"

"Some people," Lauren said, "think this is fascist."

When we made it to the street, there was fire and a mob of hundreds chanting *Bullshit! Bullshit!* gathered around the blaze. A young man in a mesh jersey was lifted above the crowd, reaching for a traffic-signal box that hung from a cable above the avenue. They lifted him until the steel box was cuddled in his arms; he dangled from it, piñata-like, as those with bottles in their hands raised them to the light.

Lauren took my arm as we watched from a distance too far to tell what, exactly, was on fire. East Lansing had brought about no drastic changes in her, not that I could tell. Her brown hair was crimped at the bangs. We were wearing flannel. She leaned into me.

"My sister's okay here?" I said.

"I think so."

Lauren kept her eyes on the crowd. Behind us a police squad in riot gear arrived, their face masks drawn, some with leashed dogs, charging toward the conflagration. When, at the periphery, a boy in a backward ball cap dug into a box of beer and the first bottle was thrown aimlessly into the crowd, Lauren and I retreated to her dorm. As we passed Caitlin's building, I counted the windows, unsure which was hers yet convinced it was one that was unlit, and that inside all was quiet.

• • •

A late-October morning, trees bare up and down the street, a season's worth of fallen leaves swept to piles at the curb; half the kitchen painted white, the other half still yellowed from years of stovetop fumes; the gas heater getting its first chance to prove it worked and doing a fine job, warming even my lair in the basement. Our new home: shaping up and in working order. Mom and I: housemates, grateful exiles. Everything seemed to be coming together slowly but coming together nonetheless, and this was the state of things in general when the psych ward called.

The band had just returned from a two-day jaunt through Canada. I was coming around after a heavy sleep in the basement and could tell from Mom's voice—monochromatic and blunt in the kitchen upstairs—that everything was not at all in its right place.

"And she's safe? She's okay?"

Usually I rose from the mattress in a doltish, uncaffeinated trance, but I tore off the sheets and dressed frantically, calling up the stairwell to my mom, who wasn't answering. When I entered the kitchen, she stood clutching the phone.

"I thought this was over," she said.

She relayed the news as though she'd already spoken it a thousand times: Caitlin had been driven to the hospital by a girl from the dorms, had said she needed help and didn't know what she'd do if left to herself for another minute.

"I've got to talk to her," Mom said. "We've got to bring her home."

Dainty, five foot four, her forearms slender as chair legs, my mother had the ability to quickly galvanize for emergencies: Dad's fluke 1981 heart attack, puddles of vomit, my childhood hernias and gashed limbs, Ozzy half dead and bloody eyed after being hit by a Cadillac. She'd move swiftly, with sheer focus, dirtying her hands while projecting a certainty that everything was soon to be okay. Ozzy would be stitched like new. I'd be healthy and healed, ready to live again.

Then came the crack pipes, rehabs, divorce papers, and a new mortgage, all of which she'd managed with a grace I'd spend my life trying to attain.

Caitlin's plunges into despair were what left Mom aghast. Her gentle ways had never consoled my sister to the extent they did me, nor could she interpret Caitlin's wounds with the second-sense accuracy she could mine. My mother's love for us was so wide ranging that the question of comparison, of whom she loved more, seemed irrelevant. Only years later would she and I agree that the unspoken closeness we shared simply could not, no matter how we tried, expand to include my sister's whorl of feelings. In this way, my sister spiraled beyond us. Caitlin's fits bore closer resemblance to my dad's wild moods, and there was no changing that: the stuff of which we were made.

"I knew something was wrong," Mom said. "She couldn't tell me, but I knew."

She dropped the phone to the kitchen floor, coughing until her eyes watered. These hacking spells had begun with the divorce proceedings and were worsening, attacking during the climaxes of made-for-TV movies, as she skimmed the *Free Press* Metro Section. I'd rarely seen her cry but had watched a hundred times as she coughed herself to tears.

She retrieved an inhaler from the cupboard, huffing on the mouthpiece as the cartridge hissed. I couldn't bear to tell Mom the shape Caitlin had been in when I'd seen her weeks before. I stood drawing heavy breaths as if they might soothe her lungs.

"I just need a month," she said. "A month of nothing. A simple, boring month."

My sister's sorrow wasn't a mystery to me because I sensed it vaguely in myself.

But I feared her pain—the thought of it turned me into a coward.

"Is she gonna drop out of school?" I said.

This was no better than my response two years earlier when Caitlin swallowed a bottle of pills and leaped from her bedroom's second-story window, landing in the shrubs before she returned, scuffed and lazy eyed, through the front door of our Ridgewood Hills house. Mom had rushed her to the ER, where the medics pumped her stomach and fed her charcoal, and if anyone asked, we claimed she'd had an episode with her heart. Much easier to imagine: my sister's young body on an operating table, her delicate heart repaired like new. What I'd never be able to picture was Caitlin opening that window, the look on her face as she passed over the sill.

MOM PULLED UP THE driveway with Caitlin in the passenger seat.

The station wagon was crammed with furnishings from my sister's dorm room—lamps, radio, a beanbag, garbage bags stuffed with clothes. All of which I carried to her upstairs bedroom and set in places I thought they belonged. Caitlin lay in bed a few days, sulking downstairs in the evening to watch TV in a medicated slump. Someone with a diploma had bandied about the term "manic depression," about which I knew only what Hendrix had sung in his '67 single of the same name. Mom tried every solution she could think of—scheduling therapists and buying mood lamps—coming home on lunch breaks to check on my sister. She sat with Caitlin through the evenings, watching television as the sitcoms aired one after the other.

None of us knew what to say, but we were together again.

Seeing the light in Caitlin's bedroom window when I'd return home during the witching hours would assure me she was safe—reading late or having gone to sleep, yet to master her fear of the dark. If I checked on her, the bedroom door would be cracked enough that I'd see her legs, lumped beneath the bedspread. Other nights she'd appear in the kitchen to share a glass of water with me, passing the cup back and forth, always sparing me the last sip.

"You take it," she'd say, sleepy in her nightgown. "You finish it."

As if the kitchen faucet couldn't have poured an ocean's worth if we'd wanted.

7

Autumn was ending with an unseasonable chill. On Halloween, the trick-or-treaters arrived white lipped with their costumes tied over winter coats. Frost a week later. In spite of the cold, Caitlin had become a stickler for energy conservation, turning the thermostat down to sixty degrees no matter how often I readjusted it. She'd bury herself under afghans before depleting the world's resources, and I took it as a sign she was recuperating. Making a stand on this single ideal, another was sure to follow, and before long she'd be taking steps each day toward better things. I didn't mind if my toes went numb while I slept in the basement. I'd conserve with her. Together, we'd spare what could be spared.

In the mornings, once Mom left for work, I put on my coat and sat beside Ozzy, massaging his lumps before heading to the record store. The mutt had grown tumored and oily furred, was gassy and anxious and skeptical of everyone but my mother. The minute Caitlin descended the stairs, he sulked away, and I'd watch her check the thermostat before taking her place on the couch.

The television awakened at the touch of a button.

Then the sound of her crunching cereal as she flipped though the channels. Her froggy voice, asking, "Why're you looking at me like that?" if I stared too long.

I waved good-bye as I left, holding open the front door, pretending to shudder at the first nip of cold. With the breeze coming through the open door, Caitlin sank into her blankets, tapping a finger against the remote, turning to smile or sometimes staring ahead, zapping the pictures as they flashed across the screen.

THIS WAS THE SEASON Will and our good friend Andrew were moving in together a couple miles east on Michigan Avenue, an event bearing strong implications for me and where I'd spend my evenings. The three of us had recently outgrown a dimwitted phase in which male affection had threatened our sense of dignity. Since returning to Dearborn, I'd been greeting them with hugs and openly calling them my best friends.

Andrew was a handsome outsider who gave two shits for music but had warmed to Will and me over the years. We admired his genuine loner tendencies because they made us feel inferior, the coolness with which he set about doing whatever the hell he chose. Andrew's friendship was earned quietly and with time, and to understand its nuances was to keep company with a dude of rare character. Caitlin had always been smitten with Andrew's mysteriousness, as had Lauren and most other girls around town. His eyes were brown, his hair dark blond and self-cut in a careless style. He was exactly my height but endowed with a warrior gene. I'd seen Andrew manhandle local black belts, psychos of numerous stripes. At twenty, he'd declared himself a Libertarian. Own property, he said. Never trust the stock market. His dad ran an electric-paneling business and bought houses on the side, fixer-uppers. Andrew had been given charge of a two-story duplex: a featureless, box-shaped compound where he'd manage the tenants downstairs and use the three-bedroom upper flat as he pleased.

Never mind the cold nights, I enjoyed my basement hideaway. I'd taped posters to the walls and arranged recording devices to surround my mattress. The room was dark at any hour, with just a smear of natural light coming through a small block-glass window. I believed I'd altered myself to fill the room, simplified my being. And these changes were for the better. I wrote music at all hours and slept peacefully, waking in darkness each morning to spin a record with no concern for the weather outside.

But on principle, I begrudged Andrew for having asked his cousin Ralph to join him and Will in his three-bedroom flat. I wondered if it was a demotion in our friendship. Will insisted he'd remedy the details. "One month," he said while I helped him move his giant stereo into his new quarters, a tight room overlooking a strip mall. "I'll smoke Ralphy out and get you in here."

Will's devotion touched me, but I refused his offer to hang that afternoon and left, returning home in time to hear the phone ring, which I hoped might be a further attempt to prove his loyalty.

"Yeah," I said.

"'Yeah'?" My dad—calling out of the blue, as seemed to be his way. "Since when do you answer 'Yeah'?" I could tell by his voice that he was in a state.

"I thought you were someone else."

Slack manners peeved him, but he had no wind to pursue it.

"Your mother fainted," he said. "We went to court today, you know?"

I didn't. But as he narrated the scene, I could picture it: a courthouse, downtown Detroit. Mom stands to state her intentions, termination of her till-death-do-us-part oath, as the judge recites his piece like he's done a thousand times. And, like that, with her right hand raised, Mom faints on the courtroom tiles.

"Scared the hell out of me. She was out cold, white as a ghost."

He sounded beaten, unable to say the word "divorce" aloud, though it was now official, on file with the state. Yet as he spoke about Mom's fainting, his voice betrayed the slightest hope, as if their parting was not meant to be. Part of me believed that, too.

"She's not hurt?" I said, a question that caused us to linger.

I hooked the cordless around my jaw, poking around through refrigerator for the sake of not thinking. Dad had been stopping by the house to check on Caitlin, but I'd been ducking him. For a change of subject, he reminded me to keep an eye on things. "You gotta pay rent," he said. "Help out around there." Then, softly, "Why don't you stop by? There's plenty of room over here."

I'd seen his new place once, a barely lived-in condo on a treeless plot of land. Our old furniture helped fill the condo's emptiness: Our plaid couch, on which I'd spent so many sick days. The oak table we'd eaten at for years, imprinted where Caitlin and I had pressed childish cursive into the lacquer while doing homework.

"Okay, yeah," I said.

"Come on over. I'll cook dinner." That meant pizza, a microwaved something or other, steaming in a plastic dish. Then he said, "This is your home, too." And I said, "Uh-huh," trying not to express what we both knew: that my home was anywhere but there. A fact that was new to us and stung so badly we'd only begun to feel it.

I LEFT THE HOUSE in a daze and walked to Telegraph Road and stared at the traffic tearing past the gas stations and barbershop, a hundred cars blurring by and not one other person afoot for as far as I could see. I thought of my mother, that courthouse scene. And I told myself that everything happening was Life, tried convincing myself that this was the harsh, impenitent reality of how it was. Then I switched off. And walked away. And within four hours Andrew and I were on a couch in Ann Arbor smoking bowls with a guy named Randall, this wildcard we'd known in school.

I'd sort of woken up there, understanding I'd been meant to see Randall.

One of the band's songs was about him, something with the words *Nobody loves him, Randall is dead.* We'd been toking for an hour inside his one-bedroom apartment when I handed him a copy of my twelve-inch record, and with no further ceremony he slipped it onto the turntable.

"It's for me?" he said, tuning his ear to the screams. "I can't understand a word."

Randall had dark eyes, black hair parted down the middle. One of those haywire cases who'd been in and out of trouble since his teens. Jails, cops, hard drugs and guns, money buried in coffee cans—once Randall got to talking, you'd believe every word or have a sense that if he was lying, then there was probably a worse true story he was saving for some bender from which you might not return.

The record revolved beneath the needle. *Stolen moments become his life* went another line, though only I knew this. Andrew wasn't much for my music. "Wild shit," he said, just basically waiting for it to end.

Then I spoke up and announced, "My dad's on crack." I said it studiously, as if reporting some scientific oddity. "He's been full blown for a while."

"Dude," said Randall. "That's deep."

Andrew had played hockey with me and knew my dad as the wisecracking, good-natured workingman, tie undone after a day at the office, a stiff handshake after a game well played. In certain spheres my dad's one-of-the-guys swagger had shone favorably on my own total lack thereof. "Goddamn," Andrew said through the haze, once he realized I was serious. "You're blowing my mind." But if there were any weight to our conversation, none of us was about to acknowledge it with our faces. Randall, after all, was blackened around the eyes and looked not to have slept for years.

"Crack," he said, touching the flame of his lighter to what resin remained in his blown-glass pipe. "I know about it. Dirty shit." Then he dropped street lingo, terms I had no idea about: "runners," "stems." He said, "There's all kinds of white boys smoking that stuff. Shit is wack."

You couldn't tell if he was boasting or if the snarled look on his face had to do with an aching flashback, but at least I'd put it out there: Dad's drugs. Being near Randall consoled me, inspiring a list of interventionist schemes that all seemed to lack some essential component, but still . . . A row of cabinets stretched above the sink in Randall's kitchen, on top of which stood a collection of emptied liquor bottles. When I asked how many of those he'd drunk, he pointed his finger as if to count each one. "All of 'em," he said. "I'd rather drink all them bottles than start smoking rocks."

• • •

I'd been twenty years old a matter of hours as I peered through the still-undraped windows of Mom's house to see Will walking toward our doorstep dressed as an angel—a garish, ill-fitting costume he'd scored at a thrift store. Mid-November and the lawn was already ice crusted. Will's brown hair was greased and furrowed from a violent combing, accentuating his regal, darkly attractive face. A halo of wire and tinsel jaunted above. He'd scissored the words HAPPY BIRTHDAY from a sheet of wallpaper and had taped each of the paisley letters to his chest.

Ozzy yapped as the doorbell rang.

"I'm your birthday angel," Will said, dancing into the living room the instant I cracked the door.

Despite his musical obsessions, Will had never taken up an instrument. Lately, he'd been referring to himself as an artist without a medium, expressing his creative intensities through improvisations that required neither stage nor set list. For this purpose, he'd been collecting women's clothing, rubber masks, and penile-enhancement devices, storing these props beneath the seats of his Ford F-150 so he could transform at moment's notice. Weeks earlier he'd been dressed in drag at a downriver house party, provoking one local roughneck to punch him in the mouth, cracking a molar. "That river rat blindsided me," he'd said, pulling at his lip to reveal his capped tooth. "But how about if I'd have kicked his ass dressed in a gown?" Once my laughter dwindled, he'd reiterated his latest adage, urging me to give a whirl sometime: "All that's in the past now, brother." You could wake up every morning and console yourself with this knowledge. "Last night is the past."

In Mom's living room, he pranced toward Caitlin, shimmying and strutting until she gave his costume its due regard. She liked him, in the way most people did—with some degree of appreciation for his absurdity. Between them, there'd occasionally been an air of mutual taunting. I hoped Caitlin might see the humor in Will's getup rather than how tightly the fabric clung to his pelvis.

She sat on the couch enduring the spectacle, uncertain whether he was screwing with her. She'd been sleeping less, walking through the house in her shroud of blankets, avoiding the world outside as if it were a barren, treacherous proposition. With the early freeze, her hibernation seemed all the more justifiable. Now that daylight saving time caused darkness to fall by five o'clock, the days must have seemed forgettable: spans of gray light that passed the windows without ever beckoning her outside.

Will didn't know about her, why she was there on the couch or anything else. He rubbed his palms together, a fricative sound he augmented with a growl.

"Is this what you guys do?" said Caitlin.

When I'd told Will about my dad's problems, he'd asked questions I couldn't answer: *How long's he been on it? Where does he get it? How does he keep his job?* Questions Caitlin probably wanted to ask me, just to say the words aloud and have someone else hear them. Will inched toward her, making a playful swipe at her ponytail. As if on the outskirts of a joke she had no way of taking part in, Caitlin smiled dutifully, causing him to laugh in a way that somehow accounted for all of us.

AT WILL'S DEMAND, HE and I took my minivan for a birthday drive. He was fixated on my Ford Aerostar, an earlier, decaying model of the automobile that nearly pummeled me in Ridgewood Hills. The heater was useless. Worse, the cassette deck had malfunctioned. The interior was smeared with an orange funk and crusts when I bought the wreck off a dirt lot that spring. As I drove, Will basked in the grime. He fingered every reachable stain, toying with knobs on the dash to see which worked. I fretted about the transmission, which clanked as though the underbody were being bludgeoned. The cold whistled through. Buttoned to the neck was my Carhartt jacket, a brand of work coat the band had begun wearing as a proletariat, antifashion statement.

"Freezing in here," Will said, warming his hands with his breath.

His halo jittered. His bare shoulders were exposed through tears in the lacy sleeves. The garment had refused to zip in the back, leaving his spine exposed. He was, indubitably, an angel. A birthday seraph. Beside him in the van, I felt his love for me.

We drove past the auto plants, our old junior high and the baseball diamond where I'd beaned poor Moe. Mister Donut. The Ford-Wyoming Drive-in. The fact of my return altered each landmark, rendered it new, as though we'd staked some claim here. We might spend the rest of our lives tooling those roads, which on a day like that didn't feel so bad.

"Let's go see Andrew," Will said. "Give him a look at my outfit."

Since learning about my dad, Andrew had been inviting me over for meals. Though I wasn't a proper resident at his apartment, I'd been spending a good deal of time there, acting like I was.

Will parked the minivan. I followed him through the front door and up the staircase, intruding on Andrew, who was in the living room, engrossed in a science program. His boots were unlaced, his posture a postwork slump. It took him a moment to appreciate Will's efforts. He winced as the angel began to prance and gesticulate.

"What do you want from me?" Andrew said. "For your birthday?"

"Nothing," I said. "Just this."

Will twirled and clapped his hands.

"I'll come up with something good," Andrew said.

But I was home, and the day was really just beginning, and that was more than enough.

TWO WEEKS LATER, A full-on December sleet storm was tacking against the windows as the three of us sat in the apartment, chugging from plastic milk jugs filled with Andrew's homemade alcoholic cider. Outside was chill and ice. Mom's path to the garage had frozen over after I forgot to shovel, and Caitlin had agreed to raise the thermostat several notches. Mailboxes had frozen shut. The booze went down like lava.

"Yum, yum," Will said. "That's a heavy taste."

You never knew where you were with one of Andrew's home-brewed potions. Sometimes a few bottles of his experimental wines barely did the trick. That night, my senses were sawed after a mug or two of cider. The brew had been fermenting beneath his sink since Thanksgiving, and Will had sampled it daily, insisting, "No, no. Not before its time." Tonight, finally, he'd nipped from a jug and proclaimed it was ready.

"Let's take a walk," Andrew said. "Enjoy the weather."

We were halfway through the second gallon. Will had opened a third for himself, raising it with both hands to pour it down. His flourishes dominated the apartment. He'd nailed flea-market wall hangings above the mantel: a nautical lighthouse scene that twinkled when you flipped a switch, and a framed, kaleidoscopic portrait of Christ.

"Beautiful," he said. "Just imagine you're yachting and praising the Lord."

He'd also taken advantage of my position at the record store, once barreling through the theft alarm with an armful of LPs on an evening when I had run of the place. A Stooges LP was the soundtrack for a silent screening of *Pink Flamingos*; Marquis de Sade sat next to the King James Bible on the coffee table. Andrew's cousin Ralph, a suavely violent, cologne-dipped Italian I'd seen terminate a house party using a single watermelon as ammunition, was revolted by Will's sensibilities and never seemed to be around.

A thick sediment had collected in the bottom of my mug.

"Drink the scum," Andrew said. "The good stuff."

I tipped up, swallowing the grime.

"Go for a joy ride?" I said.

Night driving was standard procedure. It raised the odds that something great or awful might happen, anything but sinking deeper into our chairs until we no longer had the wit to flip the records once they'd finished. Will gave a single clap of his hands, and we gathered our coats.

SMUGGLING A JUG OF cider into Andrew's work van, we slid onto an empty, iced-over Michigan Avenue. Andrew steered. There was no radio, only the sound of the heater rattling and the scrape of the tires against the ice. On the van's floor, I sat surrounded by toolboxes, copper piping and hardware. Andrew had been working as a handyman, installing granite counter-tops and rewiring outlets, tearing apart kitchens, saving his pay for solar panels he intended to affix to the upper flat's roof.

Andrew braked for a red, and the van shimmied beneath the traffic signal.

I'd maneuvered the Orgasmatron through the worst midnight rains, but I had no interest in taking the wheel. I grabbed a crowbar from Andrew's arsenal and tested its weight. Toolboxes, hammers, levels—they made me think of my dad. We'd not spoken since the season changed, and, concerning him, my confusion had grown lopsided, bottom heavy. I'd remind myself to give him a call, but then, from below, bitterness would surge. It wasn't the drugs or the divorce or any obvious griev-ances that repelled me but his desire to know whoever it was I'd become these past few years. Though his love for his son—flesh and blood—was innate, unconditional, he hadn't bargained on dealing with an actual person, a being whose desires and feelings could break so starkly from his own.

I'd vacated his sightline, jumped off a cliff to escape his worldview. He now seemed to be peering over the edge, calling my name, realizing I was almost lost to him.

Idle moments—a night drive or sitting in a movie theater just before the lights dimmed. That's when my father loomed, different versions of his face arising. To fend off these visions, I'd think of my mom fainting and the nights I'd searched for him. Then I'd feel the righteousness of an orphan, as though I'd been unchained, set loose and on the run.

I drummed the crowbar against the van floor, clanging out a rhythm. As we reached Dearborn's outskirts, Andrew braked hard to skid the van across the open road. The toolboxes chattered. A jug of antifreeze rolled and sloshed.

"That was weak," Will said. "Do it again."

A thought arose, a wasp sputtering from the nest, the words coming to my lips as it materialized: "Let's go see that fuck who pulled a gun on me."

"To do what?" Andrew said. "It's twenty miles from here."

I'd told them the story more often then they'd cared to hear it: Will's bat, the gun, the showdown in Ridgewood Hills.

"You want to get even," Will said. Perhaps as a sympathetic gesture for all that had gone wrong with my family, Will had begun calling me "Our Boy." He turned to Andrew. "Our Boy wants to get even."

I raised the crowbar, imaging what blows it might administer to that red minivan.

"The guy deserves something," Will said. "You don't pull a move like that on Our Boy."

From the back of the van, I watched the windshield being

washed by the streetlights as they passed above, lighting up the pane, the cracks and road-salt scum coming into view. "You really want me to drive there?" Andrew said. "Because I owe you—for your birthday."

HE DROVE CAUTIOUSLY ON the highway, finally veering up an exit ramp that met a country road. The tires glided as the van braked. Sleet rained down, yet the night sky possessed a blueness you could see beyond the drizzle.

"Spin it," Will said. "Spin this thing out."

Andrew laughed, giving the wheel a playful tug.

"This van," he said, "would flip."

We were nearing Ridgewood Hills. I'd not been back since I'd moved and had no interest in seeing the old house. Twenty minutes west, it was a world so much darker. A streetlight here and there, the moonlight reflecting off the ice that covered everything. Andrew turned onto Ridgewood Drive, between the wooden signs marking the subdivision's entrance.

"Take a left," I said, at the same three-way corner where a year and a half earlier I'd nearly been smeared into the concrete.

"You sure you know the house?" Andrew said.

"I know it."

We were there. I told him to turn the van around and park, giving us an exit strategy.

"That's it." I pointed.

The red minivan was parked in the driveway as though only the seasons had changed. The halogen path lamps I'd watched the man stalk past were unlit, iced mushrooms lining the walkway. Shortly after midnight, the neighborhood appeared barely conscious, the porch lights like burning oil through the falling ice.

"What do we do?" Will said, getting down to business.

Through the years—Dumpster fires, breaking and entering abandoned psychiatric hospitals—we'd conspired like this many times, wanting to prove to each other we had the guts.

A large bay window of plate glass stretched across a good part of the home's street-side facade. "Let's take out those windows," I said.

"Why don't you slash his tires?" Andrew said. "There's razors back there."

"Nah," I said. "The house. Do the house."

"Our Boy wants to get his. Don't you?" said Will. "That's a lot of glass."

I needed my friends to witness something inside of me. What that was, I didn't know. I dug through the van's clutter, handing Will a tire iron. He clanked it against the crowbar in my fist, and there was nothing left to ask.

"I'll wait here." Andrew killed the low beams.

Will and I passed the jug of cider, chugging before stepping out of the van.

"Start the engine," I said, "soon as you see us coming back."

"The engine's running," Andrew said.

Walking up the pavement, I heard the fabric of Will's down jacket grating against itself. Our steps broke loose small bits of ice in the street, scattering them across the sheen. Sleet tacked against our shoulders. The universe was watching. The holy spirits, all of mankind. For a moment we saw ourselves anew through their eyes: we were avengers, we were cowards. This much we knew.

"Go slow," I said. "We'll walk up and count to three."

We marched over the front lawn, crunching footprints into its ice-crusted surface, right up to the darkened glass. Peering in, I could see through the house and out the back window to where the world glowed blue.

Will looked the street up and down.

I counted *one, two.*

On *three* we swung, and the leaded panes shattered with deep, clattering gusts. Thick glass came down in slabs. After our initial fully cocked blasts we tapped rapidly, hammering fast, reaching high and low for any shards that remained in reach. We moved across the window, each of us destroying a portion, cracking away until the screams of children came from inside.

"All right," I said, and we were running.

Fast, shallow breaths. My thighs pumped. The crowbar's weight propelled my hand up and down with each stride. Andrew hit the lights, and as I neared the van my feet slowed too quickly, skating several inches before my heels jutted forward beneath me. Then I was plunging backward—that instant when your feet leave the earth, and there's just enough of a second to realize you are gravity's bitch.

My head conked the frozen street.

A hard crack. The kind you hear and do not feel.

I saw nothing except the blurred sky above, as a familiar taste came to my mouth: like batteries, pennies beneath the tongue. The prepain shock of a bodily wreck, in which you ask yourself whether you are mortally wounded or suffering only a momentary oblivion.

But there was no time for that.

Will dragged me to my feet and into the van as its tires spun, carrying us back through the storm.

IN THE MORNING I awoke with a gelatinous bulge, tender in a malicious way. The hair covering the swelling was stiff with dried blood. A dark red stained my pillowcase. Whether it was the head wound or the aftereffects of Andrew's cider, the thought of standing was wretched.

I yelled for Caitlin. Once, then louder.

Ozzy's nails clacked over the floor upstairs.

Cloaked in blankets, my sister came to the basement to get a look, returning a moment later with cubes of ice wrapped in a hand towel, pressing it gently to my head. She wiped the cold drips from my neck with a blanket and asked what in god's name I'd done this time.

"Like a truck hit you," she said. "That's what it looks like."

And I didn't feel good, but I'd felt worse.

"You guys were acting stupid last night, weren't you?" she said.

At which I laughed. Because what about last night?

Last night was the past.

8

Mom had spoken of Christmas's approach the way you might a surgical appointment. Yet when the time came, she met it with every bit of cheer she could muster. A wreath on the door and electric candles in the windows, candy-cane cookies and stockings hanging from the mantel—the simple things were what she lived for. Now that the carols played on WQRS, I could tell she was longing for the years when we'd bought Christmas trees from church lots and taken family portraits once the ornaments dangled from the branches.

She smiled sadly but had no intention of Grinching out just yet. "I guess we won't be hanging your dad's stocking," she said. "We'll make it nice. Do it our own way."

For my part, I insisted that the season was an act of consumerist warfare. Spiting commerce and sentimentality and the hidden tenderness I, too, felt for Christmases past. And while the abrasion on my head no longer stung, a mysterious bulge remained—a hairy egg that, each time I ran a comb over it, left me guilty about the shattered windows and screaming children.

Caitlin began badgering me to hack off my chin-length mop of hair, thinking, perhaps, that a change of image might spur me toward other progressions. A bout of wicked sadness had not, she seemed to insist, left her blind to my hygienic shortcomings. When she said, "Why do you want to be a dirtball?" I knew it was a very good sign, her investment in my business rather than her own worries. She'd also reclaimed enough of her wits to suggest we do away with presents and donate to a needy family.

"We don't need anything," she said. "Look around."

My mom agreed. So did I.

Four days before Christmas, the three of us drove to a west Detroit neighborhood named Brightmoor. A short way east of the band's practice space, Brightmoor was one of Motown's crack-shack havens. Along with Randall and countless others, I'd commuted there to buy booze from stores where, behind bulletproof glass, the clerk didn't ask for ID but rang an extra buck to the bills of white boys like us. Evergreen Road, the hood's central thruway, was an unbeautiful strip offering none of the ruined grandeur found closer to downtown.

Mom piloted the station wagon, keeping an eye on the unfamiliar signs. A pile of gifts was next to Caitlin on the backseat, nailing to a tee the wish list she'd acquired from a local charity. We had an address and vague directions. A rotisserie chicken sat in my lap.

I'd been detouring through Brightmoor after band practice to study the blocks of boarded-up houses. After dark, the streets were empty but for lone figures who emerged only to shepherd those freaky hours. They appeared ageless in the shadows. On even the coldest nights, I'd seen them lurking or wheeling by on bicycles, locking eyes with me through the windshield, turning to watch as I passed, in case my brake lights flashed, which meant something in those parts. Every fourth house seemed to stand defiantly kept amid the vacant, burned, and graffiti-covered Cape Cods. The ones I paid attention to had faint lights glowing behind drawn shades, a car with tinted windows and chrome rims in the driveway, and as I passed I couldn't help searching for my dad, dressed in his suit, walking into these places.

"This is a rough area," I announced as Mom braked for a red.

"How would you know?" Caitlin said.

I'd been asking around. All it took was a pocket of quarters, slipping them to hustlers working outside Detroit clubs. *You ain't no cop, look at you. What you wanna know? You want some shit just say so.* I'd learned from Repa how to jive with these folks, to slap hands when they throw up a palm and feel that toughened skin. That's when I'd look into their eyes, set like marbles in bone-dry sockets, expressing only a starving, animal plea for one more hit. Brown teeth and gray-skinned lips, maybe a duffel of unidentifiable salvage they're desperate to hock. I knew half of what happened to you was luck, good or bad—the circumstances that leave one person with a place to lay his head while another scrounges for coins.

"This," I told my sister, "is crack town."

"Not everyone's on crack," she said, but I'd become prone to the terrible, witless suspicion that yes, yes they were.

I tried feeling wise, as if I were in the know about Brightmoor's goings-on. Pay a runner or a hooker or street-side creep five bucks to get in your car or—if it was a guy on a bike—caravan with you to meet the man. Smoke your shit in a by-the-hour motel or then and there in the dealer's home or on the street or at a stoplight as you convinced yourself you were never going back for more . . . then again and again . . .

This was the extent of what I thought I knew.

Also that crack and grass could be rolled together in a joint, because I'd accidentally taken a hit off one outside a gig in Pontiac. That's if I was to trust a guy named Jason Heck, who'd coughed and said, "Don't mind the rough spots, it's just a little crack." I'd sucked it, back and forth with Jason Heck, until it was gone, and when the band hit the stage I threw the microphone into the crowd and screamed at the floor, and no one there seemed to mind.

MOM HAD GONE OVERBOARD with the gift wrapping: curly bows, streamers and shredded ribbons. The packages were more elaborate than anything inside the small green house we arrived at. Mom and Caitlin wore skirts. They'd showered and done their hair. A woman held open the door, saying, "Don't worry about that," as we began removing our shoes. Her children sat on the couch, three shy-faced eyefuls whom I couldn't imagine setting foot in their own front yard.

The living room was a tight unit with barely space for all of us. In the corner, a strip of carpet appeared burned away, and in the lukewarm air was a smell like wet, dirty towels. This was when I knew that, whatever my family had been through—whatever we'd go through—we had it easy.

The children approached us meekly, accepting the gifts. That was the most ludicrously white I'd ever felt: inside those walls, hoping they trusted us. Caitlin smiled as the children shook their packages. I was planning to meet the band in an hour to load the van and head downtown for our final show of the year, and I slipped into a vision of the impending performance—the set list and the strike of the first chord. Otherwise, I stood beating back every feeling that arose.

The children's mother nodded as they opened their presents: that season's popular dolls for the two girls and, for the boy, a pastel, machinelike squirt gun capable of serious battle. Taped to the walls were crayon drawings of black Santas descending to a puke-colored abode.

"Santa asked us to deliver these for him," my mom said. "He's busy this year."

"Oh, no," said their mother. "Santa's stopping by. He's comin'."

"Four days away," Mom said, by way of recovery.

The boy clutched his toy, mimicking the sounds of gunfire as the girls waved their dolls' limbs at Caitlin. She waved back. I knew what she was thinking because I'd begun to think it, too: how impossible it seemed that there was not a thing more we could do. As we drove away, waving from the station wagon, Caitlin began crying without a sound. Though I knew they'd meant well, it was easier to pity my mom and sister for their sloppy goodwill than it was to extend my own feelings. Evergreen Road passed outside the windows. Mom set her palm on my knee, squeezing gently, as if meaning to console my sister, who sat weeping in the backseat and just out of reach.

THE FOLLOWING MORNING I climbed the basement stairs with a full-body ache, twitching each limb and rotating my neck to assess the damage. My arms were dotted with welts, my lips swollen with bite marks. Postshow mornings felt like I'd been mugged, and I reveled in each twinge, as if it fulfilled the idea that I could not be easily destroyed.

Our year's-end gig had gone savagely well.

A punk in a Santa Claus hat had roamed the crowd, the red triangle of his cap sharking amid the bobbing heads. I'd done what I could to eject my soul from my body, and between songs Repa pulled a buck knife to carve his forearm—two or three slashes. Iggy Stooge, David Yow, GG Allin—the maim-yourself routine had been done, but what hadn't in the name of rock and roll? Later someone told me that with each crack of Repa's drumstick, the blood that had drained onto his snare was sent flying, speckling the audience. It could have happened. What's certain is that before our final song, once the time was right, he'd licked his wounds and made it known that the taste—it was good.

In the kitchen, the coffee was still warm. A note taped to the pot, the one place I'd see it: *Out on errands. Love, Mom.* I drained a mug and took a second to the upstairs bathroom for a marathon shower. Once the water went cold, I pulled open the curtain to find nothing to towel off with. I shouted for Caitlin. When she didn't answer, I limped naked into her bedroom to scavenge in her laundry hamper.

There was a note placed on her bed. I snatched it, the stationery darkened by my wet hands. After the first few lines, I understood.

Tugging my jeans on over damp legs, I charged through the house, calling her name. Ozzy ran in circles, yapping while I checked every room—the basement, the closets. Outside, Caitlin's car was nowhere to be seen. I passed through the kitchen, slapping the garage door opener on my way out the back door. Fresh snow had fallen. I was shoeless, shirtless, still damp as the aluminum door rolled up to reveal Caitlin's white Escort. The exhaust pipe vented blurry fumes as the car idled. The driver's seat was reclined, but I could plainly see my sister. She wasn't moving.

I yanked opened the car door.

"The hell you doing?"

"Nothing," said Caitlin, perfectly alert. Pure embarrassment crossed her face. The kind of expression you see in someone who's been caught lip-synching pop songs in the mirror.

"Go back inside," she said.

"Hey," I said.

She knotted her face, glaring, annoyance being the sole

emotion she was an expert at faking. Blonde wisps escaped from a stocking cap pulled tight over her head. She'd bundled up. Mittens. She appeared wholly rational. We might have been arguing over a carton of leftovers I'd devoured without permission.

"I found your note."

"I'm sorry," she said. "I can't do this anymore."

I reached across her and cut the engine.

"Don't tell Mom," she said, huddling into the seat.

"This is selfish," I told her. Then I aimed for something profound, making a lame speech about all those who had less than we did, limbless and crippled people, starving, in other parts of the world.

"You don't think I know?" she said. "I think about that all the time."

She was looking past me and toward an escape from this day. It must have seemed easier to sleep forever than to carry whatever diagnostic branding she'd been given, whatever humiliating dormitory episodes were playing in her mind, and to begin reintegrating into the wide, wild world. My wet hair hung in my eyes. I decided that, if it might make her happy, I'd let her trim it any way she liked.

"You want my coat?" she said.

"I want you to knock this off."

"You don't know what it's like. Everything comes easy to you."

I laughed the way you do when nothing useful comes to mind. She saw it that way—my easy life—and she might have been right.

"Everything hurts," she said. "I hate it."

"What's so bad? Nothing's that bad."

Even now, nearly eighteen years on, I'm not immune to fantasies of revising the past and altering the course of things to come. I envision myself there with Caitlin, filled with the knowledge of everything I was helpless to understand then. I'm able to fix her without a word. And she sees it in my eyes, the irreducible love that I'm no longer afraid to give—even if it would mean reliving those strange days one by one, starting from that moment in the garage.

Next she told me something awful that had happened to her, swearing me to secrecy before I'd steadied my pulse. "Promise you'll never tell," she said.

And I did.

A vow I'd never break, which made me feel as though the weight of all she'd said had landed squarely on me.

I went brutish; it was all I knew. I grabbed a hoe and gnashed several times at the cement. There were unpacked boxes on the ground, and I booted them around until Caitlin slammed the Escort's door and began to cry.

"Don't," she said.

"All right. I'm sorry."

"You're not gonna tell," she said.

I slung my arm around her. My skin was a sheet of warmth, immune to the cold. I hugged Caitlin to my ribs, and she clutched herself as her head pressed against my chest. She refused go limp in my arms, but I felt her elbow beneath her jacket, her hair on my bare shoulder—proof she was there with me. We waddled together into the house, where she sat at the kitchen table as I prepared lunch. Turkey sandwiches, a bland, scarcely garnished specialty I'd perfected.

Caitlin stared at the stack of bread and cold meat on her plate.

Did I actually think she was going to enjoy this?

An Advent calendar stood in the center of the table, a cardboard structure housing twenty-five perforated rectangles marking the days leading up to and including Christmas.

Behind every numbered flap were small plastic trays of candies, most of which had already been torn from the calendar. I punctured the paper seal that read *23* and gobbled the pebblelike confection in an attempt to make her smile. It cracked between my teeth. I opened another panel, the one for Christmas Eve, stuffing tomorrow's treat into my mouth.

Caitlin shook her head.

As though she were on another, unreachable channel, she said, "I wish I knew guys like you and your friends."

I couldn't tell if this meant she wanted to tag along with my band or if it suggested her hopeless crush on Andrew, whom she'd always adored. But we were wrong, I thought, all of us: me and my friends and my band. Wherever my sister belonged in the world, I believed we should come no nearer to it than I was at the moment: grinding the sugar from my teeth, fingering the crusts of her sandwich and urging her to take a bite, thinking it might be enough to renew her.

The first day of a new life.

9

I OPENED THE DOOR of our rehearsal room, and there was Repa swinging a claw hammer, pounding out a rhythm on a piece of sheet metal. Three or four salvaged televisions flickered behind him. Ethan sat on a garbage-picked couch, nodding along to the performance. They were waiting on me. My minivan had stalled countless times on the way over, poisoning my mood and leaving my fingers cold and brittle. I'd need a minute before my hands would be able to fret a guitar.

"All right," Repa said, whanging the metal sheet, "Kristopher fucking Kringle."

Christmas Eve rehearsal was symbolic, a test of our commitment. We were also sorely in need of fresh material. A new label had arranged to release our album-in-progress, news to which Warden had responded by calling us traitors, defectors from the CTW cause.

I blew into my hands, relieved to be inside our windowless room. The space was bare of the inspirational knickknackery most bands enjoyed. Adorning our white-plaster walls were scribbles of psychotropic poetry and a xeroxed photo of Warden, his forehead marked with a pentacle. A liquor-store clerk we'd named the Christ Figure had been visiting us with plastic jugs of vodka and econo-sized bags of peanuts. Empties and crushed nutshells littered the floor. We'd been admitting select colleagues into our rehearsals: Repa's anarchist admirers who'd rechristened themselves things like Squirrel and Star; an unequivocally likable paraplegic who bore Iron Maiden tattoos and insisted we call him Gimp; a half-Irish, half-Japanese long-hair who played along on an unamplified guitar, occasionally exposing his pierced urethra. After three months there we'd barely written a minute of new music, but we were still drawing an audience. One fifty in Detroit, a hundred or so in Chicago, ten to forty people anywhere else. They came for the antics: Ethan mauling his amplifiers. Repa pulling his buck knife.

He hooted with each drop of the hammer.

Ethan sat, eyes closed, absorbing the sounds in a spiritual fashion. This was Repa's new music—farther and farther from anything you'd call song.

"All right," I said. "Fucking hell."

"What?" he said. "You don't like it?"

It was a titanic noise that cut straight for the bowels. I was jealous that I'd had no part in its inspiration. Repa stooped to lift one of the televisions to his chest, then heaved it to the floor. A crash and a scream: the inevitable finale.

"That was wild," Ethan said.

Repa stared at the wreckage. His arm was bandaged where he'd knifed himself two nights prior. "There's no more booze," he said, thrusting forward a mostly empty forty-ounce bottle as if it evidenced a crime. "Let's frickin' practice."

He walked to his drums, swallowing the last of his beer and then urinating in the bottle before taking his throne. Ethan and I plugged in our guitars. Mine was rigged with duct tape, encrusted with blood I'd never clean because I thought it looked rugged. Without another word Repa clicked his sticks, and we began a song we'd rehearsed hundreds of times. Among our sector of musicians, Repa was alleged the best drummer in Detroit, but tonight his signature beats stupefied him. His hair had grown into a shawl of dark waves, veiling his eyes as he struggled to keep time. Before we hit the second verse he leaped up and shoved over the vintage '83 Pearl customs he'd once polished daily. He flung his crash cymbal across the room like a discus.

Ethan and I carried the tune a measure or two longer before letting our guitars dangle. Repa had taken us by surprise, which was something of a coup. Knowing this, he lifted his warm 40-ounce bottle to his mouth, making a show of a long, gurgling slug.

"Gotta be alcohol in there. I've been drinking for days." After another pull from the bottle he coughed a spray of urine. "Tastes horrible."

If he couldn't carry a beat, Repa was prepared to give us a thrill. He tugged down his jeans, grunting and lofting his buttocks over his drums.

Ethan laughed. "Man," he said. "Man, oh man."

We'd taken pride in these moments, even as they were occurring, believing they proved our band was deranged, legitimately. "Let's take this shit to outer space," we used to say.

Here we were.

"Nothing," said Repa, squatting, craning his neck to witness any turds he may have achieved. "I got nothing." With his pants at his ankles he clambered over the spill of drums, mumbling, "Gotta be some liquor in this place."

He was in character, Repa the Terror, tossing empties and

stomping the floor. His eruptions were nearly joyous, freeing him of pains he'd carried years too long. He had a way of screaming and laughing in an entwined, circulatory torrent, and this was the sound he repeated. I'd witnessed it all before, in half the states in the country, yet he now seemed over the edge—gone in a performance that couldn't be switched on or off at will.

And it was beautiful, and horrible, and wonderful.

"Not a drop to drink," he said. "On Christmas Eve."

"Try the garbage cans," Ethan told him.

Our rehearsal room was one of a few dozen in the building. Many renters were metal bands or lowlifes who'd moved in with junk-store guitars and used the spaces for narcotic getaways. Across the hall, a wrestling company had filled a room with a regulation-sized ring. Beastly, shirtless men in tights stalked the hallways, asking you to get inside the ropes with them to see for yourself how fake it was. The bathrooms were often puked upon. The garbage bins lining the hallways—large knee-high drums filled with the waste of a hundred low-rent hobbyists— were presumed toxic.

Ethan swung open the door.

Repa crawled out toward the nearest receptacle, nosing through it for bottles before stuffing a handful of discarded French fries into his mouth. He turned to us with the yellow mash between his teeth.

"Aha," he said. "That's right." `

The hallways were unusually quiet. Not a note was being tuned. The only sounds were Repa's snarls as he dug deeper through the trash, so when a tattooed guitarist we knew rounded a corner at the end of the hallway, he came into view like some preyed-upon species.

The guitarist slowed his stride, squinting as if to validate what he was seeing: Repa's jeans rumpled around his shins,

black underwear thonging his buttocks. I sensed him winding up for a blitzkrieg of pent expression so awesome it would
threaten everything we'd worked for. Not now. Not tonight,
but soon.

"Watch out," Ethan said.

Repa faced the intruder on all fours, growling and crawling
as fast as he could. The guitarist turned and dashed while Repa
scrabbled up the hall, hands pattering, rounding the corner like
some malfunctioning toy. Once he'd vanished, I locked the
door of our room and told Ethan we were going to need a new
drummer.

He laughed at me as if I'd suggested matching haircuts, zoot
suits.

"It's Repa," he said. "No one can play like him."

10

Two or three jabs landed on my shoulder before I awoke with the realization this was no dream but a real fist. The room came slowly into focus, and standing above was a familiar presence, out of place in my basement domain but exuding unmistakable energies. Another soft punch and I was almost conscious, just a twitch or two away from offering up a word.

"Merry Christmas," Dad said. "You're living like hell down here." He smiled down at me. "I could smell you from the kitchen."

Decorating my room were posters of punk rock heroes and jazzmen from the sixties. A Black Flag flyer depicting a cop with a gun inserted into his pouting lips. Dad glanced at the empties, the cables and snapped guitar strings, with a wary concentration that suggested he knew he was trespassing. Two years earlier he'd have had me at attention for a lesson in self-presentation. Things considered, his touch had softened.

And get a load of his tan suede jacket, new for the season,

a middle-aged sleekness he'd never before experimented with. His hair was trimmed. A decent-looking man. Friends' mothers had told me so, but only now that I observed him with a tinge of postrehab, postdivorce sympathy did I recognize how he'd weathered in a becoming way. Coronary surgery, his many scrapes with life—these hadn't stolen the natural dignity in his face.

He didn't look like an addict. You'd never guess.

"Let's go, Bozo," he said.

Following last night's foiled practice, I'd visited Will at the upper flat, where we'd spun records until the sky turned green. Afterward came three, four hours of sleep—something like that.

"Life's in session, boy. Suck it up."

I'd not seen Dad for weeks. To hear that he could still joke like this was a comfort. He snatched at the bedspread, attempting to tear it off in a single motion, and I fought to keep covered. I'd gone to bed naked for no reason other than that I disdained doing laundry, which left me with little more than the pair of jeans I'd toss beside the bed each night. There was a brief tug-of-war, during which I used all my strength, until Dad laughed and said, "We're waiting on you."

YEARS BEFORE, DAD WOULD have been up late Christmas Eve sanding and hammering, gluing together the last seams of wood. Before dawn, Caitlin would have awakened me to creep beside her into the living room, where we'd find his homemade presents: A gymnast's beam. A hockey net. A clubhouse replete with screen door and shingled roof. We'd tested their construction, running our palms along the sanded grain while Dad sipped coffee, watching over a leaf of the *Free Press*. So many hours he'd spent drafting plans, leveling the beams, stapling shingles and fastening the hinges. His gifts had an aura—his touch. Mom's would be hidden in the branches of an ornament-cluttered Douglas fir, and we'd pretend to be unaware until the moment she said, "I think I see something in the tree."

She'd always enjoyed a good-hearted disdain for artificial Christmas trees, wincing at the idea of these gaudy impostors. "Plastic trees," Mom would say. "It's just not the same." Yet upstairs in her new home stood a fresh-from-the-box synthetic green imitation, its branches plugged into an aluminum rod. Caitlin was zoning on the television when I emerged. Dad sat beside her on Mom's flower-print sofa, appearing out of sorts. Mom worked the kitchen stove, calling, "Almost ready," with the impenetrable courtesy she'd perfected dealing with special-needs students.

On the living room floor sat a keyboard, a disposable, toylike contrivance.

"Your mom said you want to learn piano." The excitement in Dad's eyes hit me like a slug to the kidneys. What on earth might he have built me by hand? He'd patronized the local instrument shop instead. "Tickle some ivories?"

More and more, it was jazz I was listening to. The atonal, mind-bending variety that did away with melody. The pianists—McCoy Tyner, Cecil Taylor—were my favorite. Their pounding, backward-sounding chords. I'd hardly touched an actual piano but must have mentioned wanting to.

"Thanks," I said.

"It'll work?"

The plastic instrument was dreadful to look at it, far from being anything usable to conduct the furious sounds I was after. The keys might shatter the moment I pounded. "It's great," I said, squinting to read the short catalog of electronic tones the thingamajig might produce: Organs. Bassoons.

Mom served waffles and fruit, and we sat in the living room

holding our plates. She asked Dad if he'd like his coffee warmed, the kind of gesture I'd seen a thousand times, but watching Mom repeat them now, caution in her tone, seemed to actualize all that had changed.

"Thanks, Cyn," he said. "Cyn" instead of "Cindy"—which he alone called her on family road trips, as she sat beside him with an atlas; on a summer walk, asking for a napkin to wipe ice cream from his fingers.

Dad dug into the pocket of his jacket, which he'd yet to remove, and passed a card to my mom. Sipping coffee, I pretended not to notice as her nail pried open the envelope and she began to read. It appeared to contain a lengthy message, causing her to nod slowly as she read. Dressed in sweatpants and an oversize T-shirt, Caitlin sat unmoving, her eyes ticking back and forth from the television to my parents.

"Well, you always wrote nice cards." Mom perched the card atop the coffee table, and I had to wonder if it would wind up with the others arrayed on the mantel. "I guess it's time for your stockings," she said.

Then I noticed them, across the room on a chair, so overfilled they couldn't be hung from the mantel. Mom rose and carried them over, mine and Caitlin's and my father's. Stuffed inside were odds and ends. Breath mints and Chapstick. Lotions and soaps for Caitlin. Razors for me and my father, and aftershave, the brand he'd always worn. We regarded the items duly, Dad unable to get to all of them without closing his eyes, breathing fast and hard. He nodded toward my mom. When he reached out his hand, she took it.

I was content to carry on business as usual, but this weirdness became too much for Caitlin. "I thought we weren't doing presents this year," she said.

"Just a little something," said Mom. "Nothing much."

Before Dad left for his parents' condo, where their version of Christmas was soon to unfold, I watched through the windows as he circled the house, surveying its exterior. He poked his head through the front door. "The foundation's low on the east side. The basement could flood. You want me to look into it?"

Mom said, "I think we'll live."

Caitlin was already deep into whatever was on the television. A pink sweater sat folded at her feet on a bed of torn wrapping paper. After Dad drove off, I plugged in the keyboard and toyed with the sounds, dialing up a synthesized flute. I performed an easy, bittersweet melody as Caitlin and Mom took their time dressing. Imagine the sounds moving through them, with them. For an instant I lost myself, changing octaves before deciding upon the violas, playing that simple phrase again and again.

CAITLIN AND I DROVE together in her Escort, trailing Mom's wagon and parking directly in front of Dad's old house on Evangeline Street. The Arabs who'd moved in hadn't hung a wreath, possibly the reason Caitlin huffed out an unenergetic, "Weird," as she turned off the engine. Everything was changing, but there, on the other side of the road, were my grandparents, holding open their door.

"Happy holidays."

Grandpa—Papa—wearing a Santa cap.

There'd be no talk of drugs or divorce here, only the charred gingerbread men and bowl of punch, the wood-paneled television and gas fireplace. Though I caught something in their eyes—my aunts' and uncles'—a rapid-fire sorrow transmitted through handshakes or a quick rub of the shoulder. Mom and Caitlin might have liked to talk all night with a listening ear, but I only hoped that sympathy would help them overlook my

lack of plans and shabby Carhartt jacket, taken by my grand-
mother and hung in a closet beside the peacoats.

Mom's tribe was unpretentious, people of work, family, and
church. Papa was a window salesman; Lady Grandma a home-
maker of forty years. Mom's brothers and their wives seemed
living proof of sanity's attainability. I liked them a great deal, as
much as I felt shameful and alien among them. I avoided mention of myself, and especially of my band.

"Music's good," I said, when they asked. "Pretty good."

"Do you play any Christmas songs?" said my grandmother.

BEFORE WE SAT DOWN to dinner, Caitlin excused herself and
left to visit my dad's family while I stayed behind with Mom,
pickled inside a sweater I'd outgrown, filling my glass with my
grandpa's Lauder's scotch as many times as I could. My grand-
mother's jellified roast beef oozed onto a platter next to a bowl
of canned beans. As we ate, she asked if I'd be willing to sing for
the family, once the meal was over. "I'll bet you have a beautiful
voice," she said. "Though you wouldn't have gotten it from this
family. We sound like strangled cats when we sing. We shame
the whole parish."

My mom gave me a pitying smile.

"That," I said, "is exactly how I sound."

• • •

Caitlin had already returned to Dearborn by the time I arrived
at Lauren's parents' house, just a few streets over from Evangeline. "That was fast," Mom said, seeing my sister's Escort—to
Dad's and back in a matter of two hours—parked at the curb in
a line of cars that stretched down the block. Mom braked the

station wagon in the middle of the street and we both stared at the house, an industrious four-bedroom fort strung with bulbous multicolored lights. Lauren was home for the holidays and had asked Caitlin and me to come by. Only now, with a head full of scotch, had I decided I might. Mom urged me out of the car, saying, "Go ahead, don't worry about me. I'm so tired—you guys should just enjoy yourselves."

When I knocked, Lauren swung open the door and pulled me inside with a hug. Caitlin stood close behind. From the look of her, shadowing Lauren and possibly smoothed over by a nip of wine, nothing awful had come of her visit with Dad's family.

"Hey," Lauren said, giving vibrato to the syllable. "You're here."

Her smile involved every portion of her face, such a thorough expression it appeared painful to complete. It didn't take a holiday to put her in the mood of love, but inside the house was a nauseating cheer. Sing-alongs and gut-ache laughs, everyone red faced, happily schnookered, pecking cheeks beneath scraps of mistletoe. A feast of Polish meats in the dining room. I'd never known people so purely in touch with what it meant to celebrate their togetherness, who invited you in and offered you the best seat at their table. My arrival was a terrible mistake.

"How's rockin'?" someone asked, and I shrugged sophisticatedly, understanding that bands were foolish, child's play.

Lauren mustered joy enough for both of us. "He's too humble," she said. "His band has a CD."

Caitlin held a constant, thin-lipped smile, meaning to apologize for the fact she was too shy to speak. She followed us room to room, awed by the scene. Awed, no doubt, to experience this new "like-family" upgrade to her relationship with Lauren, the cool-but-kind role model about whom Caitlin had expressed a wish for future sister-in-law status. "Hey, hey," Lauren sang to each passing relative. She was stoned, I could tell, in her eyes a sexy glaze. Her dad kept a sack of weed from which she and her siblings furtively pinched.

When no one was looking, she made a grab at my butt.

"Stay awhile," she said.

Her long brown hair was a stupendous thing, shiny against the tight redness of her cotton sweater. She was womanly, larger boned than me, and I was never more aware of this than when standing beside her, jittery and winter pale, inside her parents' home. At first chance, I began buttoning my Carhartt, trying to slip out while the scotch was still on my side, looking forward to the mile or so trudge back to Mom's.

With her eyes Caitlin seemed to say, *Yes, it's good to be here.*

"I've gotta go," I said.

Lauren and I had been through this. After four years, I remained a nearly hypothetical creature to her family.

"Fine," Caitlin said. "I'll drive you."

"Caitlin, stay," Lauren said. "I'll take you home."

There was no better place for my sister, no better company— I could see that, but not my place in any of it. Intending to communicate this, I shrugged and made no eye contact with either of them. "I'll call you tomorrow," I said, taking Caitlin's keys and waving as I left them in the doorway.

BY ELEVEN I'D SLUGGED down several bottles of wine Mom had bought for holiday guests who'd never arrived. She'd gone to bed, leaving our fake tree aglow, burning electricity, but Caitlin might let this one slip, let it shine. In the basement, I blared records, selecting each platter and letting it spin, cranking the volume for half a song before pulling the needle and tossing the disc to the floor. John Coltrane. Joy Division. Not even the greats were helping. When Caitlin returned, she clomped downstairs with an intensity that announced she was undeniably pissed.

"Are you nuts? It's too loud."

She'd pulled her hair into a ponytail, rolled up the sleeves of her blouse. In her hand was the cordless phone. Any clear-thinking person would have remembered that, days before, she'd sought the big sleep in an exhaust-fumed garage. At that moment, it seemed ages ago. The fibers of my personality rearranged themselves each time I drank, and like any other lush, I knew it and reveled in the spinning moment, wishing it would never end.

"Idiot," she said, a rare bite that raised the stakes. "Why are you boozing all the time?"

In place of an answer I snapped off the stereo.

"Have you heard from Dad?" she said.

"No."

"Call him."

She dialed his number and handed me the phone. A few rings, then his answering machine, a voice approximating the tone of a happy man: *Hello, I'm not home.*

"You think he's using?" Caitlin said.

"How was he when you saw him?"

"It was weird over there. Why'd you make me go alone?"

She sat beside me on my mattress as I guzzled wine, phoning my dad every few minutes. With each call, I increased the hostility of my messages. I goaded him and challenged him to a duel. I was totally cooked. I'd keep dialing until the batteries died.

In one message, I attempted to flaunt my lyricism: "Smoking that shit like the world's on fire. I know you. I know where you are."

"Dead man" was all I said after a while.

Caitlin said, "Stop it. You're being an ass." She went upstairs in hopes, I was sure, that Mom might intervene.

Dead man. Dead man.

When Caitlin returned, she snatched the phone, hurling it at the wall. "Who are you?" she said.

The receiver's plastic casing had split open, its wires and nine-volt battery a mess too complex to consider. Seeing the pieces, I began putting together an idea about what I'd done.

"I've gotta erase that shit."

I stood. By some metabolic gift of my Irish heritage, I could manage a good deal of spirits for my five-foot-eleven, one-hun-dred-sixty-five-pound physique, but at that moment the floor felt to be revolving beneath me. I concentrated on each step before plucking my jacket from the floor.

"You're not going anywhere," Caitlin said.

I imagined my dad listening to the repeating messages, alone. Dead man.

Heading upstairs, I was already feeling new wind.

"He's drunk," Caitlin yelled.

Mom appeared in the kitchen wearing her blue robe as I was tying my bootlaces. It'd been all she could do to survive this holiday, and here I was wrecking its final minutes. If she saw anything of a man in me, it was enough that she'd given up arguing with me about most things. Her eyes were puckered from sleep, the lack of it. "Why don't you drive him?" she told my sister. "Take him over there if he wants to go."

WE TOOK CAITLIN'S ESCORT west on Michigan Avenue, past the Wayne Assembly Plant where the car itself had been built. After that, the road widened near the airport, and there was only the neon of topless bars and the silhouettes of farmhouses. Metro Detroit's outskirts looked, for a short distance, nearly rural, before the sprawling shadows of the subdivisions a few miles ahead. Caitlin drove slowly and steadily, catching every green light along the way.

"Real stupid," she said, hands on the wheel.

The wipers yawed, scraping the ice at the bottom of the windshield. Caitlin had scrubbed the makeup from her face. This was how she appeared most like herself, waiflike, her thick brown eyebrows making unusual sense on her round face.

She said nothing more about her visit with Dad's family, but I knew what I'd missed: my dad's father in a red vest, dealing out jokes he'd pilfered from the Knights of Columbus, telling yarns that reeked of legend. My dad, too, could sell a myth: stories of the Everyman—unsung pilots and center fielders—who'd conquered fate in split-second decisions. When telling of my grandfather, it was as though he were speaking of a long-begotten hero I could hope to know only in another, more significant life I might lead. The Buffalo gangs. Grandpa's career as a crooner and a minor-league pitcher. I'd heard it all numberless times but had begun to wonder: Where were the news clippings? The seven-inch single?

The things Dad never told me about his father I'd learn much later, leafing through his rehab journals while attempting to glimpse the murky past from which he'd heaved me into the world. A bloodline dosed with its fair share of poison. Fathers' fists. Whiskey stashed beneath the sink. Delirium tremens. Children abandoned in orphanages at the turn of the century by people who'd otherwise left barely a trace. All of it a curse I'd try to pin on those who came before, and before, an old pain that had yet to be healed and was now mine to behold. At the time, I barely sensed this, or sensed it only as much as I believed there was something exquisitely fucked up about me.

The road rushed toward the windshield, and I convinced

myself that my no-show had been what set my dad off on a bender. Felt at once a wish to reverse time and arrive at the garlanded door of his parents' and also a desire to change my name and move to a distant coast, where I might write a thousand songs about it. My drunken fantasies swarmed like gnats, swept away with each saw of the wipers. Caitlin veered off Michigan Avenue. With a turn or two still to go before Dad's condominium village, I switched on the stereo, knowing Caitlin would do what she did a moment later: slap it mute, never taking her eye off the road.

CAITLIN HAD A KEY. As the door opened there was something—an infallible silence, total stillness—assuring us Dad wasn't there.

She snapped on the lights.

He'd done some decorating. Framed pictures of Caitlin and me, our graduation headshots, propped beside his desk. The Serenity Prayer tacked on the kitchen wall. Beside the phone were NA and AA texts with bookmarks jutting from between their covers. I played his messages on the machine, all of them from me, tapping the delete button as rapidly as I could.

Dead man. Dead—

My recorded voice slurring into the kitchen sounded like the dirty work of some other person, a bastard who'd ceased to be once the last recording was erased.

"So, there," Caitlin said. She appeared frozen in place, having possibly never before seen someone so hopelessly and scarily shitfaced. "Let's go."

A clock I'd fashioned in eighth-grade woodshop hung on the kitchen wall, its hands reading that the hour was well past midnight. Stalking down the hallway and pulling on doors, I found that the last opened to the attached garage. No car in sight, but leaning against the concrete wall, next to a rake, was an aluminum hockey stick. I carried it back inside.

"Put that down," Caitlin said. "You always gotta get crazy."

In the living room, I rummaged through a desk drawer searching for evidence: Pipes. Guns. Receipts from the drug fairy. Best I could find was a note on Ford Motor stationery, a woman's curvaceous handwriting: *Let me know if you need anything.* A number printed beneath—a clue, a narcotic cryptogram—which I punched into his phone with a light speed reminiscent of long-ago nights spent dialing for concert ticket giveaways—caller number 69 when the first notes of "Welcome to the Jungle" grind across the airwaves.

After several rings, a tiny voice answered with the singsong tone of a child: *Hello, we're not home. Leave a message.*

"He's dead," I said, and hung up.

By now my limbs had fully revived. I made a hearty chop with the stick, shattering the frame that held my picture. Next I went after the desk chair, cracking its legs with the aluminum shaft before stomping the collapsed seat.

"Stop it," Caitlin said. "Knock it off, freak."

She stood, arms crossed, with a frown that seemed the mask of what she thought she should be feeling. In instances like this she was not dramatic. It would be days, months, later, after she'd held the moment and squeezed it into a million shapes, that whatever she felt would appear on her face.

I was nearly lucid, lacking any hint of true rage. My outburst had been a cowardly, lazy spectacle, and I felt drunk again, cottoned mouthed and exhausted. With the toe of my boot, I pushed broken glass across the carpet.

"I'm not touching that," said Caitlin.

"Okay," I said. "I'll go on and clean this up now."

I got right to it. Swept the glass and splintered wood into

a dustpan and gathered up the chair legs with an air of duty I hoped might serve as an apology. Once I'd collected the debris in a garbage bag, I walked outside, crossing the street to a site where another condo was soon to be built. Only the foundation had been dug, in which cinder blocks were arranged on top of one another. I tossed the sack, heard it slap the ground.

Across the street, in the doorway, Caitlin's face was feature-less beneath the porch light. She might have been any kind soul, taking one last breath of the holiday night. I couldn't be sure, but I felt I'd acted for both of us, as if she'd needed to know where I stood. That I felt it, too: our fear of where all this was going.

Or maybe I'd wanted her to console me. To hold me in some way or pull me together; had I fallen into her on my way back through the condo's front door, she would have.

Instead, I returned the stick to the garage.

I redialed the number I'd found in the desk, waiting for the child's cute message.

"I'm real sorry about all that," I said. "Merry Christmas."

PART
2

1

Wrong way up was how I first noticed her.

I hung from the ceiling, gripping a metal rafter that stretched the length of the venue. My body halved like some deranged gymnast's, jackknifed, a guitar dangling from my neck by its strap. Someone there had a camera with a blinding flash; another spectator would later say that, upon seeing me upside down, he'd considered socking my face. Blood rushed brainward as my unattended guitar's full-volume feedback took on an expression of its own. I didn't want to let go. Every few beats, I pumped my thighs to kick upward at the ceiling. Dust clouded down. The crowd cheered, and she stood front and center, not bothering to plug her ears like the pretty girls usually did, if they watched at all.

We'd booted Repa thirteen months earlier and had since enlisted several replacements. This latest drummer was surprisingly good, pounding out a frantic syncopation, a war-dance backbeat. My business with the rafter was their cue to improvise. Ethan's bass sounded as though he was ripping the strings from it, possibly with teeth. The bodily demands of our shows had inspired me to work off my beer flab through a regimen of calisthenics and barbells. I felt strong, ready to dangle there for hours.

The lights warping and my temples like blinking fists.

Her eyes seemed to dare me to hold on, a little longer.

Rushing the stage, a middle-aged hippie donning a purple tank top held the microphone to my lips. His face peered at me from a bizarre angle. People called him Pharaoh, and Repa had once woken on a couch to find him licking his neck—but that was old news. With each buck of my legs, I screamed.

That's it. Let it all out, Pharaoh seemed to say, following my mouth with the mic, astonishment crossing his face like he'd long ago hallucinated this particular instant.

I howled again. Pharaoh nodded: *Yes, yes, yes.*

We'd booked tonight's show as a benefit concert to pay for damages we'd done the last time we'd played this venue, a place known as the Bastard. Once again, my knuckles were chalked with drywall plaster. Ethan had pounded a scar into the plywood stage. The PA sounded blown, so we'd indulged in a compensatory freak-out attempting to transcend fidelity, as often was the case. As the years wear on, what characterizes my memory of those performances is murkiness. I think of them and feel shameful and sad and amazed at the way my body behaved in accordance to the sound. Sometimes I feel a jolt of pride, a longing to experience that music one last time, though I'm glad I no longer have what it would take. But I'll never forget how she deadeyed me, a look that said, *I know exactly what you mean.*

Like she'd seen all this before.

Pharaoh took no notice. He was ecstatic, feeding me the microphone. Helping me ride it all the way.

My strategy was that when someone in the audience glared, I'd attempt to match their eyes. The tough guys would glower hard for a minute, a staring contest, until they'd realize our aggressions had little to do with them. The crazy ones—the sex offender who'd been arrested on channel 7 news while wearing one of our T-shirts—would lock eyes the entire show, desperately, implying we had secret business together.

I'd never seen anyone like her, here or anywhere.

Standing at the edge of the light cast by a single bulb above the stage, she wasn't turning away until I was sure she had no fear of me and whatever problem I was flailing to exorcise. Through my tunneling vision I saw enough to know that she wore a black halter. Her hair was dyed red, darker at the roots. She was short and delicate, calm in the way of something with nuclear potential.

In the venue's bathroom, I made a long examination of my face in the mirror, as though I might rearrange certain features. I'd had my hair cut short. With my fingers I combed the sweat from it, a hackjob from a six-dollar barber on Ford Road. Outside in the parking lot, the crowd was leaving, and I found her bundled in an oversize peacoat, holding her breath as if to keep warm. January 1999. The final year of the millennium had only begun. For the sake of touching her, I pressed my hand to her back and felt the wool of her coat.

"Have a good night," I said.

The cold was a cleansing thing. Beneath the streetlights, the heat rose like mist from my skin.

"You, too," she said, half smiling in a way that kept me guessing.

She walked off with our drummer, the second since we'd booted Repa the previous winter. I watched her climb into his car, which was rusted and covered on all sides with bumper stickers and punk rock decals. This was in poor taste, you'd know, if you understood anything about hard-core aesthetics. A harsh line was drawn between the mall-punk tourists and those who believed punk wasn't a sound and a haircut but an ever-evolving defiance of conventions. Our band was struggling to preserve a degree of integrity to which our newest member, Blaine, with his earrings and studded belts and sloganeering, posed a dire offense.

As they drove away, Ethan appeared beside me, saying, "Look at that fucking car, man," and I said, "What do you think of his girl?"

Women—we still rarely broached the subject, a threat to the singleness of our purpose. Ethan had yet to meet Lauren—or Caitlin, for that matter.

"She's all right," he said. "But, I mean, she's with him." You would have thought he was talking about a virus. "So what does that tell you?"

It was obvious that Blaine was a shape-shifter who'd joined our band for local status. Punk rock points, some called it. He was nineteen, two years younger than I and six younger than Ethan. Brown eyed and brown haired, he had a smooth face that was never in need of a shave, but he could play anything, even Repa's parts—albeit half as loud. A big label, Relapse Records, had gotten in touch with the band, and we were counting on Blaine to play a tight set when the time came to impress.

But, about Blaine's girlfriend—

Watching his hatchback vanish, I decided her business with him was a naïve misfortune. One of those self-prescribed disasters people bring upon themselves as a ploy to excise their worst selves, communing with what they least desire in order to orchestrate their triumph over it.

That was her case, I was sure.

With Blaine it was something else. He'd gotten lucky on a scam and wound up with her in his passenger seat.

THE BAND HAD A whiff of parody without Repa, an element of farce. Ethan knew it, and so did I. We played songs Repa had blacklisted, knocking them out too easily, the notes too precise to be true. He'd been our offbeat heart. I'd have begged his return, but he'd put his drums in storage. Japanese was Repa's new obsession, and after a year of language tapes and caffeine pills, he'd moved to Okinawa. He was capable of unpredictable feats—I'd only begun to understand. For months after we sacked him he'd refused to speak to me, and in his absence I taped a photo of him to my amplifier, which I turned up twice as loud. Some shows were practically memorials to our ex-drummer and to what we'd been.

He and I patched things up one night before he left the country. I'd arrived at his Ypsilanti apartment, where he greeted me from a folding chair, a mountain of flash cards at his feet. Not moments before, he'd seen a witch tornadoing around the light fixture. "Right there," he'd said, pointing to the ceiling as fresh tattoos, some glistening with ointment, stretched across his forearms. One resembled a sickle; another brought to mind the tree of life.

"On a broom?" I'd asked.

"Nah," he said, "just spiraling around the lights, all crunched up in a ball."

He'd bought a chopper, too, and stenciled a biker logo on the back of his leather jacket, a one-man gang. Through the blurred early morning, I'd clutched his leathered ribs hard as he sped us across Ypsilanti on his black-and-chrome hog, both of us screaming "Bonsai!" when he yanked the handlebars for a pathetic wheelie. Then and there, trusting his every pop of the clutch, I'd felt our love liberate itself from the music we'd made. He was on his way, the sweet freak . . . he was gone.

By turn, we hazed Blaine, feeding him drinks until he'd keel on the rehearsal-space floor. Someone nicknamed him Mr. Personality, and our scene of cronies and hangers-on put the name to use. Blaine seemed to it take as a compliment, grinning, pulling from behind his ornamented earlobe a Marlboro Light he'd stuck there for such occasions. Will considered our newest member a personal insult and protested Blaine's third performance by walking onstage, miming the universal sign for cutting one's throat.

"If he can play, that's what matters," Ethan said.

Blaine rarely spoke of his girlfriend. When he did, he seemed to be excusing himself for future betrayals by saying that she lived two hours away. I assumed she'd escape him soon enough, so that I'd never see her again.

After a mid-winter rehearsal, I raided Blaine's car, digging through his cassettes and chucking across the parking lot the ones I found objectionable. Hamburger wrappers were littered on the backseat, drumsticks everywhere. A Polaroid was taped to the sun visor. Her eyes—green, I could finally be sure—dominated the photo. I wasn't one to covet what I couldn't have; fear of rejection often made me pretend I wanted nothing at all. But I despised Blaine for having touched her, tainting the silvery feeling moving through me as I stared at her face. I considered snatching the image, but it was theirs: her eyes were shining for him.

2

Will was naked and prune fingered, so he said, in the midst of taking a long bath. It wasn't the first time he'd phoned me from the tub, and he always seemed a touch sentimental once he'd been soaking awhile. Through the phone came an unending racket, a swish of bathwater followed by a metallic clang.

"What's that sound?" I said.

"Andrew's rifle," he said. "I talk to it when I practice my words. It helps me orate."

Too often I forgot that Will was a stutterer. Only when ordering food or asked his phone number would his voice lapse into a repetitive, locomotive stammer. His name, its dreaded *w* phoneme, was particularly troublesome. In rare moments, he'd be brought to tears about it, describing strategies he used to avoid "tight spots" where he'd be cornered with no choice but to struggle for minutes on end to produce a string of three mangled words. His diversionary tactics were masterful enough that few people recognized the wickedness of his condition. Lately, he'd been practicing, reading aloud the works of T. S. Eliot into a handheld cassette recorder and, when inspired, spouting free verse dredged up from the most infernal areas of his discontent.

"What's on your latest tape?" I asked.

"Everything," Will said. "Everything on my mind."

I didn't want to imagine.

"And, by the way," he said. "You're moving in. I told you I'd smoke Ralphy out of here."

I avoided Ralph. He'd blindsided me at an ice rink when we were kids and these days rolled with types you might encounter amid a strip-club brawl. He wore skintight blouses and was tanned year-round, which somehow magnified his unpredictable energies. To take over his room could mean rough stuff down the line.

"How did you do it?" I asked.

Will had no regard of any sort for Andrew's cousin.

"I think he heard one of my tapes was what did it," he said.

The day before, Will had left for his latest job at a nearby Oriental-rug shop, accidentally leaving his cassette deck on the kitchen counter. After hours of flipping Persian carpets and the whole lot of nothing he did there, he'd returned home to recite a new monologue and discovered the tape had been rewound. Not only that, it was cued to a particularly incensed passage, which, Will insisted, could only mean Ralph had taken a private listen to his recordings.

"Now he knows," he said, "something he didn't before."

I took it to be true because when I stopped by to survey my new room, even Andrew seemed puzzled by Ralph's desertion. Without explanation he'd fled the upper flat in a single February afternoon, evicted by the powers of verse.

IT WOULD TAKE WEEKS to make my move. The record store had just gone under, and Will had convinced the Armenians who owned the rug shop that I'd be a great choice for their new repairman. The hours were steady, and I was to arrive early each day. Caitlin had agreed to wake me each morning so that I'd be on time. "No snooze button," she warned. "No *Wake me in ten minutes.*"

For fear of shaking things up, I was hesitant to announce my plans. The year in Mom's house had passed with relative ease, and our lives were going placidly enough. We'd survived another Christmas, this time without incident. Caitlin was half-way through winter semester at a local college and waitressing at a steak house after classes, while Mom had a never-ending list of home improvements she intended to make. Now and then, Dad called to report on Red Wings scores and life at Ford Motor, offering us the option of believing he was sober—and I took him up on it.

Following my Christmas night chair-smashing inside his condo, he and I had gone half a year without really speaking. We'd finally reconnected over the past summer while his father was dying of heart failure and decades of unacknowledged alcoholism. Everything about my grandfather seemed wounding, a darkness behind closed doors, a source of lifelong damage resting heavily upon my dad. The night the old man finally died, I drove to Dad's condo and listened to him crying hard, saying, "You know, he never threw a baseball with me, not once."

We never mentioned the chair and picture frame that had gone missing from his place. We took a long drive and found ourselves outside of the rusted batting cages on Van Born Road, where Dad led the way to the experts-only section, a smiling-and-crying look on his face, saying, "Whoever whiffs the most buys dinner," as he chose a bat and dropped quarters into the slot.

I'd been there many times, in that very cage, but not for years and never with such a desire to impress. I swung desperately at the fastballs, redeeming myself with a crooked line drive as the machine coughed up the last of its pitches.

"You still got it," Dad said, stepping inside, stretching in a professional way before crushing most of the balls to the far end of the chain-link dome. "Looks like you're buying," he'd said, slugging my arm.

Afterward, I'd sat across from him at a diner, thinking of his heart as the greasy plates arrived but saying nothing about hardened arteries or my grandfather. Dad snatched the bill when it came, looking ahead toward a harsh night and somehow telling me with his eyes that he wanted badly to discover who I was before time had its way with him, too. Ever since, we'd been meeting Tuesdays at the diner, which was where we were, eating hamburgers one February evening seven months later, when I told him I was moving out of my mom's place.

"Andrew's gonna cut me a deal," I said, my essential concern being that he, or anyone, would see it as a failure on my part to be the man of the house now that he wasn't around. "I've got the new job sewing rugs, you know?" I said. "I'll come back and do the lawn, shovel the snow."

But he didn't seem to think much about it, pulling out his wallet and passing me some folded-up bills.

"Nah, nah," I said.

"Don't worry about it," he said. "Just remember to take your old man to dinner when you're rich."

A DAY LATER CAITLIN accosted me in the kitchen. I walked through the back door to find her brooding and waiting, a look on her face that meant business.

"So," she said. "You tell Dad before us, huh?" She opened the refrigerator and began pushing around milk cartons, leering as if everything inside had spoiled. "That's what I hear."

Her hair was dyed extra blonde, hyperblonde, the color of sunlit hay bales. She'd plucked her eyebrows into fierce, angular crescents, the skin beneath the tweezed hair a shade paler than the rest of her tanned face. Throughout our first year in Mom's house, she'd remained unnaturally bronze. The slight baby fat she'd carried for years had vanished, and when she spoke, it could appear she was trying to settle into her new face. My sister was changing. Tanning booths, hours at the gym, an ill-advised attempt at modeling—it didn't seem like her, not so much. Not to me.

"Moving out," Caitlin said. "Just like that."

She huffed into the refrigerator, mumbling about a block of cheese I'd neglected to wrap. "It's a good deal," I said. "One fifty a month."

"Are you and Willy Wonka gonna get stupid?"

When Mom returned from work, she said, "Well, you've been living in that basement awhile."

She was taking everything in stride, joining book clubs, enrolling in Irish-dancing lessons. Like me, she worried after Caitlin and was cautious about probing too sharply, not to jar loose any old miseries. Any perceived analysis of her emotions wounded my sister. She refused to talk about her weekly therapy. She hid her medication in a makeup case. Though I'm not sure any of us believed in depression, that it was the mysterious beast some people claimed. Mom spent workdays helping students with true disabilities, paraplegia and obsessive-compulsive disorder, Asperger's, fetal alcohol syndrome. She'd become a specialist in assisting autistic teenagers who on bad days could barely speak a comprehensible word, but she listened, and they invited her to birthday parties and spelling bees. They mailed her letters long after graduating.

She'd also begun helping Will with his stutter, giving him private lessons and cooking him dinners. I'd come home to find him at the kitchen table, picking at chicken bones, both of them laughing as though I'd narrowly missed a joke told at my expense. Over the summer, Mom had tamed the backyard into a fertile garden. The snapdragons and lilies reaching for the scant sunrays that leaked over the garage. All the flowers seemed to lean eastward. You'd have thought they'd been there all along, but it was Mom who'd planted them, who spent all winter looking forward to the thaw, the slow-blooming life.

Having announced my upcoming move, I sat down to dinner with Caitlin and my mom, wondering why we hadn't done so more often. If I was abandoning them, no one accused me, and I convinced myself I'd come by often to put myself at their disposal. Once we'd finished eating, I gathered our dishes to wash them.

"That's a first," Mom said. "What a nice surprise."

"You're never gonna come by here anymore, are you?" Caitlin said.

"It's a mile away."

"Yeah, but I know you," she said. "I know you."

WITH HER NEW LOOK, Caitlin seemed to gain a new confidence. Some days she was chipper, jamming the booty-bang dance music her coworkers had hipped her to. At any volume, those were sounds that injured my faith in humans, but when I'd barge into my sister's bedroom intending to cast insults, I'd see her midtwirl, arms raised, clumsily regaining her footing before she'd stick out her tongue and slam shut the door. Working at the steak house, she'd made friends with the kinds of people Will and I had long ago sworn oaths against, clubsters and thugs, left-behind Dearborn roughnecks and barroom shrews who'd done a semester at Henry Ford Community College before joining the local workforce.

"Morons," I'd tell her, though I knew none of them personally.

But my suspicions were strong, and she knew it.

"Can't you be happy I have friends?" she said.

Days before I moved out, I answered a knock at the door to find a guy in a sleeveless T-shirt looming on the porch. It was a sunny early March afternoon, yet hardly warm enough for the beach-party garb he wore. His arms were gargantuan oars, and I couldn't see his eyes through his sunglasses.

"Is Cait home?" he said. It was as though he were requesting someone I didn't know, until my sister nudged me aside, muttering, "Bye," as she passed through the doorway.

All I knew of this stud was that he was nicknamed Turbo and grilled rib eyes at the steak house while on leave from the Marines. Caitlin jumped in his pickup, and I assumed she'd taken pity on him, had agreed to counsel him on some other girl, a randy vixen who'd temporarily wrecked his ego.

She'd been spending hours on the phone, listening as her new friends poured out their troubles. If Lauren called the house, it was usually for Caitlin, and their talks were long and hushed and of matters they both referred to as deep. These depths, I wanted to presume, gushed with touchy-feely whispers and pseudo-poetic analyses of love and life; many years later, though, I'd be forwarded several letters they'd exchanged during this time and would meet a side of my nineteen-year old sister I'd only imagined. A girl who wrote artfully about her own suicide attempts, oscillating between images of having her stomach pumped and lucid observations of the snow falling outside whatever window she'd sat before while penning those messages: *It's so beautiful how every flake falls down to earth and is then just kind of absorbed . . . Lauren, I grazed death physically but inside I felt truly dead. When the ambulance brought me to the hospital they parked me next to a man bleeding all over from being shot, and I don't remember any of it.* Her handwritten tone that of someone desperate to confess her burdens but fearful of the implications: *Don't think I'm psychotic, though; it was a part of my growth and a part of who I am.*

And the part that hurt most:

I feel like I know more about you than I do my brother. We were close once but it's like he's become like a stranger—a claim Lauren wouldn't have argued against. She and I had agreed, by then, to break up once and for all. Which didn't end my hope that she'd be the one to guide my sister away from the many horrible choices available to attractive, confused young women. Choices like Turbo, about whom the only further insight I was able to offer was a useless but universal, "Fuck him."

Not that I didn't try to imagine the young man who might have suited Caitlin. I liked to think he existed, perhaps in some nearby town: a steady boy whose head was screwed on in a way mine wasn't. Desirable strangers did exist, I knew, because I'd recently had a few dates with unusual girls from acculturated suburbs: kind, pretty girls who made mixtapes and talked about vegetarianism. Perfect on paper. That I preferred being alone made me worry there was a problem with my soul, as though my constant thoughts of Blaine's distant girlfriend were my way of avoiding women altogether.

WORKING AT THE RUG shop, I had plenty of time to mull things over. Day after day, I wore a surgical mask and pulled ancient, dusty threads from the carpets. I opened wounds and stitched them with new yarn, losing myself in the patterns. Cat urine, decades of shed skin, dander, and dirt—they were all there in each piece of unthreaded string. The fibers clouded my face, moting in the sun that came through the showroom window. Certain rugs caused my forearms to swell with hives. Will sat in a corner, sipping coffee and reading the paper until the appearance of a customer required him to flip through the stacks of carpets.

At the record store, I'd spun whatever albums I liked. That Frank Sinatra was the only music the Armenians permitted made the job feel like a type of penance. I might have quit, had Caitlin not been so vigilant about waking me each morning, making sure I'd be on time, regardless of how little I'd slept.

"Time to get up, lazy." She'd be fully dressed, standing at the foot of my mattress while stressing over a midterm or preparing for the gym. She'd grown by thrusting herself headfirst into change. And if the manic nature of this left me on edge, she seemed happier than she'd been in years.

She was sitting on my mattress in Mom's basement the day I packed up my room. A prophecy was being fulfilled: that Will and I would work and live and conspire together at all times. As kids we'd talked of co-owning a mansion, with a junglelike atrium housing endangered creatures and a private rock club, a racetrack circling the premises. The upper flat was as close as we'd come.

"It smells down here," Caitlin said, gazing around the basement. "Probably will for years."

I peeled posters from my walls and loaded my records into crates. I cleaned up anything my mom wouldn't want to discover. Caitlin was curious about what I'd take with me and what I'd leave behind. I made sure she was looking as I slipped the trinkets and sweaters she'd given me into the boxes.

"Who's gonna wake you up for work every morning?" she asked.

"I'm perfectly capable," I said, as if the wake-up calls had simply been my strategy for seeing her first thing each day, but that wasn't true. And, really, life never would be so easy to manage without her.

3

She tilted her head. She raised her eyebrows and smiled and waved me over.

I shuffled toward her until I was close enough to hear her say, "I've wanted to talk to you all weekend," to which I replied several ways in my thoughts before realizing I wasn't yet able to speak. We were in a parking lot outside a veterans' hall, where the band had just finished our set as part of a Detroit music festival. I was catching my breath, but I'd rehearsed this moment: what the two of us might say if we wound up face-to-face. Now that it was happening, the script I'd prepared seemed pitifully out of reach, a wordless flickering. She wore a green sweater. The sun had fallen, and in the light from the streetlamps her eyes were the most obvious thing in the world.

"Are you busy?" she said.

I'd screamed my throat hoarse, lending my voice a manly rasp it didn't possess otherwise. "Let's take a walk," I said, knowing Blaine would be watching.

She nodded, and we started off.

It was late-March, the last night of a three-day extrava-
ganza: bands for days, forty or so in all, packed into a Knights
of Columbus hall. I'd known she'd be there, as well as the usual
culprits: Will, gussied up like a pilgrim—his latest costume—
and the jackass fan who'd set knives on our amps in hopes we'd
gash ourselves. And hundreds more who came from god knows
where, as far as California. Warden had arrived with his hair
gelled into a preposterous afro. Inside the hall he'd fastened
a banner that read: CTW- BOYCOTT THIS MOTHERFUCKERS, which
he'd stood defiantly beneath, peddling records no one intended
to buy.

She and I stepped through the crowds. Musicians gathered
around vans. People stood huddled and smoking, showing off
the latest albums they'd scored. Some called out, "Good set,
man." They slapped hands with me.

"You know everyone," she said.

I'd come to feel lonesome at those shows. Now that we'd
gored our way into the scene, I felt no reason to be there. The
bands and seven-inch singles and T-shirts, the anarchist pam-
phlets. Loudmouths dressed in safety-pinned shreds of clothes,
spouting half-cooked politics. Caitlin had wanted to attend
that night, but I'd forbidden it. Soon enough, I'd regret not
introducing her to that world of fringe ideals and tube-powered
distortion. There were good people to be found there, dream-
ers looking for answers, but I didn't want my sister witnessing
the person I'd become away from home, the way I badgered the
audiences, blaspheming the punkish ceremony even as we were
at its center.

But once the sound took hold, everything was worth it.
Never mind the crowds—I still believed in music. That if
I learned to play with just the right touch, a new beginning
would arise, one from which I'd never turn back.

The girl at my side, that's how it felt to be near her, at the edge of a life-altering hugeness about which I knew nothing, only the lightness of my being.

"I've heard so many bands, my head's going to explode," she said.

"Mine already has."

"I noticed," she said. "It's a good look."

WE WALKED TOGETHER BETWEEN the parked cars. She stepped with her hips angled outward, a dancer's graceful sway, as we moved across the asphalt. It was officially springtime, but gray snow still lined the edges of the parking lot where the winter plows had mounded heaps. Her jeans were baggy, and beneath the cuffs were skateboard shoes, silly things. Boots—you wore boots if you wanted to be taken seriously. I was summoning my sharpest extrasensory capacities, X-ray vision and inner soul surveillance, scanning for evidence that she was a dud or an illusion.

Her face was the kind of thing you wanted to float your hand over before actually touching it. Then, softly as you could, you'd graze your fingers against her cheek, and nerves you didn't know existed would come alive in your palm, and you'd make the feeling last as long you could. After barely a moment beside her, I felt anchorless, helpless to effect whatever attitude of coolness I might have wished to carry. It was a kind of emotion I couldn't remember tangling with. When there seemed nothing left to do, I said her name for the first time.

"Well, Angela. Here we are."

"Where else would we be?"

She was shorter than Lauren, whom I'd forgotten entirely in the moment but who was present like a phantom to which I unconsciously compared Angela, the severe, unnameable differences.

She and drummer Blaine had broken up, or she thought they had.

So I'd heard.

And what else? She was an English major, a ballerina, with a twin sister somewhere. She hosted a radio show; spun good records, heavy ones, sad ones. She lived in a dormitory two hours west, in Kalamazoo.

We were getting toward the back of the parking lot. We were almost alone.

"I have dreams about you," she said. "I don't know why I'm doing this, but I feel like I have to know you."

My minivan had met a timely death outside the band's rehearsal space one winter evening. "That's my car," I said, pointing to my used Escort hatchback parked near the edge of the lot. I opened the passenger door for her, and we sat inside, holding Rolling Rocks I'd stashed beneath the seats; I'd been told it was a hydrating beer. The bottles required an opener, and as I dug through my pockets, Angela took it upon herself to twist off the caps using her teeth.

"Where did you learn that?"

"Oh, you know," she said. Then she got down to cases. "I just have this feeling about you."

"What do want to do about it?" I said.

"What do you mean?"

Whatever I felt, I wanted to pull a string and let it come down. "Let's screw all this and drive to Chicago, right now," I said, as charming as I knew how to be. My new room in the upper flat didn't cross my mind. There was little there yet but a mattress, and home, wherever that was, was not where I wanted to take her. I wanted to be as far away as we could go, knowing we might drive for days before it was all straightened out.

"Chicago," she said. "Why Chicago?"

The band had been playing there every few weeks; it was the first place that had come to mind. "We'll go," I said. "You and me. It only costs six bucks to drive there in this thing."

"I've always wanted to do what you do," she said.

Her hair was chopped short, pinned with barrettes. Her loose clothes—you couldn't tell what was beneath. All I could see was her face, a look on it like she'd traveled a year carrying a message of great import.

"What do you mean?" I said.

"When you play. Go wild, screaming like that. And then when you touched my back after the show that night, I knew there was more."

She was there. She was. She might have been the first person I'd ever truly seen. The entirety of her seemed conscious in her welled eyes, a green soul-world of things gorgeous and passionate and totally unknown.

"You look like an alien," I said.

"I think the same about you."

Like a bird crashing into a glass pane, a hand slapped the window: Blaine, motioning for me to roll it down.

"What are you guys doing? Making out?"

"We're discussing literature," I said.

"Oh," he said. "The book club."

To impress the festival crowd, he'd shaved his hair into a dismal Mohawk. The brown tuft dangled to his nose. He slapped the window again before vanishing through the parked cars toward the glow of distant cigarettes.

Music was faint, coming from inside the venue.

"I just wanted to tell you," she said.

I'd meant it about Chicago, driving all night. I felt I had nowhere else to be, ever again. Angela was stalling; maybe she didn't believe me. Maybe she was too sane to up and leave at the turn of the key, or maybe Blaine had injected his wicked intent into our first moment together.

WE WALKED BACK TOWARD the music as if we didn't know each other; but we did, before we'd spoken a word. Things like that happen, though I hadn't known it until that night. The festival was a thousand punks canned inside a banquet hall. A band from Gainesville was onstage: Hot Water Music, the last act of the night and the only one I wanted to see. The singer was a copper-bearded, sunburned badass who'd once put up my band in his Florida mobile home. He bled triumphantly from a collision with a stage diver's boot. Their music was the spiritual opposite of ours, the kind of thing to get you out of bed instead of stomping your guts. The crowd surged forward, crawling over one another, hollering the words. Battle hymns, a revival—I felt it, too. I imagined myself in their band, shouting an entirely different song.

Angela and I were parted by the crowd. We did nothing to stop it. I pushed toward the front of the stage, watching her swaying among the bodies. She sank beneath the horizon of limbs and bobbed again at the surface.

At the edge of the stage, a tall, blond, knuckleboned skateboarder I knew locked a sweaty arm around my neck and kissed my temple. With another beat we were wrestling, twisting through the crowd until we stumbled into the parking lot.

All around us, bands loaded equipment into vans and trailers.

The air was damp, but it hadn't rained—just springtime, the clouds changing form. Having come so close to her, I was wired. I would have done anything, leaped from a building or gnawed cement. I squeezed my friend's throat in the crook of my elbow, wrenching hard. When I let go, his neck was roped with veins.

"So," he said. "You wanna get serious?"

We were on that verge, where drunken, friendly sparring could go bloody.

He snatched a canvas bag filled with cymbals and hoisted it like a battering shield as he charged, slamming it into my kidneys.

"Do it," he said, throwing the sack. It hit the cement with a muffled clatter.

We took turns bludgeoning each other, laughing with each attack. Then we squatted against the fender of a parked car, massaging our ribs, each draping an arm over the other.

She was somewhere inside. Close, yet with a hundred bodies between us. If I sat there long enough, I might catch her leaving. The music would be over, and the cars would vanish; we'd be the only two left, and we'd talk for hours or stare out through the windshield like fugitives clutching this one thing it'd been our right to steal from the incomprehensible world as I drove her to wherever she wanted to be . . .

But, no, none of it happened like that.

4

Caitlin had been more or less right about my life at the upper flat, stupidity being a frequently occasioned thing, bending now and then toward trouble. One morning, not long before the sun rose, Andrew and I found ourselves standing in the beer and wine aisle of Farmer Jack grocery. It must have been the stillness there, Muzak echoing through aisles of cereal boxes and soup cans—suddenly I knew we were shit out of luck.

"Wait," I said. "It's gotta be three A.M." Long past Michigan's cutoff time.

A case of High Life was nestled beneath my arm.

"Four," Andrew said, holding up his wristwatch as if he'd known all the while.

This was his slow season, no lawns to mow and little electrical work, allowing him full-bore pursual of his self-education in quantum physics and solar energy, studies that were often aided by drink. The coolers rattled. Shelves of wine bottles stretched away from us—fifteen feet or so of gleaming reds and greens.

Andrew was pacing. It was like he was walking in a hall of colored glass. "Imagine that," he said. "Time disappeared."

For weeks, we'd been celebrating my new residency in the upper flat with beer and records and a whole lot of nothing much. Earlier that evening, we'd had an impassioned debate over natural selection, nature and nurture, and other mysteries about which we knew only catchphrases, interrupted only by the discovery that we'd run out of spirits.

Will remained at the flat, a mere two hundred yards across Michigan Avenue. A weeknight. Hugging the box of beer forced me to consider the fact I had to be at the rug shop in a matter of hours.

"What now?" I said.

Andrew walked to the end of the aisle. He wore a flannel jacket and work boots. Will had buzzed his dark blond hair right down to his thick, hearty skull.

"Now is now," he said.

With a gentle palm, he dusted the wine bottles, hearing them clack together like loose teeth. He paused, teasing a bottle neck with a finger, smiling, fingering the glass neck a bit harder, until the bottle tipped from the rack, falling end over end toward the floor. As the glass shattered, I knew we were in for something. Andrew moved down the racks with a creeping fascination as one after another the bottles crashed, spilling purple through the aisle.

Moments like that: I guess you could say we lived for them.

I was sure I heard a commotion coming our way.

What happened next wasn't a decision, exactly. I asked myself if I had the nerve to bust for the exit, and the answer arrived with a jolt to my thighs, igniting a flurry of strides. My arms cradled the chilled box. I heard Andrew chuckling behind me. As we passed the checkout station, an employee cried, "Hit the doors! The doors!"

Andrew dashed past me with a gingerly step. He'd been able to leap backyard fences with barely a running start; I'd seen him scale brick buildings—they wouldn't catch him. The automated doors had closed tight, unresponsive to our jailbreak approach. Evidently they hadn't locked, because Andrew wrenched them apart, holding them open long enough for me to get a leg through and squeeze myself into the night.

Andrew ran alongside the building's facade with the awful idea of taking cover in the woods behind.

"Aye," I said, but it was every man for himself.

I booked ass across the parking lot, cradling the beer, heading for the upper flat, which sat in plain view beyond the avenue. Halfway across the asphalt expanse, I heard the huff and puff of the vigilante gaining on me, steps away from tackling me to the pavement. A voice behind, motoring, "Mo-fucker, mo-fucker, mo-fucker."

Sacrificing our booty was my only chance. I whirled, tossing the box of beer. It skidded across the blacktop, wide of a husky, bug-eyed employee coming at me with pumping forearms and a face reddened with a need for cruel justice. I saw all this in the space between heartbeats; then fear carried me into a frantic sprint. Running with a singleness of purpose, I opened each stride a little wider, knowing that you never, ever look back until you're certain you've escaped.

WILL WAS SITTING ON the couch, lost in music, as I barged through the door.

"Andrew," I said. "He started breaking bottles."

"Yeah?" Will looked as though I'd spoiled a meal he was in the midst of blessing. There was free jazz playing, or one of his psycho-ambient records. His hair was slicked with royal jelly, the latest sleaze he was working. "You never know with Andy," he said, and Will was one of the only people who could shorten Andrew's name and get away with it. Andy Dandy—fighting words.

"Andy, Andy," he said, and went to bed.

I was spooked the way people get when they've been bedeviled by a horror flick and cannot rest until they've checked the locks, bolted the windows. I switched off the lights and lay on the couch, listening for Andrew's return or a phone call. Jail, I imagined. Bail money. This was life in the upper flat. How it would be from here on, and I was okay with that.

A half hour passed before Andrew's steps sounded in the stairwell.

I met him at the door.

"What happened?"

In his hand was a cup of coffee, steady as could be.

"I ran out back, down by the river," he said. "A rent-a-cop was on me, but he wasn't going into the trees." He sipped from his Styrofoam cup. "I would have turned his lights out."

"Where'd you get that?"

"It's decaf," he said. "Here, you take it."

He wasn't breathing heavily, not a bit. Andrew was deadpan serene, always. Even when he'd snap, come undone, which wasn't often, he'd move swiftly and methodically. Only his eyes would go feral, as if he'd stared into an eclipse and seen the end of all of us. You'd have to shake him out of it—after the fight or fire or whatever. Sometimes he'd get that way talking about the solar panels he was saving for. The sun's energy, quantum what have you. It was a good thing the guard hadn't found him.

"I threw the beer at the other guy," I said. "He almost got me."

"No," Andrew said, scanning the room like there were energies yet to be detected, as though I were an impartial presence.

I never liked it when he did that. "No," he said. "No, he didn't. You would have done what you had to."

• • •

Angela and I managed to swap phone numbers through the college radio station where she volunteered as a DJ. We talked for hours, late at night, about books and records and who we understood ourselves to be. She had depths, and wounds, and a giant need for honest love—I heard it in her voice. After I hung up, the memory of her raspy alto and exhalations of cigarette smoke kept me awake, going over whatever we'd said. When the phone bill came, Andrew circled the long-distance charges and made me cough up the fees, which I paid gladly.

Mom and Caitlin said they'd noticed a difference in me. I'd been hugging them chivalrously. One afternoon, I bought them flowers. I'd heard that when love gets a bite on you, it can blind you to your fears, and it was true that I was feeling some type of rapture. Good weather energized me. Music sounded better than ever. I'd even begun cracking jokes at band rehearsals, which I'd leave early enough to call Angela before she fell asleep. Blaine would diddle on his snare, glaring in a way that confirmed he knew what was going down.

By late April, Angela and I finally made a date. I spent the preceding days jogging and doing push-ups, being frugal with my weekly pay while enlisting Caitlin to trim my hair. "You need a professional," she said, nevertheless putting the shears through a workout, snipping until an undeniable pride crossed her face.

That Saturday, I drove two hours across Michigan toward Kalamazoo, listening to what I believed was sentimental music:

the Cure's "A Strange Day," "Praise Your Name" by the Angels of Light. It was the first time I'd taken that stretch of highway without the band, and there was something right about it, and a little bit wrong, which made me want to get there that much faster. Arriving in Kalamazoo, I became instantly lost and wasted an hour tooling around the university my mom had attended thirty years before. When I found Angela's dormitory, I called her from a pay phone in the lobby.

"I couldn't do it," I said. "I had to turn around and go back."

"You're downstairs, aren't you?" she said, magically and shockingly busting my first attempt to pull one over on her.

No sooner had I entered her room than the phone rang and Blaine's voice came over the answering machine. I stared at the device, the red dot of light that flashed as he spoke. He'd timed this to perfection. *I hope you're both happy*, he said. *It's the last you'll hear from me. I won't be here tomorrow.*

"Man," I said, "you don't think he'd—"

"He plays that card," Angela said. "You have no idea."

I'd had a man-to-man with Blaine the day before, using the tone my father took when deliberating with cops or busybody neighbors. I told him if he wanted to quit the band, it was fine by me, because my seeing Angela was something destiny had insisted on. He claimed I was breaching the musicians' unwritten code. "A band," he'd said, "is like family." Then he said that I might as well have broken into his house and ganked his wallet, which gave me a clearer idea about his conception of her.

The machine snapped off, and Angela opened her arms. We hugged for the first time, casually, except for the length of it, until the phone rang again.

"Enough of that," she said, unplugging the device.

Her roommate had left for the weekend, and the space was divided into two very different halves. Angela's oil paintings and books faced a wall on which her roommate had hung pennants and family photographs. I felt I was exactly where I should be but had no sense of what to do now that I'd arrived. Playing cool, I inspected Angela's cassettes and discs, finding a number of jewels I'd never have expected. Deep cuts—a Nick Cave bootleg, especially.

"Those are old," she said. "Are you judging?"

For the sake of touching her, I wanted to reach out and do something goofy to her cheeks. She locked the door, and we avoided looking at each other, and then we laughed because there was this feeling that we had a whole lot to say—but why rush a goddamn thing?

WE TOOK A WALK. We sat on a bench by a pond. Escorting her to dinner, I must have believed our best option to be the palace-sized Italian chain restaurant on the periphery of the local mall. Free bread and a syndicated soundtrack of *italiano* hits. I made a show of flashing my ID while ordering a bottle of the red stuff, thinking a legal drink would appear classy. I took it down in gulps, putting my stomach in knots. Angela was nineteen and had to sneak nips from my glass because the waitress had made a stink. She hardly touched her noodles and would later tell me she'd been so nervous she'd thrown up before I arrived. I'd never have known. When we stopped for ice cream on the way home, Angela raised her cone in a toast and daubed her nose with it. A vanilla gob slid down her chin as she crossed her eyes and stuck out her tongue, and in every second of her joy I felt also the most tender sadness, which made me all the more crazy for her.

Back in her dorm, once night fell, she put on a disc, the Cocteau Twins, angelic-sounding gibberish that, until that moment, had baffled me. A radiator in the corner blasted hot air. Angela pulled off her sweater. Beneath, she wore a black tank top. Her arms were taut from striking ballet poses; her skin had the smoothness of something never before touched. We smoked and clanked beers, each of which she pried open with her teeth because it made me laugh. Her manner of looking me dead in the eye caused me to mispronounce certain words. She didn't correct me—but she would, soon enough.

The stories we traded felt like they were astrological alignments or proof of our having the same rare blood type. She'd seen her father raise his fists; I'd seen my dad cracked out of his head. I told her my sister had a sad streak. Angela claimed her twin had always outshone her, which seemed unthinkable. And once I kissed her, we did nothing else until the sun rose. Fully clothed. Hands in hair. Our dry tongues figuring out every possible combination there was to discover.

Sometime that morning I broke to use Angela's bathroom, a chamber full of lotions and hair ties, where in the mirror I noticed a cable of hardened snot clinging to my nostril, twisting onto my upper lip. When I returned, my expression must have looked that of a man who'd just pissed himself midflight.

"How long had it been there?" I pointed to my septum.

"Just about all night."

"Why didn't you tell me?"

"I didn't care," she said. "I didn't want to waste the moment."

· · ·

Once the schools let out, Mom was home every day, perfecting her garden. Caitlin took full-time hours at the steak house and lamented the fact that I was rarely around. Angela came home to live with her parents on Grosse Ile, a well-to-do island in the

Detroit River that I helped her escape at every chance. At the foot of the Grosse Ile bridge some joker had raised a signpost decorated with the word REALITY and arrows that pointed away from the island and toward the industrial mainland, an apt symbol for what it felt like each time I drew near. By day Angela worked in a chiropractor's office. Most evenings I drove a half hour south to wait in her parents' driveway until she slipped out the back door. Then we'd creep through Grosse Ile's bird sanctuary or cross the bridge into Windsor, Ontario, where the legal drinking age included both of us.

Hoping to make things official, I brought Angela to Dearborn and introduced her to Mom and Caitlin. Angela shook their hands and spoke clean, eloquent sentences. The word "perverse" made its way into their small talk, as did "posthumous," and I could tell Caitlin was astounded by how unlike Lauren this dark-haired stranger was. My sister seemed to shirk away, perhaps feeling under-spruced and underdressed, except for the silver watch Lauren had given her many months prior. Angela wore no makeup at all but had added a new piercing—a steel band that clamped her upper lobe.

"She looks so young," my mom said. "A beauty."

Caitlin nodded. Though she was three months older than Angela, and an inch taller, my sister was stunted by my new love's unspoken intensity, her sharp green eyes, which looked straight at you, took in your details. Yet another thing I loved about her. And I interpreted by Caitlin's enhanced shyness that she found Angela at once dangerous and enviable. The two of them smiled at each other with friendly, uncertain faces, like devotees unsure whether their religion was one and the same.

My dad happened to drop by that evening, greeting us with a black eye and head gash he claimed to have suffered while opening his kitchen cupboards. Caitlin opted to roll with this one, letting him take the floor. His mood was all shine, and he turned up his charm, stealing the scene with a few wisecracks. "You let me know if he gives you a hard time," he told Angela. "I'll take care of it." Other than his gash, he looked in fighting spirits—I was glad to see it, to see Angela smiling as he jived away. It wasn't until later, once we were alone, that she said, "You have your mom's eyes and your dad's face."

ANGELA'S PARENTS WERE STINGY about lending her the family car, which stranded her on that island between Canada and America. They grounded her for being out past her curfew and were ready to battle at any time; in the near past there'd been fists and hair pulling, bruises and soul-burning insults of a psychotic nature. Angela was just beginning to disown them, truly and irrevocably, as I was slowly comprehending the miracle that a person like her had risen from such ugliness. Hearing about her parents inspired gratitude for my own. When the night came to sit down at their dinner table, I drove to Grosse Ile nipping a quart of Black Velvet with a wish for instant tranquility. Pulling off the highway, I took a clumsy swig as my Escort coasted along a winding exit ramp. The bitter swallow stirred my gut, and without further warning I retched a hot plash of ramen noodles onto my jeans.

Ten minutes of sink showering inside a truck-stop restroom, then spreading the crotch of my dampened jeans beneath the hand dryer, only convinced me that Angela's parents would sniff me out and know I was a wayward Dearborn shitheel. As it happened, her mother and father shook my hand fiercely, relieved to see any face in lieu of Blaine's. Angela's father offered me a beer. Her mom made a point of roasting Blaine, and I nodded accordingly, thrilled that they found me a preferable suitor. Angela scowled because nothing these people said brought her peace. And the farther she got from Blaine, the more ominous he seemed. That very night, he sat parked at the end of her street, revving away the moment I left her house. Days before, he'd trailed us to the Canadian border, turning back only once we reached the foot of the Ambassador Bridge.

"So," he said at our next rehearsal, "you met the parents."

Band life was stranger by the day, neither of us saying much more but occasionally locking eyes while we played. Ethan carried on, pounding his bass and talking strategy about upcoming tours. Blaine seemed to delight in the arrangement, as if through proximity he still had the opportunity to spoil my idea of Angela, who'd seen him parked outside her workplace and answered hang-up calls at all hours of the night. He was making it known that he had no intention of quitting. Though I'd never have admitted he was anything more than a hired gun, I felt with him the closeness one does to a rival. Our first Canadian tour was booked, just weeks away, and I saw no choice but to continue as planned. If Blaine could endure it, that was reason enough to prove I could, too.

• • •

Having worked three months at the rug shop, I knew the proper threads for any given carpet, how to dye and distress the yarn before needling it through the weave. In the same way, I'd gotten used to the unanswerable questions the Armenians fussed over: what day of the week the burger shack across Michigan Avenue served the best sliders, and who was the richest man in Dearborn. The owners lived in an apartment above the shop. We called the man of the store the General. His wife acted as a saleswoman and worked the showroom. Their youngest son, Georgie, was a failed pop singer whose job was to clean rugs.

Throughout the workdays they spoke to Will and me as though we were two waifs in need of worldly guidance. The General's wife attempted to coach Will on life management and asked little work of him. Georgie, when he arrived in the afternoon, would explain to me what it was going to take to make it big in the music business.

"You gotta have the face for it. The whole package."

Not to say that the Armenians were ungenerous, simply that Will and I took offense at their pity. Our only recourse was to pretend we were lovers, pinching at each other's buttocks and holding hands as we dusted the showroom.

"This place," Will said, "is a whorehouse of neutral energy."

I'd gripe to him, telling him that Blaine had stolen Angela's mail, that he'd sent a message to her twin sister in Ohio, attempting to turn her against me. How it all would end was a worry eclipsing all others in my mind. "You're only as good as your nemesis" was Will's advice, but that wasn't going to do, and he knew it. To make sure I was in fighting shape, we began sneaking to the back room used for washing rugs. Will would choose a rolled carpet—big ones, thirty-footers—urging me to throw jabs at the barrel-like shapes.

"Hit it," he'd say. "Give me the rough stuff."

One morning I attacked a hulking rug, a spool the size of two stacked oil drums. Will held it steady, bracing it like a heavy bag as I slugged with a sloppy wrath, punching so wildly that when I backed away my knuckles were scraped raw, trickling blood. Will held my wrists like a trainer preparing a contender for another round, scrubbing the wounds with a sponge he'd found in a pail of blackened suds.

"That a girl," he said. "We'll get you cleaned up."

When I returned to the showroom, the General called me over to teach me a new braid that was to be tied along the fringe of a rare Persian. Sitting beside him on a workbench, I watched his fingers pull the elaborate threading this way and that. Up, under, and around.

"Now," he said. "Let me see you try."

I approached the carpet with my palms upturned, but soon enough it was necessary to pivot my hands in order to loop and interlace the thread. A small bit of blood pooled in the creases of my knuckles, thickening with each pulse. I smeared it on my jeans and went on threading as the General studied my hands, saying nothing, watching me tie the perfect knot.

5

Without Repa aboard, the Orgasmatron was but a corroded jalopy, all man-stink and no charm, rattling north on the Ontario 401. I knew this route, the billboards and kilometer markers. Certain farmhouses and barns were familiar as I drove. The tour's first show was in Guelph, four hours from Detroit. We'd just passed through Windsor, where Blaine swiped a carton of cigarettes from the duty-free store. He was sprawled across the bench seat with a cap pulled over his face, and I wished he'd fall asleep.

"Our ride," I told him, "would be over if your ass had gotten caught."

"Relax," said Blaine. "I don't get caught."

Ethan sat dozing in the passenger seat.

I gassed the van.

How many fans might await us in Guelph? Twenty? Thirty?

Our prospects for a big record deal had mysteriously fizzled, probably due to a mistake we hadn't known we'd made. I'd begun taking stock of what the band was costing my life, but what kept

Ethan and me going, what always would, was the possibility of our music being remembered. Or that we'd someday taste the same inspiration our heroes had, the ones who'd truly put themselves on the line—and we'd come so close to that, once or twice.

We'd driven an hour in silence when Ethan's hand shot upward with a raised index finger. He dug through a bag of cassettes, injecting one into the boom box. "Almost forgot," he said, and I knew he was talking about what Repa called our good-luck jam. *Play it, or we're cursed*, Repa would have demanded the moment we'd left Detroit. Ethan pecked the rewind button, amending the oversight.

What was this?

Thoughts of Ionesco World Tour, 1999.

We'd amassed a checklist of superstitions: Never park on streets named after presidents. Never eat in towns advertising a Perkins Restaurant. The rare occasion we sprung for a room, it was never, under any circumstance, a Motel 6. Ethan suspected the chain to be owned by the Freemasons, while Repa had alleged the number 6 was a hex. Other traditions were pure jest. Every time we passed the west Michigan town Climax, we writhed in our seats, feigning lavish orgasms. Repa's performance had always been most euphoric: shrills and coital whimpers that lasted for miles.

Our phobias and honorary customs were the ligaments that held together our traveling creep show, and none was more important than our good-luck song: a loathing yet triumphant barn burner that repeated the line *Just can't win* with a fury that bolstered us for the miles ahead. If we were to have a legacy, so it would go. Decades later, when the connoisseurs unearthed our records, they'd hear our earnestness. Never did win—but what glorious losers. And this, I could tell, was the spirit we were now missing.

Ethan pressed PLAY on the tape deck.

As the song began, Blaine perked up to study me in the rearview. He had an eerie ability to detect vulnerabilities, sentimentalities. Behaving subtly, doe-eyed, he'd provoke tender moments in a way that contaminated them. Ethan and I grooved along, thinking of Repa across the sea, basking alone in Japanese neon.

Blaine fired up a Marlboro Light.

"What's this?" he said. "Mick Jagger on Valium?"

Ethan notched up the dial, as though in due time Blaine would hear what we were hearing. It was midafternoon. Day or night, Canadians drove with their headlights ablaze. I steadied the wheel and switched on the beams, waiting for side 1 to end.

AFTER A WHILE, YOU really do become some version of what you've pretended to be. You fake yourself straight into form. Once I could no longer recognize certain aspects myself, I realized whatever soul-exchange prophecy I'd bought into was long under way. To achieve self-invention, you first evacuate the truest parts of yourself—they were slipping from me, connected only by a fear of losing touch completely. I'd begun to sense this, an awareness that pestered my thoughts as I stared out the van's windshield or to the ceiling in an unfamiliar house.

We were playing well; that wasn't the trouble. Blaine had mastered our songs. Onstage, every beat landed as it should. Yet the shows were black holes, out of time with reality. I'd begun feeling this about my entire life, as though it had always been occurring in a dimension that existed apart from who I was. I wanted to be two different people, or three or four—none of whom I liked entirely. But I imagined awaking years later to find myself rooted in the world, clear in my sense of purpose. A doting, obnoxious uncle to Caitlin's children. I'd visit Mom, having proved my mistakes had rounded me into a dignified, honorable man. Maybe I saw a small house in the country, with shelves of books and records. Angela dancing as a record spun. And a mutt in a field, an acoustic guitar on the porch. I would have told you there was no place for someone like me, but I didn't truly believe that. I had a dream for my life, just like anyone. Yet without the music, what I was worth? To my friends? To Angela or anyone else?

Each night, after the shows, I searched the streets for pay phones. Between verses I'd been biting my gums so hard they burned at the touch of the gas-station peanuts we ate on the drives. Talking to Angela long distance, I spat blood on the cement, a sweat-through T-shirt plastered to my chest, the knees of my jeans dirtied from the stage floor.

It was through the phone, on an international call, that we first said it.

"I love you."

"I love you, too."

"Don't say 'too,'" she said. "If you have to say 'too,' then don't say anything."

Her sweet logic made perfect sense. Though her face, after a couple weeks, had become impossible to remember precisely.

"Come back safe," she said. "We have all the time we want."

A NIGHT LATER I had Blaine by the collar, pinned against the backseat. The van was parked outside a house belonging to a Toronto local who'd been good enough put us up, who was now flashing his porch light at random intervals with a purpose I was unwilling to interpret. As I shouted, my spittle misted Blaine's face. He'd buzzed his Mohawk to a military crop, which suited him well. He wasn't homely, not at all—just sneaky eyed and wolf jawed. He was taller than me, ropy and slippery, the kind of fighter who'd go straight for the jewels. His strength surprised me as he grabbed my forearms.

"Say it again," I told him. "Let me hear."

Some locals had introduced us to a potent Canadian malt called Mongoose that had done us no favors. As a welcoming homage, the opening band had given us a husk of bottle rockets we'd fired off after the show, and it was amid this—the lighting of wicks, aiming the rockets from the Orgasmatron's windows—that Blaine mumbled an uncouth something or other about Angela. A barely audible, seedy epithet he'd been saving for such a moment.

We'd been at it since, for nearly an hour, until, finally, I felt my arms weakening. I whacked his cheek, telling him to never again speak Angela's name. But he shook his head, smiling the slightest bit, seeming to thrive as I leveraged a palm beneath his jaw.

The Toronto police were on us before I heard footsteps. Their flashlights shone through the windows, and I threw up my hands to explain there'd been a dispute, nothing two men couldn't handle. "The neighbors said it sounded like murder out here," said an officer.

"Just talking," I said.

His expression never quite defined itself, miffed, but also curious at finding only us, two young men, conjoined in the backseat.

"And you?" the cop addressed Blaine, who'd lit a smoke. "You the one makin' all the noise?" To which Blaine, as I knew he would, played it smooth.

"We cool, officer. Just chillin'."

The cop gave us a warning, while the other prowled the van, beaming a light through windows. As they left, Blaine exhaled a gray plume in my direction. There were six or seven shows left to go. There was Angela waiting for me at home. The Canadian summer night, airy and quiet as I stepped out of the van. Blaine and I entered the house with bedrolls tucked beneath our arms, where inside an unfamiliar living room we found just enough space on the floor to unroll our sleeping bags and lie side by side in the dark.

• • •

I'd been back to work a couple weeks when I looked up from a rug to see my dad grinning, on his lunch break. His suit coat was slung over his shoulder. He walked casually along the aisles of carpet, making no eye contact, delighted with the awkward humor that was implicit in his arrival.

The shop was a mile from the engineering compound where he worked. Despite his rehab stints, divorce proceedings, and quadruple bypass, he'd not only held on to his career but had been promoted to manage a staff of thirty engineers. Some mornings I could hardly manage to outsmart my headache and shower in time for work, which left me in awe of his tenacity. Despite whatever rest he'd gone without, I knew that when morning came he'd be the first on the job.

The General had taken Will on a delivery. The General's wife was the only other soul in the shop. She approached my dad sweetly, with her usual pitch.

"In the market?"

"I could be," he said.

He browsed the showroom, seeming to take interest in the stock as the General's wife pointed out the merits of the rugs. Then she nodded to me, and I stood, walking over to begin flipping through the piled carpets.

I paused dramatically at the most hideous culprits, sliding my palm over the silken finish of a pink Turkish disaster.

"That's a looker," Dad said.

The General's wife was charmed, I could see, as Dad mused about a time that comes in man's life when he suddenly finds himself in need of a fine carpet. His barren condo might have actually benefited from one of those atrocities. I flipped a rug, then another. Dad and I shared a smile; he might have winked. In that setting, he appeared as sound of mind as anyone I knew, healthy and spry, with a wholesome flush to his face. His gray-ing blond hair was trim. He was clean shaven, as always during the workweek, and did his best to give me a workout.

"Look at him go," he said. "He deserves a raise." He exited with a boyish gleam and a business card the General's wife had slipped into his hand.

"That's a nice man," she said. "Go look. See what kind of car he's driving." She often asked Will and me to peer from the store's back window to identify the model and make of a cus-tomer's automobile—their spending potential.

I watched my dad pull away in his blue sedan, the brake lights glowing and releasing as the car vanished in the sun.

"Just a Ford," I said. "Nothing fancy."

DAYS LATER, ETHAN APPEARED in the showroom as I was vacu-uming the floor. Following Ethan, as if being led, lurched a dark figure in leather and denim, a mane of hair in his face. I'd slept the previous night in my car outside a Grosse Ile grocer, unable to make the drive after dropping Angela at her parents'. The morning found me pickled and passing hot gas in that painful, hungover way.

It took a moment before I recognized him. Then a bolt of excitement shocked me into commission.

"I need a rug," Repa said, to no one in particular. "Bad."

Here in the flesh, straight outta Okinawa, he evoked a dirty magic from which I hoped the carpet-strewn showroom would never recover. Rugs might have burst aflame if he'd fanned his arms. It had been a year since I'd seen Repa's giant face, which was bearded, his smile widening as we took him in.

Will began flipping through the carpets, the General scowling as Repa described each one: "Crap. Crap, crap, crap. Makes me sick."

When the shop closed, I found a note drawn in Repa's hand stuck to my windshield: *Howell's*. An old-timers' bar just up the block. By the time I entered, he was on a stool, shitfaced and crooning to the jukebox. Deep-fried skin and chicken bones sat on a paper plate in front of him. The joint was empty but for a regular or two staring into the glass behind the bar. Ethan had abandoned him to fend for himself

"This place is great," Repa said. "I love these guys."

He hugged me tightly enough that I could smell all of him: spices and beer and the briny odor only he seemed to emit. "I love you," he said, pulling from his leather jacket a red pouch on which a golden swastika was printed. A chintzy sack made of fake velvet. I opened it and plucked a number of Asiatic charms from inside, all of them tangled together in string. Beneath the lights of the bar I could see they were stamped with mystical characters and made of something like tinfoil.

"The hell is this?" I said, scratching at the pouch's fascist logo. The least intelligent animals of the punk kingdom were known to champion the symbol for its sheer obscenity, but we prided ourselves on a rigid intolerance for bigots. "The swastzi?"

"It means something different over there," he said. "It means 'peace.'"

We drank what we could, and Repa demanded more chicken,

until the barkeeper gave us the nix. Night had fallen without our knowing. Sometime during the proceeding blur of music and calls to Angela so that she could speak to my lost friend and Repa's telling of overseas motorcycle wrecks and the many ways he'd soiled the Japanese transit systems, he and I clutched fists and agreed he was in the band again.

"This time," he said. "We do it wild."

One bad idea, the best we'd had in a long time.

6

The two-dollar fare to cross the Ambassador Bridge was a better option than the Windsor Tunnel, which plunged you beneath the water through a cylinder of diesel-blown tile. From the bridge's arch you'd glimpse civilization, split in two by the Detroit River. The west bank: Detroit's garden of rust and hollowed buildings, sunrays splintering through jagged glass. To the east was Windsor, Ontario's polished chrome, the green turf of city parks, restored crosses rising from chapel steeples. Swiveling your neck left to right, it was like a before-and-after exhibit, one side imploded and the other upright and gleaming.

For the band, crossing into Canada meant pulling over to allow border patrolmen to dismantle our road cases and molest our equipment. Coming home, the U.S. guards silently waved us through with a lack of ceremony that made us feel we'd returned to an undesirable place. I'd been crossing the bridge since I'd turned nineteen, able to legally enter Canadian bars two years before the States would allow it. Windsor's pubs were unthreatening rooms with cheap pitchers and good music. Canada was a place of luxury, a nearby reprieve. Their red maple leaf stamped everywhere, on paper sacks from McDonald's drive-throughs and on the freshly painted receptacles into which those sacks were so diligently pitched. SMOKING KILLS warnings plastered to each pack of cigarettes; the Canadians' rote politeness and clarity of speech. I didn't hassle with strapping an antitheft bar across my steering column when I was there. Nothing was lurking in the corners.

There were also the Windsor casinos, which had never enticed me. By early September, though, Warden was on a monthlong winning streak, gambling the last of his record company's account after he'd been fired from his job delivering Hungry Howie's pizzas. Coming off a stay in his mom's trailer, he was living near the Canadian border in a loft soon to be bulldozed for a new Tiger Stadium. Since Angela had returned to Kalamazoo for fall semester, I'd begun stopping by Warden's cavernous new home, taking solace, imagining the glorious pad it might be if he bought a couch and arranged a stereo for communal listening. His only amenities were a mattress laid over milk crates and a formation of stuffed garbage bags containing most of what he owned. His bathtub was a trough of gray water.

I'd been there, half asleep on his floor, the morning Hungry Howie's canned him.

"Don't do this," Warden said, into the phone. "Not now."

Then he'd threatened to kill his boss's newborn son.

The craziness he'd spew—you could have had him locked up, diagnosed him this or that. A sicko, mainly. Some people wouldn't believe it, but Warden was, in his guts, a sweet man. He had no command over words; they came out of him like belches.

"You just don't talk that way," I said. "It ain't cool."

"That's how it is, man." And by this he meant I was right.

As for the bands and the scene, if they spoke of Warden at

all, it was as the ass end of joke. CTW hadn't released an album in more than a year, and his back catalog was stacked in boxes lining the walls of the loft. It gratified me, knowing copies of my band's debut sat inside that tomb, as near to obscure as one might get. A record meant so much more if you'd scavenged for it, rescued it from a place like that.

And what about Warden's undrained tub?

"Backed up?" I'd asked.

"I just get in it when I feel like it," he said. "I'm not wasting any water."

It wasn't long before Warden lost all his winnings in a single night. I accompanied him with the purpose of glimpsing his luck in action, and after a few evil spins of the roulette wheel he drove through Ontario's streets in a sad, delirious tantrum. I slouched in his passenger seat while the city spun by. The windows were open. Bad Brains was on the tape deck. The tires whined. It was one of those moments you want to stay in, where there's enough simple chaos that you're not worried about what comes next—moments Warden lived one heedless second at a time.

After fishtailing and a few more mindless turns, he braked in the middle of an unfamiliar road, shaking his hands at the wheel as if it were the brains behind his fit. Up the street a pair of headlights made themselves known, as though they'd been there all the while. When the car pulled next to us, its window rolled down. I couldn't see who it was, but the voice was a man's, someone old and impeccably sane.

"This is a one way street, buddy."

"That don't matter," Warden said. "I'm from Detroit."

WELL INTO HER NINETEENTH year, my sister had developed a fever for Windsor's dance clubs. Joints I knew only by their neon signs. Jokers. The Loop. On weekends the queues stretched from their doors, putting on display guys wearing white-gold necklaces, silken shirts tucked into their flared jeans. Women in heels and halters, smoking and snapping gum. You'd hear the bass of house music rumbling the street. Andrew and I had approached one of those dens wearing flannel to have the bouncers turn us away us on sight. The signs read: LADIES NO COVER HALF-OFF DRINKS. Caitlin had begun leaving the house with her hair sprayed up into a wickerlike explosion, her black stretch pants so snug against her curves that the seam of her panties appeared embroidered on her rear.

Canada pants—that's what they were known as in Dearborn.

Dearborn girls of a particular ilk pulled on this attire for their club lives. Seeing Caitlin in her Windsor-bound outfits, I refused to think of it as anything but a girlish fad, or a way of spiting me. I convinced myself that her benign, unworldly face would work as a shield against whatever she might encounter. The quiet girl in the back, holding up a wall . . . drifting along the schoolyard fence.

One August afternoon, she drove me to have my wisdom teeth pulled. After the molars had been yanked and I'd filled my oxycodone prescription, we took her Escort for a fast-food lunch. Burritos, I suggested, something easily chewed—though my jaw didn't hurt a bit. I'd gobbled a number of pills before exiting the drugstore. By the time we picked up our meal, I was in a self-less, fuzzy mood, teasing her about the thug rap music playing on the tape deck. Tupac as Machiavelli. Caitlin drove, handling a burrito as she steered, a fluorescent entry bracelet from whatever club she'd attended the night before dangling from her wrist.

My brotherly advice erupted in paranoid bursts, even when it was incontrovertibly true. "You gotta be careful out there. There are scumbags everywhere."

Catlin balked, dipped uncertainly into her newfound cool. "I know people who'd kill anyone who messed with me."

She proclaimed this the way someone does when they tell you they have friends in crucial places—famous friends, rich friends—her tough-girl tone frayed by doubt. Still, it was one of the only things she'd ever said that chilled my bones. I pictured a defensive line of steroid-injected beasts, mixed martial artists aspiring to cage-fighting tournaments. I'd heard of some of the maniacs she'd been rolling with, people I knew only by the local legends that preceded them.

"I can't help you when it comes to those people," I said.

This was as honest as I could be. I'd posed as a tough guy when we were younger, and she alone might have been fooled by my bluster. More recently, I'd begun thinking of myself as a crazed and feared showman within my scene of malnourished punkers, but she needed to understand I had no powers compared with these mooks she'd befriended.

"I tell them," she said. "I say, 'My brother would go crazy if anyone messes with me.'"

Even this talk of violence was new about her. Yet I was too proud—that she saw me as a foreboding protector, that anyone did—to say otherwise. I was painless. My thighs had begun a warm tingle, and there wasn't anything more I'd have asked from the day. Caitlin notched up the stereo's bass, mimicking a thuggish bravado.

"They ask, 'How big is your brother?' and I say, 'He's not big, but he'd go nuts.'"

• • •

As summer of '99 was turning to autumn, Dad became a semiregular around Mom's house, dropping in for dinner and assuming seasonal chores. Come by after 6:00 P.M., and maybe you'd find him at the kitchen table or on the stone bench in her garden, talking with her as she weeded the flowerbeds. They'd been divorced for well over a year, and while I detected no romance rekindling, Mom seemed considerate of the fact he had nowhere to be once the workday ended. She obliged my dad the way you might a bohemian uncle. To me, she swore she had no interest in finding a new man. Said she'd manage on her own—that all men her age wanted, anyway, was someone to dote on them.

Since none of us had the spirit to accommodate new worries, I was free of having to answer for much. Mom avoided asking what I was getting up to, occasionally admitting she feared to know. For Dad, that I spoke to him at all satisfied him. It was Caitlin who'd begun staging outbursts that sprung my parents into tandem action, overriding whatever acrimonies remained between them. One early evening my sister threw a fit about wanting a new car. She'd badgered my dad for a loan.

"I don't know what's wrong with her," he said, pacing Mom's cramped kitchen. "She says her friends all have nice cars."

"What the hell is her problem?" I said.

There was a lunacy among Dearborn's working-class stargazers, who hoarded their tips to lease sports cars while never saving a cent. I, at least, had a timeless record collection of first pressings and rare jazz imports to show for my spendthrifting.

"She's gotta get a grip," I said.

Dad and I had begun seeing eye to eye on a number of practical matters, like the fact that Detroit's mayor Archer was supremely more efficient than his psychotic predecessor Coleman Young, or the superior coffee available from the new Tim Hortons restaurant on Michigan Avenue, a delicacy previously available only in Canada.

I followed Dad into the living room, where Caitlin and Mom sat before the television. Something about the four of us together gave me the urge to run my mouth. As though taking a podium, I said, "All you care about is your clothes. What about charity and people with less and all that?"

"Look who's talking," Caitlin said. "You dress like a bum." She turned her face from me as if she didn't know where to begin. "Doesn't he?" she said.

My parents all but winced.

Other than the collared shirts I wore to the rug shop, I'd reduced my wardrobe to five black T-shirts, which I could tell apart by their tatters and cigarette burns. And two pairs of jeans. Those early autumn nights, I'd proudly uncloseted my Carhartt jacket, its collar stained by blood droplets from an onstage mishap with a microphone.

Without another look at me, Caitlin tromped upstairs to her bedroom.

"She's out of control lately," Mom said. "She's like a different person."

This was the part I didn't want to hear. Neither did my father.

"If she wants a new car, she can go out and bust her ass for it," he said.

Ozzy patrolled the floorboards, slinking toward my mom and retreating to the fringes each time my dad spoke. "I don't know," he said, seeming to admit he'd relinquished some jurisdictional power or that he was, after all, helpless to arrange the world to his liking. "I just don't know."

WHETHER OR NOT DAD was sober wasn't a question anyone spoke aloud. His showing up to Mom's house seemed to imply that he was. He'd also begun phoning me at the upper flat, where, at my mom's suggestion, Will had been answering the line as a linguistic exercise to help his stuttering. I'd return the calls during hours that left to chance whether he'd be home, and then it might be days before he'd get back to me. When we'd connect, he spoke with the self-deprecating insight of someone who'd undergone a severe conversion and was subsisting on only the rawest aspects of himself.

"I've gotta keep it simple" was one of his latest phrases. The lingo of the 12-step fellowships he'd been taking part in. "Do the next right thing" was another. His sponsor was a Vietnam vet who told stories of bullets whizzing through the jungle and had, my dad admitted, diagnosed him as an "insecure egomaniac."

Dad's favorite new slogan was "It is what it is." But if ever I had a technical problem—an oil leak or a question about sinking anchors into my bedroom's plaster walls—his voice would spark as he offered technical details with a confidence that made me believe he was, as he liked to say, "on the beam."

My uncle Dennis, the third youngest of Dad's five brothers, had been joining my dad at meetings. Once or twice, they'd stopped by Mom's house on their way. Dennis was a truck driver. After years hauling freight over interstate highways, he'd settled into a schedule of local routes and a modest Dearborn home with his wife and two daughters. Dennis's favorite slogan was "My drug of choice is more," and his sleeveless shirts exposed a tattoo of a bloody-fanged wolf on his bicep.

In their husky stature and thin blond hair, they were unmistakably brothers. Walking beside each other, they looked like a two-man gang, reformed troublemakers on a penitential mission. I kept a distance but figured my dad had no better sober ally than his brother. It was Dennis's wife I saw most often. Aunt Bonnie worked the register at the 7-Eleven on Telegraph Road and nodded to me like any other customer when

I'd come in to deplenish the beer supply. She had flaming red hair you'd spot the minute you pulled into the lot. Her most evident tattoo was an eagle, its wings fanning wide across her sternum.

DAD PAINTED THE WALLS of Mom's living room on an early September weekend. Will assisted, working off the speech lessons Mom had given him and leaving me with no role in the refurbishing. I waited all year for autumn. I reminded myself not to miss it as it happened. The sky was densely blue, the air perfectly lukewarm. When I came by the house that Saturday, I saw Will leaving in his paint-smeared jeans. Passing me in the driveway, he raised his brows in a way he rarely did.

Mom was smothering her nervous cough with a Kleenex as I entered through the back door. "That Dennis," she said. "Something's going on." Down the hallway I heard my dad pacing the living room, speaking a quiet gibberish into the phone. Aunt Bonnie, Mom told me, had called in a panic.

My plans that evening were to roadie for a group of friends who called themselves Wallside and were playing Grand Rapids, two hours west. We called it roadying, yet it was merely a way to tag along in another band's van, to feed the compulsion of being forever on the road.

Dad stalked into the kitchen, surrendering the phone.

"I've gotta go get Dennis. He's in trouble."

"Where is he?" Mom said. "Is he in some crack den?"

She seemed to be lamenting the fact she'd invited any of this into her new sanctuary. Muttering "What's wrong with these people?" she walked out the back door to tend what was left of her garden. Dad stood blowing gusts, the weekend scruff on his neck daubed with white paint. It was his brother. It was the poltergeist of his addiction conjured into a sunny afternoon.

Caitlin was working the dinner shift at the steak house, which was a lucky thing.

"Can't someone else get him?" I said.

I was crunching the facts I knew about the drug, bits I'd been told by rehab counselors: the abysmal recovery rates, the never-ending temptation.

Dad said, "I'm just gonna pick him up."

"How do you know where he is?"

"We know where he is."

"Where? A crack house?"

"You wanna come with me?" he said.

I could take it or leave it—either seemed an act of trust. Dad had also been inviting me to 12-step meetings, so that I might comprehend his disease. Or perhaps because he suspected I, too, might benefit from the principles suggested there. My reason for refusing any of this was not for lack of burning curiosity but for fear of witnessing my father any more closely and nakedly than I already had.

"I have to go out of town," I said.

"Don't worry," he said. "I'll get Dennis and bring him home."

WALLSIDE's '84 FORD ECONOLINE was far more hospitable than the Orgasmatron. I'd come to feel more at home with these musicians than I did my own band, and we drifted into a lazy silence after leaving Detroit, watching Michigan pass east to west beyond the windows. Wallside's music was high-decibel chaos owing nothing to proficiency, spared only by the earnestness with which they went apeshit. Their brotherly ways heartened me, as did the fact that they admired my band, read-ily admitting we were superior. Hard to resist telling them Repa would be rejoining, that we'd again be at the apex of our pow-ers. But I held out. There was a show booked at the Shelter for the end of the month—a prestigious gig for which ads had already run—and we'd need Blaine to drum one last time.

Nearing Grand Rapids—no chance of turning back—I accepted my failure to confront whatever grim passage my dad had offered to lead me through. He'd never again speak of that day, but what I imagined was specific: the front room of a Brightmoor crack house; a cinder-burned couch occupied by tweaking addicts inhaling doses of smoke. I pictured my dad extending a paint-spackled hand to Dennis, pulling his brother to his feet amid the secondhand fumes. I could have been there, could have smelled it, but I'd taken the easy trip.

Throughout Wallside's show I crouched beside the amplifiers, ready to attend to any technical difficulties. I drummed along on my knees, wishing I were playing. Their singer lost his footing and took a spill, splitting open the crotch of his pants. Before the last song, Scott, their long-haired guitarist, turned to me while standing at the microphone. "This next one's for our friend here." He eyed me through wet hair, miming a pistol with his fingers and pointing it my way. Pressing down his thumb. Bang. "One of the good ones."

A customary thing: a band ingratiating their roadie before an audience. I'd done it many times to Will, to Warden. Just then the simple courtesy crept over me like some shamanic rite, as though my friend had perceived the darkness in me as I'd stared out his van's windows.

The hiss of the amplifiers. The guitars being tuned for the final onslaught.

One of the good ones . . .

I nodded, extending my arm and aiming two fingers, firing an invisible bullet right back at him. The drummer counted off the beat, and I felt the tickle in my throat, warning that the tears were coming, which gave me more than enough time to cinch them at their source.

• • •

The night of her late-September birthday, Caitlin crossed the border, partook in Windsor's festivities, and returned with a black eye. Her purse was stolen, too, though no one would find out about it until later that week. I'd gone to see Angela after Caitlin blew out her twenty candles and hurried off to the real party. By the time I returned, her bruise had begun yellowing around the edges. It looked worse as the days went on. Caitlin spent a week on Mom's couch with her bangs brushed over her face, missing work and skipping class, reeling in her old trance in front of the television.

She was curt about what had happened, evasive—no names, no places. She said there'd been a fight, a mess of blind punches she'd tried to stop. Another day, she said it had been an accident. Once, she said something about how Dad or I would never hit a woman, but no matter how I drilled, that was all I could get out of her before angry tears clouded her eyes, one of which was hemorrhaged and bloodshot.

We'd just sat down to dinner—Caitlin, Mom, and I—when two detectives showed up with the purse. It was one of those big, black numbers that could carry a human head and then some. But nothing inside it was missing. The Windsor club my sister visited had installed undercover cops, suspecting one of their employees of snatching American wallets for their licenses and passports. They'd caught the skeever just in time, and after an international handoff, here it was, care of the Detroit police.

"You'll want to double-check your belongings," said one of

the cops, standing on the porch while I paced back and forth past the front window, wondering if I had a purpose in the situation.

"They got him," Mom said, really trying to interpret this visit as good news. She invited the men inside, a guy in his early thirties and another pushing retirement. When handed her purse, Caitlin held it at arm's length, her face not quite settled on any one expression. "Smells good," the young detective said, about our dinner, which was going cold at the kitchen table.

Both men interviewed my sister, thinking she might have information that could lead to further arrests. "You have to be careful," said the younger one, clean-cut and pleased with his role here. "Identity resale is big business."

Caitlin was terrorized, swiping at her bangs while refusing to look anyone in the eye. I also felt suspect in the presence of these men. Mom pressed the detectives for details, asking the name of the club and what went on in those places, wanting a connection between the missing purse and my sister's bruised eye. As she and the men spoke, they seemed in agreement that the youth, these days, had gone insane. The younger officer would later call the house, trying to better acquaint himself with my sister under the guise of follow-up work; that day, they left chivalrously. "You have a great dinner, now." Caitlin took immediate refuge upstairs, leaving me with a barely manageable urge to break inanimate objects. I managed the high road instead.

"This has to stop. Her running all over Canada."

Mom folded her arms. When it all got to be too much, she seemed to hold in a single breath for as long as she could— that's when she'd cough. She covered her mouth and let out several quick barks. We both needed an unthinking moment before any more could be said. Mom looked around the living room and after a deep sigh explained that my dad and Will had made a horrible mistake. They'd slathered the walls in gleaming, high-gloss trim paint instead of the flat eggshell satin finish she'd wanted.

"Oh, it looks stupid," she said. "Can't anything just work out?"

Will would hear all about their error. Sooner or later I'd tell him about Uncle Dennis, whom he'd always been fascinated by and had nicknamed the Beast. "Tell me about the Beast," he'd say. Will relished the hard cases, tough-luck stories. Sometimes I felt like a man of the world, being able to report such troubles. Yet I'd keep Caitlin's black eye to myself. I'd pound the image from my thoughts any way I could, usually with a ferocious new hatred for all of Windsor—though the memory of her wound would arise again. Not just in the days following but for years after. Blue turning brown. The busted vessels enclosed by her blonde lashes. Her hand shooing me away when I pressed for more details. The television's light reflecting on the glossy living room walls.

7

A dozen of us lounged on the street-side patio of a Greek-town restaurant, the band and a mob of hangers-on. Our table was in plain view of the Shelter, a three-hundred capacity club we'd play in a matter of hours. It would be our biggest headlining show, one to prove our mettle in a club where we'd seen some favorites. Detroit's *Metro Times*—a weekly that largely dismissed bands like ours—had run a sympathetic article, calling us "one wild ride." The poster for the evening's gig, stapled to nearby telephone poles, flaunted a photo of Repa sneering in his leather jacket. He was here, too, spouting Japanese across the table. We were all here. Ethan, Will. Warden was due to materialize any moment.

"Think anyone shows up?" I said, meaning an audience.

"Fucking rock and roll," said Repa. "That's what matters."

Blaine sat abnormally quiet, his blankness causing me to wonder if we were on the verge of an incident. Every available indication was pointing to the fact that this evening's performance would be his last with us, and he was many things but not dense.

Angela had wanted to hitch a ride to Detroit, which would have been a sure cause of trouble. Thinking of Blaine's eyes on her put me in a lunatic state. I felt prepared to duke it out with him at any moment, knowing that in a fistfight there was always the chance he might get lucky with a jab to the nose. No risking Angela being around to witness a fluke like that. Instead, I planned to drive to Kalamazoo immediately after I played. Though we'd first met at a show, I'd now cordoned Angela in with those I intended to keep a safe distance from the band's whirlwind, like my sister, who'd clipped our article from the *Metro Times* to make a point of wagging it my face: "Ooh . . . 'wild ride.' Too wild for me."

"What are we gonna play tonight?" Ethan said. He'd scribbled a set list on a napkin only to drop it in a spill of beer, the song titles wilting.

"Improvise," Will said.

Already, he was in a greasy, drunken condition, dressed in felt slacks and suspenders, topped by a black cowboy hat, which he'd graciously tipped as our waitress read his handwritten order for octopus, jotted down to avoid pronunciations. Once the plates arrived Will ate strategically, tucking bits of seafood behind his ears and retrieving them midconversation. I'd begun worrying about him. While I'd spent the summer nights with Angela, Will's public insobriety had become artlessly demented. Yet when I spoke of my new love, he'd say, "I'm happy for you," squeezing my shoulder as though I were his to give away.

To announce he'd finished his meal, Will raised his plate, attempting to smash it over his head—a hollow *tonk* and a spatter of fish oil, then a line of blood trickling from his hairline. Seeing this, Repa leaped the patio fence to climb up on a nearby Dumpster, howling once or twice before growing intrigued by whatever he saw from that vantage point.

Blaine watched skeptically. Over dinner, part of me had sympathized with him, and this was my mom's altruism at work, infused in me: her belief that the least likable people are most often those who'd gone unloved. There were traces on Blaine's face of an awkward kid who'd grown painfully into a slender, wisecracking schemer. I knew much more, too, bleak details of his time with Angela that I'd never repeat. What I understood beyond doubt was that all this—losing Angela, the band's dark hymns, Repa's howls—was a scary culmination, edging him toward his worst days.

And still, I liked him less than anyone I knew.

DIM THE LIGHTS AND leave them that way. No strobes. Nothing in the monitors but the vocal. Tell the soundman to crank the kick drum and redline the snare. No entrance music. No *Good evening thanks for coming out*—the last thing this crowd wants. We take the stage, and by the first verse, Ethan is butting the headstock of his bass into the floorboards. Someone sprays the audience with beer, a thumb over the mouth of a shaken bottle. You fret the notes as best you can, but the important part is the sound, charming the feedback like a snake. The low end is a tempest Ethan and I have on reins, and I can almost see it: coiling before the stage. The trick is to choke it silent when the stops come—on a dime, on the downbeat.

This is what we do. It's why they say we're *tight*.

Repa stood front and center with a cigarette in mouth, pumping a fist to the beats he'd written years prior. The Shelter was half full. To make an impression, I'd borrowed an extra Marshall and was pushing two hundred watts. The audience lurched back the moment we began. You saw it in their faces: windswept by decibels. Midway through the set, a bottle was smashed, and the crowd parted to watch Will drop and roll through the glass—the "creepy crawl," as it was known in California. Repa joined him on the floor, the two of them wriggling in a sexless embrace as the show climaxed.

Here is all the noise you've ever imagined. Here are your friends dancing on glass. The crowd cheered and shouted out their favorites, the ones we didn't play anymore. As our final song reared toward its end, I pulled off my guitar and battered it against the stage until there was nothing left but shards, which the audience scrambled for and further annihilated. Claiming his part in the dervish, Blaine kicked over his drums as Ethan held an ugly, sonorous note that rang long enough for me to sneak out the club's back door. My Escort was the first car to leave the parking lot, headed for Angela's Kalamazoo bedroom. One hundred and forty miles' worth of Michigan passed like nothing, my head ringing as I steadied the wheel.

Angela slept the next morning as I sat on the edge of her mattress, listening through the phone as Ethan detailed the show's aftermath. Repa had retched, and Will had kicked a hole through a wall in the club's restroom. We wouldn't be invited back to the Shelter was the general feeling he had.

"At least we'd got paid," he said.

Angela's pretty face twitched, accentuating the feeling that I alone had orchestrated the whole debacle from here in this miniature bed—phoned it in.

"What about Blaine?" I said.

"He took his drums home in his car."

One way or another, he'd known his time with us had ended. Hanging up, I should have been relieved. But later that day, as Angela and I cruised the west Michigan country for the simple pleasure of being on the move, I pictured Blaine driving home with his carload of gear, dragging on a Marlboro Light, waking alone inside his mother's house with his hands calloused from our music and the postshow whine in his ear.

THAT MONDAY, I HIT Dearborn in time to start the workweek, just a minute or ten late for my morning shift. Angela and I had barely slept, and it was days like this when I welcomed the stillness of the rug shop. Frank Sinatra's voice, crooning from the showroom stereo, serenaded the hours. The Armenians never tired of those easy, swinging tunes. And while I refused to memorize the words, here and there in Old Blue Eyes's ballads were such grandiose melancholies rising in the string arrangements—these I'd hum along to.

On my worktable, the General had unfurled an enormous, threadbare Persian carpet that awaited my care.

"It's a big one," said the General's wife. "He must trust you."

Will entered the showroom freakishly alert with a cup of coffee and news of a groundbreaking discovery, sidling up to me when he saw his chance. Saturday night, he said, he'd spent quarantined in his bedroom, blasting his headphones while high on ecstasy. "You won't believe this stuff," he whispered. "Coltrane never sounded so good."

I knew ecstasy as a designer drug, a favorite of the Day-Glo club kids who organized raves in abandoned warehouses. Techno was their groove of choice, and Detroit was touted as the genre's birthplace. The urban innovation had since been co-opted by baggy-panted, nipple-pierced suburbanites, and I despised electronic music on principle—its artificial drumbeats and garish synthesizers. The drug, too, I abhorred for its tacky connotations.

"That's all chemicals, man," I said. "Brain-damage stuff."

"I'm telling you, it changes everything."

Come Friday night, I was slithering on Will's bed, gripping

the sheets as he sat beside me blaring Coltrane's "Ascension" into headphones he'd clamped over my ears. Will worked the stereo's knob, conducting the sounds, smiling down on me. What he'd claimed was true: the music made eels of my limbs.

Will had taken a hit as well. For the moment he was content to dote on me, clutching my hand through the sonic journey he'd prescribed. With my eyes closed, the saxophones were trails of flame. My body was an orb blown from the horn—the horns, seven of them—my jaw chattering to the ride cymbal's clang, the sound undoubtedly more majestic than anything I'd heard, felt, seen blazing over the sky. Something erogenous was going on with my jaw, grinding my teeth together in a way that pleasured my entire being. So that we might trance together, Will tried blasting the music from his speakers—a feeble sound compared with the claustrophobic roar of the headphones.

"We'll trade." I plugged the headset back into the tuner. You could honestly hear my molars ripping into one another but it didn't bother us. "On and off, man, on and off, we'll choose each other's songs."

I played him the second Stooges album, their best. He responded with a Godflesh mindmelter called "Head Dirt," industrial lava taking form like devil disco.

"I love you," we said, each time we exchanged the headset.

A pile of CDs collected on the floor.

To my mind, ecstasy inhabited a precarious region of the drug spectrum: worse than acid yet nowhere near as abominable as crystal meth. I'd swallowed the pill fearing I was at the foot of some accursed road my father had ventured a long way down. But the zest, the depth of my bliss—it had been worth the risk. Lording over Will, I scrutinized his collection for what I'd play next. Just then, I believed I understood my friend's anguish. I visualized that stutter he'd never been able to tame, trapped in his throat.

I wanted him healed—I'd do it with the perfect song.

Standing to choose the next disc, I felt the drug course into whatever part of me it had yet to touch. Then it was as though I felt all the love I'd ever known and ever would condensing inside me, becoming a singular, comprehensible thing: a diamond, I held it beneath my tongue. The music whined from the speakers clasped over Will's ears, and I had an urge to call everyone I knew, to tell them I'd been cured of every bad thought I'd ever endured. My sister—the perfect words came into my possession, the truest things possible. Pure joy touched me, or I'd been returned to it. I had a sense I'd feel that way forever. And all this happened in a matter of minutes. Or it might have been hours. But it did happen, and I was never really the same.

TEN HOURS LATER, I awoke on the floor. On the mattress above, Will lay snoring in tangled sheets. My gums were chewed raw. My neck ached from whatever contorted position I'd slept in, yet an exhausted awareness of what I'd experienced remained. Lapping water from the bathroom faucet, feeling it wash through my chest, my first legitimate thought was of my mother, and I drove the quick mile to her house, calling her downstairs as I entered. Caitlin had left for work, but I hollered her name anyway. Then I sat at the kitchen table, half aglow, listening for steps overheard.

"I love you," I said the moment Mom appeared.

Something was awry—she knew me. She took a seat, reached instinctively to prune a flower stemming from the table's centerpiece. She'd begun dying her hair a conservative blonde to conceal a faint gray tint that had emerged these past years. It was pinned back with girlish barrettes, revealing more of her face than I was ready to see. Worry had lit up her eyes and turned her cheeks a flamingo shade.

"Your hands are shaking," she said.

Driving there, I'd meant to tell her our troubles were clearing up, that I'd happened upon a new way of being—and how simple happiness was, really, when you got down to it. I'd actually felt these things, but now, as she stared deep into me, my mood plunged.

"I'm so sorry" was what I managed. "I've been a terrible son."

Mom might have been waiting for a moment like that, in which I'd awaken from the sullen blackout of my youth. She began to weep as I told her of the hope that had been set loose within. That I saw what mattered. That I'd always be there for her, from here on out, no matter where the years might take us.

"The only thing I want," she said, "is for you to be happy. You were a happy kid, you know?"

Maybe I had been—memories that had embarrassed me until this very moment.

"Yes," I said.

"You remember when you used to tell me everything?"

I'd heard about ecstasy's vicious, serotonin-depleting comedown, but other than my aching jaw, this was easygoing. On the ride over, it had even crossed my mind to share the drug with my mom, that the two of us might access that euphoria together. I wanted to meet her there, to know her in that way. I reached over and hugged her, assuring her that everything would be okay. I saw clearly now: whatever needed to change was damn well about to.

I STOPPED BY EVERY day after work, washing Mom's dishes and startling Caitlin by massaging her shoulders. The two of them laughed as I put the pans and plates in all the wrong places.

Trying to repair a towel rack, I drilled a number of erroneous holes into the drywall.

"He doesn't know what he's doing," Caitlin said. "He's making a mess."

That weekend I drove to Kalamazoo, to a house Angela had moved into with seven girls, all of them bartenders. A true college squat, with empty fifths displayed like trophies and posters of pop stars on the walls and a television going nonstop. Once we were alone, I dug two pills from the pockets of my jeans.

"It's safe?" Angela said. She'd just come from the shower. Her hair was slicked. Her cheeks were pink. "I heard people get sick. I heard sex is so good you'll never think about it the same."

I set a pill in her moist palm. The blue tablets were incised with Cadillac logos, rendered with the crude accuracy of an Oreo's wafer-top decoration. Angela smirked at hers, as if wondering what basement druggist would take the goddamn time.

"It's okay," I said. "Once in a while."

We kissed. We swallowed the pills.

She'd excused herself to the bathroom when the drug began to overtake me—an instantaneous joy-wave that, as it arrived, felt as though I'd known it for lifetimes. Unable to wait another moment, I barged into the bathroom. Angela had just vomited, but I saw in her eyes that she too had become lifted. We cuddled on the linoleum, massaging each other's temples and trying out every possible way of saying we were deathly in love. For hours, we remained like that, rising only to lap water from the faucet. When her roommates pounded on the door, we locked eyes and breathed as silently as we could into each other's mouth.

Angela's earlobes turned crimson. Her eyes swirled, and I had the feeling that if I touched her imprudently she might die. Kissing would have been too much. We merely toyed with the possibility as we ironed our foreheads together and huffed into each other's lungs. "Give me air," I said. Not because I was breathless—it was ceremony, inspired by that dim-lit, window-less commode. Our tandem breathing was also the only thing that ceased the grinding of my teeth. And she resuscitated me, again and again, emptying her chest as I kneaded her hands, feeling each bone in her palms.

It was, until then, the happiest moment of my life.

Eventually, we came out. By then the house was empty, but we scurried through the hallway and locked her bedroom door behind us. I was still brimming, beginning to mourn the slow comedown while trying to think my way back to the peak. I lay on the carpet as Angela pulled a CD from her shelf and a trickle of piano began chirping through the room.

"This is the one I did a solo to," she said. "Chopin. I usually hate to listen to it."

She'd recently given up dance, something she spoke of drearily. Her twin sister had since begun traveling the world as a professional ballerina. Of the two of them, Angela was the emotional one, the troubled one. During rehearsals she'd had a grace her sister didn't, but the stage—the crowds and spotlights—was not her glory. In the bedroom, she raised her heels, balancing tiptoed while craning her arms. A sweat broke beneath her clavicle. Her face was a planet, filling up the room. And the rubbery scrape of my grinding teeth could not be stopped. I gnashed my molars in time with the piano and Angela's rotating ankles, wishing she'd never stop twirling.

• • •

Something huge was about to happen; I could feel it. I was

writing songs about it, sensing it at every turn. I took ecstasy nearly half the days of October, not to party but out of a nearly philanthropic desire to plumb spiritual mysteries. Or maybe I took less; maybe it was twice that. Maybe it wasn't the drugs at all. What I remember most is that I seemed to be living in unending low-grade euphoria that felt holy and dreamed. An exchange at a grocery store could fill me with wonder, as could the sound of my guitar traveling along the apartment's floorboards. For the first time in my life, I tried to sing instead of scream, and outside the windows the leaves were changing color.

I'd begun devising a two-year plan, the first matter being to end the band in proper fashion with Repa. From there I'd get a degree and start a new group, inspired by the spacey balladeers Angela had softened me to. I'd bought sacks of vegetables and had begun flossing my teeth, had even jogged around the high school track, feeling ecstasy's residual tingle as I walked a final, cool-down lap. And I'd bought a Chopin record, as well as a vocabulary manual called *1100 Words You Need to Know*.

Sometime during this hazy month, Caitlin and I took an evening walk, staged and awkward, but we strolled as though with a little practice we'd soon be experts.

"Think about it," I said. "People drive everywhere these days, but our bodies were meant for walking."

"Wayne County is the most obese in the country," said Caitlin. "I saw it on television."

Her hair was yanked into a rubber band. Her black eye had healed, and she'd quit the steak house, shutting herself in at night to channel her feelings into long hours of studying. She'd also been forgoing makeup and appeared so much more like herself, uncertain and guileless, a gentleness in every aspect.

Our conversation trailed off, but I knew she was glad to

be near me; that she, too, understood a great shift was taking place. I didn't intend to interrogate her; I wanted her to never look back. We were nearing Ford Road when she asked about my band.

"You think I'll come see you one of these days?"

My secrecy about the music had moved from the realm of weirdness and into ridiculousness, and now even I sensed its toll on my health and also that secret lives had to do with my own shame as much as they did protecting anyone from anything. I'd orchestrated all this, and now I was living in it. But the cold fact remained that I feared the band's sicko sound would darken Caitlin's nights, push her farther away.

"All that," I said. "I'm getting too old for it. How did we get so old?"

"Don't you ever wish you were a kid again? When there was nothing to worry about?"

Were I able to return to that walk, I'd let her know exactly where we stood: those years were harsh and confusing, but there were so many ahead of us. At the time her question seemed illogical, hardly worth pondering.

"You can't," I said. "You can't ever go back."

We'd returned to the house, through the back door.

Caitlin asked, "Do you think we're normal?"

What I wanted to say was *Why would anyone want to be?* but I instead bent low to begin untying my shoes.

"You know," she said. "You think we'll ever be, like, normal people after all this?" And with that, she lost me. I couldn't pretend to have the faintest idea.

I NEXT SAW HER on Halloween, when we met at Mom's house for Dad's birthday dinner. By then she'd burrowed so deeply into her studies that she seemed bothered to act out this endangered tradition: gift giving and a quick meal, then a candle-spiked pumpkin pie just as the costumed droves crept out in full force. I'd arrived with a paper Dearborn Music shopping bag and was pacing with it through the house, thinking about wrapping paper but not seriously. Caitlin carried on speed-reading, paying no attention to my dad, who sat beside her on the living room couch, not really saying much, just sighing like he'd had a long one—the day, the year.

"Happy birthday," I said, finally handing him the crumpled bag.

"For me?" Dad upturned the sack so that a Nick Drake CD slid out, a spare acoustic recording Repa touted as the world's finest hangover album. "Never heard him," he said, examining the song titles as if they contained a personal message.

His visits here had tapered off, not that it surprised me. Things couldn't be that way forever—his dropping by Mom's, taking out the trash, painting the walls of a home she'd made without him. Weeks earlier, there'd been an upheaval over Caitlin's black eye. From what Mom said, Dad had a full-scale shitfit before he'd sat red faced and panting on the couch. She worried about his heart. In the kitchen, she was working up a spread of salmon and rice, doing away with her tradition of preparing Dad a birthday sirloin. I noticed her making these quiet changes, as if to remind him where things stood.

"Smells great," Dad called out through the house, staring off and listening for a reply.

It shames me to admit that I'd spent time wondering if he'd given ecstasy a spin—and why not? It seemed to me that, having succumbed to crack, a man would have few scruples left. It also struck me as perfectly logical to think ecstasy's curative powers might wean someone off the darker substances.

Mom set the food on the kitchen table and called us in.

Caitlin took a few bites before pushing aside her plate to replace it with a textbook, in which she began highlighting entire paragraphs.

"Can't that wait?" Dad said, but she breathed deep and carried on.

Sequestered upstairs, Ozzy was tormented by the unending bustle of trick-or-treaters in the street below. We heard him yipping, his nails clacking against the windowpane. Every few minutes, Mom rose with a bowl of miniature candy bars for the masked children who came onto the front porch to holler through the screen door. Years earlier, Caitlin and I would have been walking Dearborn with pillowcases and painted faces. We'd roamed in different groups, me with Will and whomever else, cutting through the woods, while Caitlin kept to the sidewalks, costumed as a cat, her painted whiskers twitching as she gave thanks for each treasure she received.

This day always scared up something tender and joyous in me, memories of fake blood running from the lips, returning home after the porch lights had snapped off and the jack-o'-lanterns had faded, one year with a pocket full of hood ornaments. Caitlin sitting in the kitchen, organizing her stash. Mom and Dad in front of the television, a made-for-TV thriller playing as they lay entwined on the couch. Dad licking the pumpkin filling off his candles, asking us what good stuff we'd brought home. "Anything with peanuts?"

We'd set the Mr. Goodbars before him, which he'd eat one after the other. Any other night, Mom might have said, *Tim*, meaning he should go easy; on his birthday, he'd been free to scarf until he was satisfied.

Finishing his last bite of salmon, Dad said, "That hit the spot."

Which meant he'd soon be leaving.

Headed where? I'd never have asked.

Though Caitlin might have: *Where are you going?*

Home, he'd say, the strangest word.

After taking his plate to the sink, Dad made for the front door with a fistful of candy bars. I followed him out. As he left, he dropped the candies into the pails of the beggars who'd gathered on the porch. He kept one for himself and tossed another to me. Then he was gone. Forty-nine years old, with the whole night ahead.

• • •

THE DEAL:

We wouldn't perform songs that had been written without him.

We'd demand a seventy-five-dollar guarantee for live performances.

Warden was not to be allowed in the van, studio, or practice space.

These were the conditions of Repa's return, and I took issue with none of them. Few clubs outside Detroit would guarantee us anything, meaning our new policy would leave weekends free for me to visit Angela and keep an eye on Caitlin. Anyway, it took no more than one early November rehearsal to discover that Repa had jettisoned his skills somewhere in Japan. We bumbled through our oldest music like a reunion act. To mark

Repa's return, we'd booked an Ann Arbor show for November 20, my twenty-second birthday, which I privately decided would be the last time I screamed those songs.

None of this stopped us from practicing long and hard, same as ever. Afterward, we'd cruise Seven Mile in Repa's Buick Century, pounding the dashboard, re-creating our tunes with grunts and vocalizations: Repa beat-boxing the drums as Ethan motored his lips to approximate the bass. By some trick of the pharynx and windpipe, I'd generate a guitarish burble.

Repa goosed the engine. "Sounds real good," he'd say. Some nights we stopped in at a bar, one of Seven Mile's most uninviting facades. "There she is." Repa would nod, parking outside a paint-peeled dive where a single fluorescent bulb hung above the doorway, the neon sign cracked up like no one cared whether you entered or not. "A place like that—you might never come out again." But we did, the three of us together, a band, riding out our last days wherever they took us.

"HEY, CAITLIN'S OUT THERE."

Angela tugged my arm to make certain I'd heard her. She'd just come back from a cigarette, and now the opening act was going full blast, the singer doing the look-no-hands microphone-in-the-mouth thing and not such a bad job of it. We were in Ann Arbor, inside a subterranean venue known as the Halfway Inn—the Halfass, some called it—and I was counting down the minutes. The small room was packed.

Angela nudged me.

"Your sister's asking where you are."

It was an all-ages show, alcohol prohibited, but I was drunk enough after swallowing several rounds of birthday shots with Repa at a nearby bar. Angela had wanted to be here on account of my turning twenty-two years old today, and I worried her presence might jinx the band as we took the stage this one last time. Four years, thirty thousand miles, a hundred fifty shows. Repa and Ethan were off priming themselves, having no idea this was it.

"Caitlin?" I said.

"Outside," Angela said. "With Will."

Needling through the crowd, I exited the building to find Will with a cigar smoking between his lips and an arm around my sister. They sat on a short wooden bench beside the venue, Caitlin wearing a blue windbreaker, its hood cinched so that her chin and forehead were invisible. Her cheeks shone, saucer-like. She didn't smile when she saw me but arched her brows so that they vanished underneath her hood. Will had padded his oversize coat with twenty-four-ounce beer cans, the last of which he'd given to my sister. She held the can like some tabernacular thing, both hands cupped around its bottom. Will and Caitlin had known each other for fifteen years, but only then did it occur to me that she was the closest thing he had to a sister.

"Here's Our Boy," he said, as I came at them.

I trusted no one with my sister, was only beginning to consider that granting her access to my world at large might not sadden and terrify her. Will grinned, making an embarrassingly true joke at my expense as Caitlin laughed knowingly, which touched me, got me to thinking: Let it be. Let her be here.

Angela had accompanied me outside. Her arm was hooked into mine, and I recall so clearly being worried that my sister might see this as further evidence of the ways I'd excluded her. I knew what she saw: the pretty young woman at my side who'd gotten so close, so easily. Caitlin regarded Angela shyly, easing slowly into the understanding that I'd parted with Lauren for the last time.

No one could have known how moved I was by the fact my sister was there, myself least of all. But over years that night has become charged with meaning, the way she eyed the black-clothed spectators who loitered, smoking, with records tucked under their arms. The tentative look in her eyes, knowing she was breaching a code I'd worked hard to establish. A collision was in progress, two realms I'd kept apart.

"What are you doing here?" I said.

Caitlin sipped at her beer, one of the only times I'd ever see her with a drink. "Am I not allowed to be here?"

"How did you know we were playing?"

"I was studying in a coffee shop. I heard some guys talking about going to see your band, so I thought, If they can go see my brother, then I can, too."

And I admit to feeling proud, as if a stranger's random mention of my music might validate its seriousness in my sister's eyes. We had fans, believers.

"He's a star," said Will. "Don't you know? Our Boy's a star."

I bent to hug my sister, putting something extra into the squeeze, and over the sleek fabric of her jacket my hand slid down the notches of her spine. One of those accidents that remind you the people you love are made of bone. You can reach for them. You can touch their face, if you want—reach out and prove they're real.

I still see her there, not her disease or whatever they'd try to call it, but the timid uncertainty on her soft, young face as I stood and met her eyes. The unfinished person who hadn't yet found herself but was flailing messily toward that discovery, just as I was. All these years later, I go back in for another hug. And does everything change in that instant, flowing outward and leading us anywhere but where we were headed? Yes, it does. Because I hold on to her a little longer. I never let her go.

"Happy birthday," she said.

Angela smiled, and Caitlin smiled back.

We spent a few minutes, talking small, but I felt the earth beneath our feet and the season in the air. I didn't know where things stood, but I was aware in every sense of where we were. Every few beats someone approached us, asking how much longer until the band went on. "This is my sister," I told them.

I'd burned calories devising ways to avoid revealing myself to these people—the scene—and they acknowledged her puzzlingly, as if expecting my relatives to resemble hyenas, the mentally deranged.

"Didn't know you had a sister."

Someone held up a flask, toasting my twenty-two years. Will walked off in search of another drink, and I took his place beside Caitlin, put my arm around her. "Thing is," I said, "you gotta stay out here when we play. You don't wanna see this."

"What's the big deal? I'm too straight, like I can't handle it?"

She spoke quietly. She knew it was our business.

"You just wait outside, you know? We'll hang out when it's over."

The band onstage had finished; it was my turn. Repa, I knew, was off chanting to himself. Ethan was stretching, working out the kinks. Will came marching down the street with a plastic sack full of bottles. "Showtime," he said, enunciating like a natural, never stuttering once his mind was lubricated.

While heading in to set up my equipment, I took him aside.

"You keep an eye on Caitlin. I don't want her in there."

"If that's," he said, laying a hand on my shoulder, "what you want."

THERE'D BEEN TIMES I'D faked it through a song or two before the ritual took hold. I'd slapped myself, thrown a bottle, worked my way into the convulsion. That night, I'd given up before the first note. My shoulders were slack; I felt my hands trailing over the frets. Someone from the audience yelled, "What? Aren't you pussies drunk enough?" But there'd be no freaky stuff, no creepy-crawls, no scaling the rafters. Beyond the glare of the stage lights, the back of the club was vague, all faces obscured by shadow. As the chords rang, there was no telling who was watching.

Repa stole the show. Onstage again, spotlit, he became infused with his old voodoo. He and Ethan locked into the rhythms, oblivious to me posed inanimately beside them. I heard the sound, the odd time signatures, the down-tuned grunt of the chords. Our death rattle. It wasn't until our last song that I gave in. A long, destructive piece, one of our oldest. Only recently had I realized it was about my family, all of us. Knowing it would be the last time I howled those words, I chewed into them, giving all I could to the verse: *A thirteenth step, by love.*

WILL WAS CURBSIDE, HOUNDING postshow loiterers for a light. A cigar hung from his lips and shreds of tobacco dappled his chin. In the place Caitlin had been, Angela sat alone, fending off various admirers, some of them friends of Blaine. Had they seen it, the underwhelming end?

I clasped Will's shoulder, holding him in place for a god-damn minute. "Where's Caitlin?"

"She left, man," he said. "She was cold."

"Did she go inside?"

"She stayed out here with me, and then she left."

So it was, my sister would never experience the band. Never meet Repa and put his unforgettable face to the frenzied baritone she'd laughed at when his messages spewed from the answering machine.

"Was she upset?"

"I don't think so." Will pulled an envelope from his jacket. "She said to give this to you."

I walked up the block to open it: a standard-issue birthday card containing a multipage letter Caitlin had written on sheets of yellow paper. I began reading in the streetlight. After the first line, it was impossible to engage the message sentence by sentence. I couldn't manage any more than to scan my sister's tidy cursive: Epithets. The word "Mom." "Dad." She'd used the term "idol" to describe her feelings for me. The letter contained no birthday wishes at all but a missive about what had been lost, our closeness as children, and the present gulf between us. There was a line about how she'd parked outside my apartment, staring up at the light in the second-story window, too afraid to walk up the steps and knock on my door.

I folded the letter, pocketed it. A problem that needed fixing—another rising difficulty I'd need to solve one of these days, whenever life revealed to me the flawless, finite answers. I crossed it from my mind: the only important thing that happened that night. The crowd was leaving. I heard Repa laughing above everything. And once I fled this scene, I believed there'd be a short time before my name and the sound of my voice would be forgotten.

But I couldn't read Caitlin's words as she'd intended, not just yet.

In fact, I wouldn't open the letter again. Not until years later, once it was far too late. Then I'd read it from beginning to end for the first and only time, and it would transport me to that scrap of Ann Arbor sidewalk, beneath the November streetlight where the sweat burned my eyes. By then, everything would make perfect sense: How acutely she'd seen our lives. How well she knew me, more than I did myself. I'd see her composing those thoughts inside a coffee shop. I'd know why she'd driven there, hoping to witness whatever she imagined my music to be, hoping I'd invite her to see for herself my version of what we both felt. By then I'd know that she alone was the one who could have truly understood.

8

Caitlin knocked at the upper flat's door on a Christmastime weeknight—three uncertain raps I might have missed had I not been waiting, more or less staring at the walls. What little I'd read of her letter had convinced me I needed to be near her, whatever that took. Over the past year it had been growing, a slowly churning awareness of how dire it was that we discover a new way to connect, to transform our sibling habits. To grow up, I guess, a task that was mostly mine. We'd been behaving shyly toward each other, but, finally, I'd invited her for dinner.

"Hey," I said, opening the door to welcome her inside, where she stood idling in the apartment's front room. She'd done her hair, and I hoped it wasn't for this. A runty plastic Christmas tree sat in a corner, but there was little else in the way of holiday spirit. Will and Andrew had gone out for the evening.

"Hello," she said.

I hadn't wanted to make a fuss, didn't take her coat or anything formal. She ought to feel she was casually dropping by, that this would become a regular sort of business. Caitlin took a seat on the couch, and we settled for a movie playing on one of the channels Andrew had hijacked with a satellite dish. *Pretty Woman*—I'd never seen it before. Caitlin eyed Will's homemaking: The lighthouse scene, plugged in and blinking. The Jesus shrine on the mantel, which she was sure to find heretical.

While the movie played, I took breaks to tend the microwave. I'd become a wizard of the chicken sandwich, zapping the precooked fillets and dashing them with soul-food seasoning that didn't belong to me.

"How is it?" I said, after serving the entrées on plastic dishes.

"Good," she said. "Spicy."

An uneasy feeling, once the romance scenes heated up. Richard Gere unhooking Julia Roberts's garter. A hooker movie, of all things. An indirect expression of our sister-brother awkwardness—you click the remote, and there it is.

The R-rated images silenced Caitlin and me, looming larger and more lifelike than what we needed to say. One of the stranger confusions I'd felt, an unnecessary embarrassment about being unnecessarily embarrassed that certified just how dislocated she and I were. I asked Caitlin if she wanted to watch something else. She shrugged. The movie trailed on, without the respite of commercials.

The actress had tremendously long legs; the stud a chest that appeared to have been shaved as smooth as his ass, which the camera panned over as he thrust and bucked, but gently.

"You into this?" I said.

"Whatever's fine," Caitlin said, because the movie had nothing to do with anything. "Do you wanna turn it off?"

"Only if you do," I said, and we continued staring at the screen as if a moment we'd been trying to take hold of was being led astray. The hooker and the tycoon plummeted troublesomely into love, threatened by contrary lifestyles; yet they found their way, in time for the closing theme.

The credits rolled and I took my sister's plate to the kitchen. As she was leaving, I told her to come back soon. With any luck, I said, the year 2000 would not mark the end of human-kind, and we'd be seeing a whole lot more of each other. Then I cracked some *Pretty Woman* joke, at which Caitlin laughed and said, "It's fine, it's all good. Sorry if I'm boring."

ON THE CORNER OF Telegraph and Ford hung an ominous ban-ner above the entrance to Harry's Army Surplus: GET YOUR Y2K SUPPLIES HERE. Angela said her father had for months been stocking his basement with nonperishables and weaponry for just this occasion. At the upper flat, Andrew had taken precau-tions by storing gallons of fuel in the garage and making sure there were enough rounds for the rifle he kept hidden from Will in the apartment attic.

"Andy Dandy's ready," Will said, and the three of us laughed.

New Year's Eve 1999. We were huddled on the apartment's miniature balcony, staring down Michigan Avenue to where Detroit's skyline was a dusky apparition. A crisp evening, warm for Michigan, the final minutes of December. I eyed the twenty-four-hour Farmer Jack across the street, imagin-ing the windows blacked out and looters shattering glass to ransack the aisles. It must have been nine o'clock, and we'd each swallowed a hit of ecstasy while sipping bottles of piss champagne Andrew had bought for the holidays. Beneath us cars chugged along and streetlights changed on cue, as if to defy whatever catastrophe was about to begin.

The weeklies had been advertising end-of-the-world parties, urging Detroit to let it all hang out, one last time. Around ten, Andrew made his way to some such event. Angela had returned to Kalamazoo, where I was to meet her the next day, leaving Will and me alone with the agreeable option of blasting off to a private celebration.

He'd wired up a surround-sound system in his bedroom, a speaker in each corner, in the middle of which we sat blitzing ourselves with music. Every so often, we regrouped in the bathroom to swallow another pill, and in this way the year's change passed without our knowing. We didn't hear the ovation, the guns going off in the city—bullets shot at the moon. It was well after midnight when we realized we'd lived to see the new millennium. By then we'd gobbled our entire stash but for one tablet, which we cut in half with a razor in honor of the future.

"Happy two thousand," Will said, tucking his portion between his gums.

"How many have we eaten?"

"Your eye," he said. "It's all messed up."

I glanced in the bathroom mirror to see a contorted visage resembling what I might look like if I'd regressed to some prehuman species. The flesh around my left eye sagged lifelessly. The pupil was dilated and deadened, a fish eye peering through aquarium glass. I poked at my nose and flexed my cheeks. I'd never again reached the high of those first autumn doses, yet this buzz was exhilarating, making it impossible to worry at length.

Will stood behind me, seeing what I saw. "My god," he said. For a minute, he couldn't turn away. Then he returned to the music, and I called Angela to wish her a good year. Next, I called my mom. I said the same things to both of them, jabbering while massaging the flesh below my eye—speaking of love and all the great things ahead. And next came a stretch of minutes so spectacularly oblivious I might as well have lived them in a place like heaven, but one thing I'm sure of is that the sun hadn't yet risen when Caitlin knocked at the door.

By then I'd polished off the champagne. Sweat slicked my lower back, and I'd changed into a white T-shirt because my black one had attracted vicious energies. There was no name for the ride I was on as I danced toward the door, swinging it open with an insane, impersonal friendliness.

"Happy New Year," I said, before I could really comprehend her.

It seemed impossible to view my sister entirely. I took in square inches: Blonde locks. Deep-red lips with that blotted end-of-the-night smear. For months she'd been holed up studying, but this evening Caitlin had hit the town wearing her finest nightlife clothes. Black pants, a white blouse. Heels. She was wrapped in a peacoat as I hugged her into the room. I might have asked her to dance. From Will's bedroom music blared down the hallway, and in this late phase we'd reached for the funky sounds: James Brown. Curtis Mayfield. I'd been dancing away the scary ideas that began to creep in each time I stood still. I was afraid to stop.

"Are you rolling?" Caitlin said. "Your eyes are all weird. Why are you grinding your teeth?"

Hearing this sobered me for an instant, realizing my sister could identify ecstasy's teeth-gnashing effects.

"No way," I said. "I'm drunk. We're Irish, you know?"

She took a seat on the couch as I continued a soft shuffle about the living room.

I did the Travolta. I fluttered my hands, clacked my heels. The funk was still thumping when Lauren showed up with a HAPPY NEW YEAR badge pinned to her sweater. Caitlin had asked Lauren to meet her at the apartment—for what purpose I had no mind to consider. A year had passed since I'd seen Lauren, yet without a word I took her hand, prancing to the backbeat as she shimmied along, smiling as if nothing had changed. The tenants below arrived home to pound on their ceiling, but the music was in Will's hands.

Lauren and I grooved awhile longer, until the wallops beneath the floorboards began rattling the windowpanes. Then she headed toward Will's bedroom to see about the noise while I sat beside Caitlin, petting her shoulder with an undivided concentration.

"Something bad happened," she said. "I just wanted to see you."

Christmas had been unmemorable in an alleviating way. Easy. We needed to keep everything smooth and easy, but Caitlin curled into herself and began crying hard.

I actually don't know what I said next, or how long we carried on that way. By morning, Lauren and Caitlin were gone. Will and I awoke spooned on my mattress, dressed in ski hats and winter coats, and throughout the apartment every window had been opened wide. Apparently we'd decided that an evil had been turned loose; our only hope had been to cleanse the air as we lay shivering beside each other, awaiting the first light of the century.

TWENTY-THREE DAYS LATER, I walked into Oakwood Hospital's psych ward with only a book to offer, an Oscar Wilde novel Angela had given me for my birthday, encouraging me to read. Will said of dud records that they made him "throw up in his mouth," and I'd lasted mere pages with *Dorian Gray* before feeling similarly. Yet of the books on my narrow shelf, it seemed most precious, the safest one to hand Caitlin as she lay in a hospital bed on suicide watch.

"These people are terrible," she said, giving the novel a courteous once-over.

If she in any way expressed relief at seeing me, I do not

remember. Others things are crystalline, but not that. Though I wasn't surprised to be there, or couldn't feel the surprise, and whether that was a mistake or a failure or a lapse of heart, it was the worst of my life. "You might like . . ." I said, yet to speak a full sentence. I meant the book.

It was a late-January afternoon. I'd just punched out at the rug shop. The night before, Caitlin had swallowed a month's worth of her antidepressants and passed out in her car after calling Mom, who'd rushed her to the ER in time to have her stomach pumped. Mom had been at my sister's side all morning. Dad was the one who'd called me, saying, "Your sister. I don't understand."

Hospital policy was that attempted suicides were to remain under psychiatric evaluation for two weeks. Caitlin would spend the days lounging in a paper gown, doing arts and crafts and group therapy with junkies and neurotics. Needles stuck out from her hairless arms, held in place by strips of surgical tape. Bags of fluid dangled from a rack next to her bed. Her heartbeat was displayed on a monitor that glowed silently above, but I saw no dark circles beneath her eyes or any obvious signs of agony.

"Everyone here's a freak," she said, when I hugged her. "Can you get me out of here?"

I felt her shame and her near-total surrender to it. A shy, becoming twenty-year-old girl locked in a nuthouse that demanded she announce her every trip to the restroom. Only later would I consider the mealtime slop being served or what crossed my sister's mind as she showered, her nightly routine, before laying her head against the hospital pillows.

"These doctors walk in with their students," she said. "They talk about me like I'm not right here in front of them."

The supremacy of doctors—I still trusted that they must know what's best.

"Can you relax?" I said. "Get some sleep?"

"Sleep," she said. "You try it here."

She then went on to tell me what had happened on New Year's Eve. That a friend's brother had dragged her into the bathroom at a party and sexually assaulted her. Caitlin spoke in an even tone, as if reading aloud a police brief, warning someone that life was full of danger.

"Who?" I said. "What friend?"

"I don't ever want to see them again."

I kept a gentle voice, prodding her until she explained that two days earlier she'd finally confronted the guy and his sister, Sheila, who for the past year she'd been calling best friend. Sheila had eaten dinner at Mom's house. She'd taught Caitlin how to dress for the clubs and made her tapes of booty rap, club bangers. Nice enough, but I'd never had much to say to her. One of those Dearborn lost girls who seemed beyond the scope of my social graces.

"I just wanted an apology," Caitlin said.

Sheila and her brother had thrown Caitlin out of their house. They'd called her a liar.

"They had the audacity to yell at me."

Whatever her troubles, my sister was not oblivious. In a way she saw things too distinctly and felt them too immediately, without filter, without defense. So susceptible to heavy feelings that she was bound to endure many, sometimes at the hands of people whose nature it was to prey on all things fragile. Her face wasn't sufficiently angry, just burdened, like she'd been told it was entirely her fault for letting people treat her this way.

"But what happened?" I said. "Tell me what happened."

Months later, I'd investigate the incident from numerous angles and be told that Sheila's brother had pulled Caitlin into a bathroom, that he may or may not have shoved her to her knees. Unzipped his fly, wagged his thing in her face. Almost certain is that a crowd of drunken Dearbornites gathered at the stall door, chanting, "Suck it!" Mom would tell me that Caitlin had described the way her heels slipped across the bath-room's tile floor as she tried to struggle free—a detail that would become the crystallized, indisputable bit of evidence I'd cling to when I began stalking Sheila's house in the early morning, devising ways to murder her brother without being caught.

In the hospital, Caitlin elaborated no more than to say the guy had done something "messed up." When I said the word "rape" she said, "No, he's just a jerk because his mother left when he was young." I didn't yet know his name or what he looked like, only what I'd heard: he was a trained boxer and a male stripper across the border in one of Windsor's male entertainment clubs. I knew Caitlin had bought him a gift that Christmas and that her checking account was overdrawn.

"Sheila wasn't even there," she said. "She was off with some guy."

A nurse observed us, seated feet away, half engaged with a magazine. She appeared to be assigned to Caitlin. A privacy curtain hung on metal rings, clamped to a track in the ceil-ing, separating us from the activity of the ward. The lights were dimmed. If there were windows somewhere, you couldn't tell. Other people were nearby, but I couldn't see them—could only hear their shoes clomping on the linoleum. The sounds of foot-steps and televisions surrounded us. Who in their right mind would get well in a place like that?

Caitlin said, "I just want to start over."

"You can," I said, having no idea what that meant.

But I knew it wasn't just New Year's Eve that had delivered her there. Trouble sniffs out people who are lost the way we were; or else we'd marched toward it, expecting to find ourselves.

Caitlin had gone pale, or I'd just noticed.

I'm not sure I even took her hand in mine, which is the kind of thing you spend the rest of your life trying to forgive. What did I know, barely twenty-two? Absolutely nothing about anything in that very moment, or what the moment itself meant.

I said, "I love you." I said, "You just have to make it through."

Caitlin looked anywhere but at me.

My senses were shot—the adrenals, the emotion cells. Just then I was vaguely sober, but there'd been a hazy run since New Year's Day. Instead of calling Caitlin that first morning of the century, I'd met a dealer at 7-Eleven. My wonky eye had snapped back to form, but ever since, my face had felt like mashed tinfoil. There was a sickness in my mouth that could not be rinsed away. A few days into the millennium, a pain vibrated through my chest, radiating up my neck as my organs ceased manufacturing whatever mojo I needed to be sane. I'd wedged a chair beneath my doorknob so that Will and Andrew wouldn't catch me bawling with an unspecific dread that felt as permanent as the sky. I'd driven to see Angela twice, to hide in her bed. I'd slept five hours at a rest stop on I-94. Nothing had helped until I saw a doctor at a walk-in clinic, who, with a glance, wrote a script for a tranquilizer called Ativan. Enough of those, and the days had passed as dreams, because the thing about being in a spin like that is how quickly the world blurs on by like some bogus marvel you'd had no desire to see.

"Are you all right?" Caitlin said.

"Me?" I said. "I'm always all right."

Standing beside her in the psych ward, I remembered little about having been alive the past weeks. And I'll never recall exactly how I left my sister in Oakwood Hospital, or where I went next, only that she sat propped on a stack of thin pillows, thanking me for the book.

WHEN I ENTERED THE rug shop the following morning, there was a look I'd never seen before in the eyes of the General's wife. She hovered near the doorway, her dainty figure electrified as if expecting a visit from a saint. She stammered through our routine: "Good morning, how are you?" Then she walked to her desk and sat down. Will wasn't around. He must have been on delivery with the General.

"Your mom's friend called," she said. "There's been a change in your sister's status." She began twiddling with a spool of new thread. "She said to stay put. She's coming to pick you up."

Mom had never been inside the rug shop, let alone called me there. Someone must have gone to the trouble of looking up the number, which even I didn't know. All of which was strangely wrong, because for what ridiculous purpose would I need to be chauffeured anywhere on any occasion?

"Is she all right?" the General's wife said.

"It's her heart." Our euphemism for Caitlin's past attempts. "She has a condition."

I was out the door.

Oakwood Hospital was a couple miles from the rug shop, across the street from Stout Middle School where Will and Caitlin and I had done time. I'd skipped class to steal desserts from Oakwood's cafeteria. Caitlin had been born at Oakwood; I'd had hernia surgery there before I knew my name. Pulling into the hospital driveway, I couldn't imagine what change could have taken place. Yet I was familiar with the emotionless calm spreading through me. Behaving with a mind of its own, my car circled the block-long complex twice before the visitor parking area loomed ahead.

From here you could see the building my dad worked in: an old engineering compound surrounded by a cement fence, the slope of a Ford Motor test track rising above the barricade across

Oakwood Boulevard. He'd driven Caitlin and me up that hill in a premarket Thunderbird; his crew had been updating the car's transmission system. He'd gunned the engine, handling the machine as if he'd scrapped it together by hand, Caitlin and me cheering as he hugged the track's corners.

Dad walked into the hospital not long after I did to find me wandering the hallways in a panicked search. Caitlin had been moved from the psych ward. I hadn't wanted to ask for help, but Dad badgered the staff as though every second mattered, shouting, "Where's my daughter?" He wore a suit, was sweating around the collar. Seeing him in a jacket and tie allowed me to cling to the sense that there was still order, an official procedure.

We were led to an elevator, then into a conference room where Mom was seated at a roundtable of nurses and doctors. No one said a word. Behind us, Mom's friend barged in short of breath and, seeing that I'd found my way, composed herself.

We all looked to one another like we didn't want to know what might come next. I could tell Mom already knew more than anyone. She was dressed in public-school attire: a dark blue blouse; clip-on earrings, in case her autistic students were inspired to snatch them. Her fist was pressed to her mouth. She turned her head the slightest bit, saying hello to me with her eyes.

"Cyn," my dad said. But he didn't ask.

I felt Mom guiding my thoughts, assuring me this wordless prelude was necessary.

Dad and I took our seats. Then Mom related the details.

Caitlin had rolled her IV into a private shower that morning, pulling the needles from her arms and using the plastic tubes to tie a noose, which she fastened to the shower rod as the water ran. By the time the nurse burst in, Caitlin had been down for ten minutes.

She'd been "down"—that's how Mom said it.

I chose then and there to picture my sister on the floor, silently collapsed. To this day I picture that, only that, but for horrific split-second frames that flash unbidden like lightning. And then, I see only partially.

"She's alive, though," I said, insisting it.

Dad wheezed, staring at nothing, like a man blinded by a punch to lungs.

"Caitlin's unconscious," Mom said. "But they're doing all they can. To restore brain activity. And the only thing we can do right now is pray for her."

Next, a doctor spoke. Caitlin had been moved to intensive care. They'd revived her pulse and were feeding her oxygen. There'd be tests once the swelling in her brain subsided. He gave no indication about the odds of survival, but that didn't alter my belief that she'd come to. I'd seen movies about this sort of thing, where a person awakes from a comatose sleep, instantly restoring harmony to the universe. She'd open her eyes. She'd laugh an exhausted laugh, and we'd cry our faces dry, and the idea of that sweet moment of relief was my only endurable thought. I couldn't feel my fingers.

Dad's bottom teeth protruded, the sound of air sucking through them audible as he breathed quick and shallow. All essence had drained from his eyes. He appeared clenched inside his creaseless black suit. I didn't know it then, but the delusion of being immune to life's consequences was the most significant thing I'd inherited from him. We were both immersed in a similar kind of self-important denial. It was about us—about what we had and had not done. Yet it was the technical details, the mention of tests and the chemistry of Caitlin's brain, that became too much for him to endure. He moaned in a way that shook his whole body. When I reached out, he grabbed my hand.

Mom asked the smart questions: about the science, past cases, medications, the neurological assessments, the strategies. She said, "I want you to make sure the person who found her doesn't blame herself. We want them to know we don't blame anyone."

The nurses and doctors bowed their heads.

Which was when I realized that Caitlin had been trapped in a place where her guardians had failed to protect her from herself—the one thing they were supposed to do.

ANGELA ARRIVED BY TRAIN the next day. I met her at the Michigan Avenue station, a couple hundred yards up the track from where Will and I once set pennies and homemade explosives on the rails, waiting for the trains to pummel them. Angela's eyelids were swollen; she was buttoned inside a peacoat and carrying a schoolbook. We'd loved each other less than a year, but she was there completely, gripping my arm, ready to follow me through.

On our way into the ICU she met Lauren, who was sobbing hard after having seen Caitlin strapped to a gurney, a ventilator pushing air into her chest. "She's pretty," Angela said, once Lauren had walked away, covering her face with a sleeve. The silver watch she'd given my sister was now stowed in a plastic bag, along with her clothes and shoes and the Oscar Wilde, which I'd never open again.

For two days, the ICU was crowded with a revolving cast of the people closest to us. My dad's eight siblings came and went, as did two of Mom's four brothers. Her youngest brother's wife was due to give birth any day in Pittsburgh; her oldest brother, whom I'd met twice, called from Arizona. Those who visited brought bagels and soda and flowers. There was a clutter of roses and a small feast arranged in paper bags inside Caitlin's hospital room, where Mom sat in a plastic chair, clasping the hand of everyone who approached her. Their eyes glazed over, and what they saw of Caitlin turned them gray, but few wept in front of us. They wanted to offer strength or were acknowledging that if anyone was allowed to go to pieces it should be us. When Dad could bear to stand inside the room at all, he held Caitlin's hand and swept the hair from her face. Never lasting more than a few minutes before he'd collapse against the wall and stagger out, the power of his sobs echoing down the hallway.

Eventually, Will and Andrew arrived. They hugged my parents. I'd never be sure what they said to me or how long they stayed. There was no logic, no order to what I saw or heard. My mind chopped the hours into hunks of imagery I might or might not remember, each memory unsequenced, out of time in the fluorescent hospital glare.

I peeled open Caitlin's eyes, in which blood had coagulated like red mucus. I stared into them as deeply as I could. Minutes would pass, and I'd begin to feel I was floating in the blue of her irises—I'd heard that, like snowflakes, no two were the same. Caitlin's were flecked with gold. I brought my face within centimeters, micrometers, searching for life, then swimming deeper into the blue, pleading with her soul, trying to coax her from whatever darkness she'd been lost to. Mom might have sat there behind me. Angela might have been on my arm, but I wouldn't have known. Caitlin's eyelashes grazed mine. I whispered to my sister, right into her temple. I told her I loved her. Again and again, like a promise.

AFTER FOUR DAYS, THE doctors announced that a neurological assessment would be made the following morning. The evening before the tests, I wound up alone with Caitlin. All this time she'd been propped upright in a seated position, her head elevated to allow for proper blood flow. They had it ice cold in there because she'd been sweating with a high fever. I was several feet from her, wearing my coat and sitting in a chair near the door. Someone had placed a pink flower in her hair. Her bruised throat was exposed and looked to be straining from the tubes inserted between her chapped, purple lips. The hospital was silent but for the machines.

Mom must have been at home, showering and feeding Ozzy. I didn't know where Dad had gone, or Angela. We'd all been in and out, seeking the relief of the world outside once the hospital left us boneless and morbid. In the ICU, we were scavengers of faith, bottom-feeders for god's mercy. Privately, we offered ourselves in place of Caitlin—gracelessly, shamelessly. Except for my mom, whose strength seemed fortified by whatever endless prayer she was reciting.

A bottle was nestled between my legs. I hadn't eaten, but I'd been buying beer from a drugstore up the street. I stared at Caitlin across the room, over the ridges her toes formed beneath the blue sheets. You pray at a time like that, whoever you are or whatever words you use. Your mind speaks a madness to itself, a barely subliminal chorus doing everything it can to become thoughts. You doubt the laws of the natural world. You could convince yourself of just about anything. I was terrified to approach her, but I did, and then it was the two of us. The only song that came to mind was "Pretty Woman," and I sang it softly, the few words I knew, and it was the closest I'd felt to her since we were children.

When a nurse arrived to administer another round of

medication, I awoke with my head on Caitlin's stomach. I'd fallen asleep on my feet.

"Talk to her," the nurse said. "It helps."

I sang as the nurse injected something into the IV. It wasn't minutes later that Caitlin gurgled and her eyes flashed open mechanically, two dilated black marbles staring away into nothing as I grabbed her wrist and called her name. I thought a miracle had occurred, that it had been my doing. Then her eyes closed up, and she gasped several times, a low, wet, chalky noise rattling out through her unmoving lips.

"What is this?" I said. "What's happening?"

And the nurse said, "It's okay . . . she's not in pain . . . I just now gave her plenty of medicine."

I remained there in the morning, slumped in a chair beside my parents as a neurosurgeon explained that the tests had failed to reveal brain activity. None of us believed it entirely because there was Caitlin's heart, blipping on the screen. Her bare hands, colder than usual but so soft they felt like new. The scant freckles on her throat, her chest, rising with each huff of the ventilator. Her living body, the girl whom I'd tickled to tears, piggybacked around the yard; who used to lick her finger and stick it into my ear—this is what I suddenly remembered: two of us in the backseat of a car, her wagging a glistening finger and grinning, awaiting my move. Yet I was being asked to understand it's merely science, synaptic activity inside her skull that determines whether or not she exists.

THE HOSPITAL GAVE US as long as we wanted to decide what would happen next. The following day, after another surgeon ran more tests and explained the situation in precisely the same way, there was only one decision to make—about which my parents consulted me, as though we had a choice.

Before the machines were unhooked from Caitlin's body, we each took our time saying good-bye. I'd been told that when someone dies, their spirit exits their body and hovers above, witnessing all that is happening below. Much later, my mom would tell me she'd fallen asleep one night in the ICU when my sister was wrapped in cooling blankets, running dangerously high temperatures—erratic blood pressure and a pounding heart—and that she'd been awoken from a dream by an uncanny feeling of peacefulness. She'd watched Caitlin's vitals changing swiftly on the monitors, her heart rate calmed by something unknown, her body relieved of suffering. As I hugged my sister, prying wide her eyelids and wringing every last wish and prayer from my mind, pushing them through my eyes and into her hers—I worried she'd escaped before any of us arrived. If she'd floated above, I was almost certain she'd done so alone.

• • •

From the steps of Howe-Peterson Funeral Home, the upper-flat apartment was nearly visible in the distance, three blocks west on Michigan Avenue. The weather was January muck, a dusky sky in which you couldn't tell morning from noon, and what Christmas lights remained dangled unblinking from the nearby storm gutters. Andrew and I were standing there, staring across the avenue, when I said, "Sun looks like it might poke out here soon," because a feather of light appeared to be scratching through.

"Crazy, that light we're seeing happened eight minutes ago," he said.

And I said, "Yeah," because all those people gathered inside—lost friends and old neighbors, elementary-school teachers, nieces and nephews, my parents' coworkers, Lauren and family, Lady Grandma and Papa, shivering although it was not cold—all those impossible minutes within the funeral home, they were like that, too: figments that had happened at some other time and were now flashing before me, reflections of another dimension that hadn't been meant for anyone.

A wake—some called it a memorial service.

None of it seemed real.

I had the pure and sincere feeling there might still be an alternate route, a loophole through which I might travel in order to rearrange events. Inside the chapel there was no music, only the drone of sad whispers. I'd been drinking, not eating, and had lost almost entirely any notion of time. My parents spoke in alien tones I'd never before heard, greeting one by one all who arrived. The room fell silent whenever one of us made our way to kneel before Caitlin. Some broke into tears as Dad kissed my sister's head; his brother Dennis led him shaking into the hallway. Mom told stories about my sister's childhood, reminding us who she was, trying to honor her daughter's life any last way she could.

Who she was, who she'd been . . .

Caitlin's body was displayed in a lavender sweater, a white scarf wrapped around her neck. Flesh-toned makeup caked her face. A rosary had been woven between her fingers. But whatever had happened hadn't really happened just yet. Even as I touched her hand, nothing could convince me.

Warden had arrived as early as anyone, wearing a cable-knit sweater, his hair damp with what looked to be Vaseline. From the band, only Ethan showed, hurrying off after sampling a buffet outside the visitation room. The members of Wallside bought me pitchers at a pizza joint across the street. Whenever I looked for her, Angela was at my side, pretty and winter pale in a black dress. Will and Andrew were there in shifts, one of them always nearby.

Late that afternoon, Caitlin's friend Sheila entered wearing black. She had two-toned, crimped hair and firecracker eyes, kind of like her father, whom I walked toward, staring as if he held the only available truth inside that room. Caitlin surrounded us: in collages and framed portraits, crayon drawings our young cousins had placed near her coffin. Sheila's father gazed uncertainly back at me. He might not have known a thing about New Year's Eve, but I noted that his son was not among us. Sheila covered her eyes with a tissue. And when the moment became so bizarre that I felt uncertain of who he was, or where we were, I told him I'd like to have a word with him and his son, once all this was over.

A day later, Mom's arm was hooked into mine as I escorted her down the aisle of the Dearborn church she and my dad were married in. Dad walked to my left, a hand on my shoulder. And when Mom stumbled I braced her, urging her forward as she said for the first and only time, "I can't do this." The eulogy she read was sweet and specific, a vastly different vision of Caitlin that in the end amounted to pretty much the same as mine: her kindness, her force of soul—keep it with us as long as we live.

CAITLIN'S ESCORT REMAINED AT the curb outside Mom's house. On the windshield was a bouquet of pink flowers, the stems tucked beneath a wiper. One morning, lying with Angela on the living room's pullout bed, I watched through the curtains as Lauren walked to the porch and set a care package on the doormat, along with the first of many cards she'd leave there over the years. Dad slept a few nights beside my mom, and what would have been their twenty-sixth anniversary came and went. In the early morning, he could be heard mindlessly singing Beatles songs or weeping at the sight of bobby pins and winter hats. Intending to make arrangements for my sister's headstone, he barely opened the phone book before he began attacking it in the living room. He flailed among the torn pages as I sat on the couch, the two of us alone, dozens of flowers cluttering the windows.

"Stop," I told him, because I couldn't stand to be there, or to leave his side.

Dad took his hair in his fists, wrestling with his grief, which soon left him annihilated on Mom's fake Chinese rug. "I don't know how much longer I'll be alive," he said, curling on a side. "But at the hospital, I promised Caitlin I'd never use a drug again."

Over the course of these days, Angela was getting to know these stunned versions of my parents, who were grateful to know she'd be with me through the nights. She held me in a severe new way. She looked me in the eye without hesitation, saying the kindest things, whispering, because the house was otherwise silent. Once Angela returned to Kalamazoo, I spent weeks lying in my sister's bed, examining the contents of her drawers and staring into her portable television. I caught up on every mind-numbing program I'd missed over the years, and each time I'd think of Caitlin, there'd first be an instant in which I schemed to bring her home—springing her from the hospital, taking her by the arm as we charged out the doors.

Mom kept busy writing thank-you notes and taking phone calls no one else would answer. She mailed a congratulatory card to my uncle Steve. The day Caitlin was pronounced dead, his wife, my aunt Tina, had gone into labor in their bathtub. Beside the tub, clutching her hand, Uncle Steve called 911. Told the operator he wasn't going to budge, that the medics should break down their front door—which, with the assistance of the Pittsburgh fire department, they did. By then my newest cousin was already wrapped in a towel, in perfect health. Uncle Steve had once scared Caitlin to tears wearing a Wolfman mask; he'd spent years making it up to her with birthday gifts and kind jokes. He was her godfather, her favorite, had seen her baptized as an infant. Years ago on a day of heavy spring rain, he'd taken us joyriding in his pickup truck, impressing me with his coolness, tearing through puddles as Caitlin clutched my hand.

"Don't crash us," she'd said.

She laughed when it was finally over, a beautiful sound.

My aunt and uncle named their newborn daughter Emily and were interviewed on the Pittsburgh nightly news, hundreds of miles away. And I thought about all this every way there was to think about it. And none of it made any sense, except when it did: somewhere, someone was smiling, hearts were beating, and, in spite of predictions, the end of days was nowhere in sight.

PART
3

1

The purr of their small motors was the most peaceful sound I knew: two box fans running day and night, whenever I was in the bedroom, which was a good deal of the time. Soft, cool static. They helped with the ringing that had begun in my left ear but also with the heat. Summer of 2000 had arrived with one long, humid swipe, giving the overused couch a grimy feel and gumming up the layers of old paint inside the East Lansing house where I was living with three young women.

I'd moved there in May, after Lauren offered to share her bedroom with me. We'd been talking, hugging, spending days together, magnetized by our shared memories of a recent time when living seemed easy. She didn't mind the box fans or anything else, and it was, I hoped, the end to a scary five months of flamed-out nights and quitting music and breaking things off with Angela. Lauren had graduated with a teaching degree and planned on returning to Dearborn that fall to put it to use. I reckoned that I, too, should be making my way and intended to trick myself into a new lifestyle. I threw away old clothes jinxed by past mistakes. I sold my albums to record stores, remembering where I'd scored each one as the clerk blew on the vinyl, checked for scratches. Gone, too, were my amplifiers, and on a nervous high I'd enrolled in summer classes at the same school Caitlin had escaped on psychiatric leave two years earlier.

When I'd arrived, Michigan State's campus was in its vacation-season lull. We lived on a block where many houses were empty, awaiting fall tenants. I'd brought along a couple trash bags full of clothes and the stereo Dad had given Caitlin that Christmas, a nifty, toaster-sized Sony. You inserted a disc into a slot and watched it spin behind a clear plastic guard as music played from miniature speakers. Who needed vinyl? The music cube sat on a coffee table in Lauren's bedroom, next to a fleet of dwarf cacti. In a corner was a futon that tipped when either of us rolled too close to its edge. A window allowed a slab of light to cut across the walls, which were decorated with tapestries Lauren's oldest brother had shipped home from the Peace Corps.

The house itself smelled like bananas that had begun to turn black. It had been that way for some time, though the girls had yet to locate the stench's origin. Lauren and I had to creep through someone's bedroom in order to use the sole bathroom. Inside was a cramped standing shower with a spigot that drizzled ten minutes of hot water before going cold. The only way the stall contained the two of us was if we entwined. In her early twenties, Lauren had grown more voluptuous. Over the past months, I'd lost ten pounds of good weight—the muscle and girth of my shoulders I believed had made me capable of a hard day's work.

Lauren wrapped herself around me as the water came down. My face pressed against the slick of her bronze, unfreckled shoulders. Her waist was larger than mine. She was tanned from head to toe.

I avoided comparing her with Angela, whom I'd not seen since May and whom I was trying unsuccessfully to forget. Every move I made was toward forgetting—the past, the present as it happened. The little things were the worst dangers, because in every mundane detail there arose a memory of my sister. She was in the kinked toothpaste tube and the breakfast cereal, in any particular shade of sunlight. In the color of a stranger's shirt or the scent of cut grass, and in any fleeting instances of happiness because they could not last without her.

The shower was a vortex, one space so misted and confined there seemed only the elements at hand, the inevitability of our bodies. Drizzling shampoo over us, Lauren clenched her eyes as the suds rinsed down. That's when I'd kiss her, to watch her eyelids twitch as her mouth fumbled for mine, becoming a smile when I pulled away.

Toweling off, we snuck past our housemate, who'd always pull the sheet over her head as we left wet footprints on the worn beige carpet. And if I crawled back onto the futon or drank and slept for days on end, Lauren said nothing about it other than "We need each other right now."

The box fans rattled loudly enough to conceal the sounds of the housemates and their boyfriends. You could feel the air toiling, lifting the tapestries from the wall. Sometimes, a moment of peace. Lying there in the whir, I'd begin to hear songs, phantom melodies I believed were my own. Now and then a tune playing on the stereo would remind Lauren of Caitlin. She cried giant tears as I held her in the breeze, feeling her arms pulling me in.

LAUREN SPENT EVERY MOMENT she could beside me, walking along the Red Cedar River or standing in the backs of bars or taking long drives around the university's horticulture farms.

She fixed me up with a job at the bookstore where she worked, and we held hands and talked about ideas that would take us far from where we were. My friends had seemed to scatter, all but Will and Andrew—and Warden, who urged me to keep after the music. I hadn't laughed sanely in half a year, but Lauren didn't mind. Something new had overtaken her, a need for us to bare ourselves entirely, miseries and all. She began avoiding her many friends, choosing me instead, and I worried that she was following me into the fugue. The sun banged through East Lansing. Her friends tossed Frisbees in the streets and drove to lakefront beaches and threw backyard parties that went all night, but she chose me instead.

A corny old saying: "Everywhere you look, you find yourself." In a way, it was true; there was death in everything I saw. A game of hangman drawn on a napkin, one table over at Peking Express; a hospital, an ambulance; a blonde stranger as she passed. There was no pause, only variances, the sound of an outdated Seattle band singing through the open windows of a pickup truck *Love like suicide*. I saw my own life: beginning and ending, taking its course. Eighty, ninety years began to seem like a short while, and I believed I'd come to understand the impermanence of life's gig. Even the sun, the moon—to be one day pulled through a knothole in the universe, just like Andrew always said.

During shifts at the bookstore, this type of thinking caused me to chuckle at inquiring customers, the names of the dead novelists rolling off their tongues. I felt inspired to lie relentlessly, for reasons I'll never understand. One day, I informed my boss I'd urinated blood, because I'd dreamed it the night before. I told a 7-Eleven clerk I'd witnessed a murder in Tampa, because I'd read about one while touring through. These elaborations flew out of me before I had much chance to consider them. I could make it all up on the spot. And what did it matter, eternally?

Some days, stripping naked in the street was what made sense. I'd peel off my clothes at the slightest whim as Lauren laughed herself hoarse. Yes, she was still a laugher. She was there with me, picking up my jeans and socks from the concrete. Knowing what I knew. This crazy life—it was happening with or without us.

I hadn't yet spoken my sister's name.

Lauren reminded me to call my mother. I thought of her constantly, but getting Mom on the phone was a task. She slept long hours and often turned off the ringer. I'd leave demanding messages, three or four in a row, until she'd return my calls with a small, croaky voice. We'd mention the weather and books. Mom was reading texts about grief and warned that people tended to make foolish mistakes in the wake of a traumatic event. She talked about being in shock. A tricky thing, she said, because you can't tell it's happening.

I allowed this to explain what happened when I drove back to Dearborn one weekend to visit with her. No one envied Mom having to live in that house, but she'd kept it in fine order, all but the refrigerator, in which there was barely enough food for lunch. After we ate, she fell asleep, and I found myself cruising Michigan Avenue, overcome by a sublime delusion that it was possible to banish Caitlin from the past. To carry on, as though she'd never existed. It was as though my chemistry had altered, just so. A cog lifting, a paradigm shifted.

And she was gone, the very essence of her.

I could no longer remember her face . . .

A spell that lasted ten minutes, until I pulled up Mom's driveway and drove my car into her garage door. I'd hardly recognized it was happening, my foot tapping the gas instead of the brake. I checked the rearview mirror—no one was watching. The creak of expanding aluminum as the car reversed and yanked its fender from the crumped door. I almost expected Caitlin to storm into the afternoon wagging a finger as I tried to explain everything.

Inside the house, Mom lay asleep on the couch with a book opened across her chest. When I woke her, she couldn't be bothered to look at the damage I'd done. "Don't worry about it," she said. "As long as no one's hurt."

THE BOOKSTORE WAS SO easy and uneventful it left me anxious. I began filling cardboard boxes with books I figured I should read, stories that might turn me toward one of the many new lives I saw myself living. Using the store's mail system, I shipped the packages to the upper flat, where Will and Andrew would stow them until I visited. The guilty thrill passed my working hours: browsing cautiously, pulling the spines from the shelves and sneaking them to the mailroom, slapping a label on the cardboard. First class to Dearborn, Michigan.

The books I stole were things Angela had mentioned, sleek novels with austere jackets and poetic titles: *The Unbearable Lightness of Being. The Fire Next Time.* I admired her passions and fine taste; yet when I thought of Angela, I made sure to remind myself me she'd hardly known my sister. I charged this against her, wincing away the memory of how it felt to be near her. Her whip-smart language, her soft hands and knowing face. How certain songs reminded her of colors—*I hear green, blue.*

That February, I'd driven back and forth across Michigan to see Angela and Lauren, believing they each held some fragment I couldn't be without. I'd told neither of them about the other as I left one college town for the next. They were, both of them, stronger than me, capable of real love. One of my greatest blessings is to have had them in my life; at the time it seemed another fix I'd put myself in. Eventually, I'd called Angela in haste, telling her straight out that I needed to be with Lauren.

"Why?" she'd asked.

I hadn't been able to say. Many nights, I'd closed my eyes, hoping to be guided toward the right decision. I'd asked what Caitlin would have wanted. I'd envision the rest of my life, wondering which of these women would remain with me until we were aged and incontinent. Who would carry some piece of Caitlin with them, year after year, on even their happiest days? I'd see the silver watch Lauren had given her—my mom had set it on Caitlin's nightstand, the place she'd always leave it just before drifting asleep.

Over the phone, I'd mentioned none of this to Angela. I blamed it on circumstances beyond comprehension. "I don't know how things got this way."

Angela said she was losing her grip. Flunking classes. The nightmares, she said, were working her over. "Everything we went through, and that's it?"

"I can barely think," I told her.

"You don't love me?"

"I do," I said, because it was true.

"I told myself in the hospital that I'd be with you no matter what," she said. "And I need you to know that I would." When I had nothing useful to say, she told me Blaine had begun harassing her again. He'd gotten her number from a college directory and had been calling at all hours. "I don't even want to tell you," she said.

"What?"

"He whispers her name into the phone."

"Whose name?" I said.

"Caitlin."

RETURNING FROM AN AFTERNOON at the bookstore, I walked into my new bedroom to see, perched on the dresser, a framed picture of Lauren and my sister. In the photograph it was winter, the snow reflecting sunlight. Their arms hugged each other's shoulders. They looked to be on the verge of laughter. A stocking cap was pulled down to Caitlin's eyebrows. She appeared as happy as I'd ever seen her, but I couldn't tell where they were. I didn't intend to look any closer.

Lauren lay on the futon, reading, wearing cutoff jeans and a T-shirt. There was absolutely nothing unpleasant about her. She looked at me and smiled huge.

"Could you put that away?" I said. "I'm sorry. I can't see that right now."

She knew what I meant. She stood to remove the frame from her dresser, moving quickly. Then she held it, not knowing where it belonged.

I left the room to take a shaky walk around the block, and when I returned the picture was nowhere in sight. Lauren stood wiping her face with her wrist. And there it was: how terribly she cared. Enough to make my sister disappear when I asked; enough that she'd tried to keep her here with us in the first place.

THAT JULY MY PARENTS arranged to meet with a world-renowned spiritual medium. After years of communicating with dead souls of every variety, this particular seer had narrowed his specialty to working only with parents who'd lost a child. He'd been interviewed on talk shows and national news stations, though I'd never heard his name.

"I know it sounds hokey," Mom told me, over the phone. "We're gonna try it. He helps people in our situation."

They'd booked flights to New York for their session, which gave me the hope they might get back together. In that way, things were looking up. That they were divorced, conspiring to share a hotel room—who'd judge them at a time like this?

Mom offered to buy me a plane ticket, but I didn't consider it. Any mention of my sister could send me into a tailspin, so I smothered my need to believe that she might be reachable somehow, somewhere. Instead, I offered to drive back from East Lansing and keep an eye on Ozzy. After dropping my parents at Metro Airport, I turned around every picture of Caitlin in the house, hardly glimpsing her face as I pointed the frames to the wall.

For months, I'd been investigating Sheila's brother. The boxer. The male stripper. Into almost every memory of my sister, he'd sooner or later intrude—this vile, faceless presence I wanted to cut down to nothing. I'd jotted his address inside the cover of a *Tropic of Capricorn* paperback. Once I'd memorized the information, I crossed it out and stuck one of my ex-band's decals there, for fear my notes could be used as evidence. While my parents were in New York, attempting to commune with my sister's lost soul, I planned to use Mom's house as a base for surveillance.

It was a Friday morning when I parked Mom's station wagon a few doors down from the house he lived in with Sheila and their father, a small, unassuming Dearborn Heights bungalow, one thousand or so square feet, on a block with twenty like it. I staked out the scene as the sun was coming around. I'd sipped my way through a cup of coffee and sat deconstructing the Styrofoam rim, wearing an old Tigers hat and a pair of women's sunglasses I'd found in the glove box. Ridiculousness did not occur to me, only this terrible worry that felt like violence and made it hard to breathe.

At my first glimpse of him, descending his porch, it was difficult to believe he'd existed all that time, so close to home.

Surely we'd crossed paths at a drugstore or a gas station, a bar. He strutted toward the street, an athletic shrug with each step. Can the blood roar and pound so hard that it rises to the tongue? Something tasting of alkaline tickled the back of my throat. My hands felt featherweight, like those dreams where you're being assaulted and can't raise a limb in defense. He was tall. Sturdy and tan, with a large, solid jaw. By the way he threw open the door of his pickup, I knew he'd be able to manhandle me in a street fight.

His truck faced me head-on, about thirty feet off, windshield to windshield. He fussed around in the cab and started the engine. We might have been staring at each other as I awaited his approach, but I couldn't tell. As far as I knew, he'd never seen me before, either, though I believed he'd experience a freezing premonition, some dark recognition of my nearness. But he pulled fast into the driveway of his house, swiftly reversing the truck and revving toward the opposite end of the street without noticing me at all.

EVERY POSSIBILITY HAD CROSSED my mind: black-market guns, screw-on silencers. I considered a sword, so there'd be no bullets to trace. I'd concocted a plan of mailing him what would appear to be a free sample of a muscle-building fitness drink—a mix-with-water powder, unidentifiably laced with a deadly poison. This would require chemical research in libraries I'd visit once and never return to and graphic-design techniques for the packaging, tricks I'd learned from putting together album covers. But how to test it to make sure there'd be no chemical tang when he swallowed?

Or maybe just a sword.

But what if he screamed? Maybe a gun—a gun was the sure bet. A pistol, tossed in a Great Lake afterward. I'd drive straight there once I'd blasted him in the heart. To the Mackinac Bridge, five hours north, then toss the weapon into the Straits of Mackinaw: Lake Michigan flowing into Huron in the gap between the peninsulas. Never to be found. There was a maniac or two I'd met downtown who I imagined might have a beat on stolen firearms.

But who could be trusted?

I told no one about any of it: That I returned later that night to find his pickup already parked at the curb. How I monitored the house, noting what time the lights went out—early, too early. And what about his dad, and Sheila? There appeared to be a side door, but I'd have to survey the backyard, too. Or I'd just nail him as he's coming out of whatever deadbeat bar he drinks at, just turn out his lights and run. These strategies were live wires, sparking through my thoughts. Taking up serious minutes of my days and haunting nights that were already restless. Not that I actually and truly intended anything, but merely gesturing toward harming this stranger made me feel like I was doing at least one goddamn thing to honor my sister's name.

THE NIGHT BEFORE MY parents returned from New York, I cruised past his house several more times before heading to Gusoline Alley, a cramped bar in the city of Royal Oak frequented by people I knew, musicians. After a couple of hours on the stool, I ran into Scott, the ex-Wallside guitarist. He'd very recently been playing in an illiterate radio-rock band with Blaine—who'd abandoned his drums in order to strum a guitar and sing songs he'd written about Angela.

Of course, Warden was doing their record.

But Scott had just quit, I'd heard, after Blaine slept with his girlfriend.

"Dude's a fucking rat," Scott said.

He was slender and bearded, dressed sharply in a ruffian style, a plainspoken chain-smoker with the word LIES tattooed inside his lower gums. A genuine nut for music and all that came with it. We'd toured together, traveled the continent, but I'd recently disowned Scott for his Blaine connection. Now we had an enemy in common.

"He's got it coming," I said.

Blaine was the easy target, a patsy—it didn't take long to convince Scott to arrange a setup. He might have thought he owed it to me for having stood onstage and played those god-awful love songs about my girlfriend. "Call him right now," I said. "Tell him you want to meet and talk things over."

It was 1:00 A.M., 2:00 A.M. Blaine and his cell phone—the first satellite fiend I ever knew. I was sure he'd answer.

Scott dialed from a pay phone.

"There's a party downriver," he said as the phone rang. "He's probably there."

If Blaine hadn't picked up, I'd have let it go that night. Getting my hands on him wasn't something I looked forward to, but my daily visualizations of doing so were vivid enough that anything short of bloodshed would confirm my lack of spine. Angela had heard him whispering Caitlin's name, I believed that—though I could barely conceive of anyone so heartless, the prank was undeniably his, carried out in his cheap-shot style.

Scott talked inaudibly into the phone while I stood on a curb breathing deep and flexing my wrists. "He wants to meet at our practice space," Scott said, once he'd hung up. "He's going there now."

"Good."

We took Scott's Ford Contour downtown, talking about

nothing, headed for a warehouse on Trumble and Holden, an industrial hub where a number of bands rehearsed. One dark, desolate corner of the city where crack merchants huddled across the street, sometimes doubling their wares to include as many bootlegged pornos as could be fit into a trench coat. There'd be no one getting in the way.

When we pulled into the lot in front of the warehouse, Blaine was sitting on the gravel, leaned back against the grille of his car. The lot was fenced in on all sides. Our headlights washed over him. He was alone, with a beer between his legs. I leaped from the car while it was still moving, and there was an instant when Blaine's eyes understood what was under way—as I ran toward him, just before I booted him in the face and heard his head wallop against the fender.

I was weak. I felt the hollowness of my fists as I hammered down.

But I worked on him for a good minute, slugging at his forearms, which had covered his face once he'd curled into a fetal lump. I told him he was sick—a sick animal. Scott stood between his headlights, pecking his cigarette. When I looked up, his smoking arm was trembling, but his eyes didn't say one thing or the other.

They'd claim I'd jumped Blaine. Suckered him. Even in the heat of things, I felt the need to defend myself.

"He's a rapist," I said, because I didn't think it was below him. "He's rape waiting to happen." Scott seemed to understand. Then I kicked Blaine's forearms and spat these words at him, "You say her name again, I'll kill you."

Though I didn't say her name, I was the last person who could.

Blaine was mostly conscious, but he lay balled up and unmoving, playing dead as we drove away. The tires crunched the gravel, and there was a long drive back to Royal Oak, where I'd left Mom's station wagon. And I didn't feel well, but I'd done something. One small shift of dirty work no one else was about to get busy with, though it was far from over. The signs blurred on the highway; then came a stretch where I picked the torn skin from my knuckles.

"He deserves worse," I said.

"Maybe," Scott said, "he'll learn his lesson."

He continued smoking, staring ahead like he was ashamed of what I'd done but agreed that some things—you just don't let them slide. You can't live with yourself until you've done all that you can.

• • •

The spiritual medium had felt the presence of a girl. It was very hazy, he said—unusually so—but he'd intuited something having to do with gasping for air, a lack of oxygen. A drowning? No, that wasn't it. Hard to get a sense. She was awake, but not awake.

"He sat and thought for a long time," Mom said. "He said it was an odd case."

The man had addressed my mother for the entire duration of the appointment, conveying certain images and energies, telling her my sister was sorry. Very sorrowful.

"Do you want to hear about this?" Mom asked me.

I was in bad form on the living room couch, a short matter of hours since I'd assaulted Blaine. The night before remained with me in the soreness of my hands, the taste in my throat.

Dad had carried Mom's bags to the porch and declined to come inside.

"He's upset," she said. "The man didn't say anything to him. Not a word. Barely even looked at him."

I had to wonder if they were losing touch with the unalterable facts of this life. I'd grown more certain than ever that our souls were merely chemicals swirling inside our craniums. Science. Synaptic combustions—the mental fires that trick us into believing we are who we are. But for the Catholic mass and their belief in the Virgin's mercy, my parents had been levelheaded skeptics, realists. Unmystical. Unfazed by reports of UFOs, ghosts, psychic encounters.

"I don't know," Mom said. "It was good to get away."

Ozzy assaulted her with affection, patrolling the room to make desperate swipes at her legs. The poor beast—I'd forgotten about him the night before and he'd vomited on Mom's fake Chinese rug, refusing to break his housetraining.

"Why did you turn all my pictures around?"

"I can't see that stuff right now," I said.

I did nothing to hide my tattered knuckles as I reached for Mom's luggage because she wouldn't notice. There were a lot of things we weren't noticing. We were forgetting to pay bills. We were letting the plants wither. We ran our cars out of gas and walked to filling stations, startled by how quickly the minutes passed. You're one place and then another, with so little memory of the walk, the drive, the workday.

What did it say about our minds? How we'd manage to leave our wallets in the refrigerator, the milk carton in the cupboard.

Driving back to East Lansing, I missed the exit for Okemos Road, realizing it only after the highway veered south toward unfamiliar towns. When I finally made it into the house, Lauren was asleep on the futon. By then I could hardly remember Blaine's crumpled shape or if I'd truly intended to slay Sheila's brother. One moment, my anger overran every rational thought; the next, all I longed for was a pillow. I slid onto the futon, the frame teetering until I rolled near the center. Lauren wrapped her arms unconsciously around me. Just before I went under I said a silent word or two to my sister, up toward the ceiling, thinking that perhaps she'd arrive in the night-blue air above the bed, twirling in the wind of the box fans. Her spirit. Her ghost. And what was it she'd be trying to say if she were there, whispering down to those of us listening?

2

What can be said about that year that is kind and forgiving and proves we were learning to survive? I've gone back time and again, trying to remember the hours when the sun shone or a crow was set loose from the attic or a stranger took my hand and walked with me until I'd remembered my name, all of which happened, yet the truth of those days is something else—awesome and strange only in the sense that we are no longer there.

Will spent the first half of August binging hard before his body collapsed. He was nearly comatose by the time his dad carried him from the upper flat and drove him to Oakwood Hospital. My mom called with the vague details, "He's in the ICU," and I hurried off the phone and sped toward Dearborn, where Andrew was in the weird zone of a multiday fast during which he'd been drinking only water. Living in a room just feet away from Will, he'd been too deep into a state of hunger-induced transcendence to notice anything amiss. Since I'd left the apartment, they'd been using my old room for storage.

Weeks earlier, Will had been jailed in Iowa after an incident of public disruption. He'd returned to Michigan with a copy of his mug shot, which he mailed to me in a heart-shaped envelope days before his hospitalization. Crazy—the currency of our old joy. I couldn't see it then, but Caitlin's death had ripped through the lives of my closest friends, driven them a little crazier than before. Andrew and Will didn't speak about having seen my sister on life support or the fact that she was gone. Not long after her funeral, Andrew told me my dad was the saddest man he'd ever seen, and Will said he'd had a long cry at the rug shop—which was just about the end of us talking about that week in January.

I cringe to imagine how I'd have handled things had I been in their position, if I might have hijacked their grief for my own musical themes. We were young, too cut off from ourselves to reach for one another. But no one really knows what to do about a mess like that: a young girl dying.

I'd called Will the day his mug shot arrived in Lauren's mailbox.

"You see those stripes?" he said.

In the booking photo his eye sockets were darkened. He stared upward, holding a placard with his name and arrest number. The Iowa sheriff's department had him dressed in a black-and-white horizontally striped shirt that looked to have been worn daily for a number of decades.

"I thought that shit was from the movies," he'd said. "You get a look at those stripes?"

WHEN I ARRIVED AT Oakwood, Will was laid up a floor below the unit where Caitlin's life had ended seven months prior. A psychology course I'd taken that summer had informed me that the average onset for mental illness is between the ages of twenty-one and twenty-five. Antisocial tendencies, delusions of grandeur, seeking meaning in chaotic patterns, messages divined from rock albums—I'd come to see the potential in nearly everyone I knew.

"I got diabetes," Will said as I entered his hospital room. "I brought it on myself. They said another day or so and I'd be dead meat."

The space was partitioned by a blue sheet. Whoever lay beyond the curtain had a gnarly cough. Will raised his brows and hissed at every sound the man made. To see him, more conscious than not, relieved by degrees the clenching inside my head, my neck, my lungs.

"Isn't diabetes hereditary?" I said.

"That's what they say, not what I say."

He was thin and greasy. It was in his beady blue eyes, mostly, the illness.

I clasped his hand. Will wriggled his finger lasciviously in my palm, giving a sleazy tickle so that I flinched away. Now he was grinning, and so was I, shaking my head.

"You talk to Andy?" he said. He had his headphones beside him. CDs, the great escape. "He saw a shoot-out. In the street, right in front of the apartment. You should go ask him about it."

INSIDE THE UPPER FLAT, Andrew sat on the couch, pale and vibrating with unfinished theories. The shades were drawn and a Joseph Campbell videotape played on the television, something about the masks of eternity. Andrew acknowledged me with a nod, as though I'd just returned from taking out the trash. I'd never seen him so docile.

"Not gonna visit Will?" I asked.

"I called the hospital," he said. "They wouldn't put me through. Tell him I love him if you see him."

He was soul deep in a malnourished meditation. His eyes bulged. His face looked thinner. I got the idea that he didn't plan on leaving the couch until his spirit voyage was complete. Perhaps he dreaded returning to that hospital, where he'd months before seen Caitlin—not quite alive, not yet dead.

"The mind works so fast when you're not polluting it with food." Andrew stared at the television. "It has so much energy," he said. "I'm learning things."

The daylight outside was brilliant. A slab of white sun crashed in as I opened the door to the balcony and peered down at the street.

I hollered across the living room, "Where was the shootout?"

"Right out there," he said. "One of those suicide-by-cop things. The cop was real smooth, man. He bent down behind his car door and took the guy out. They're trained for that. I helped them search for stray bullets after it was over."

"What? The guy gets pulled over and started shooting?"

"I don't know. I heard shots. Maybe the cop shot first. The cop probably shot first. It's all part of everything."

"You gotta eat."

"I need to make it eleven days. Eleven is the number."

Andrew pulled a scrap of paper from his jeans. I walked over to have a look: *Eleven*, the word and numeral, scratched on a receipt.

"What's it mean?" I said.

"Some hooker downtown. I told her I'd been thinking about eleven, and she said she'd been thinking the same thing. She wrote it down."

"You didn't do her, did you?"

"No, man. It's not about that. None of this is about that."

"Today? How many days is today?"

"Today," he said, "is nine."

ONCE EVERYTHING FEELS LIKE madness, there's so much room to wander, to dabble. You're not nine-to-five. Your family is not nuclear. The earth throbs beneath you, urging you to get busy chasing every arising whim, never mind tomorrow's cost. I wondered what people did in the days before psych wards and emergency rooms. You got one shot at a meltdown. You saw god as you withered in the desert. You waded into the ocean and let the riptide take you all the way.

I had nowhere to go. I had my Escort and half a tank of gas. Standing in the street below the upper flat, I was clobbered by a vision of driving to Kalamazoo and showing up at Angela's. Beside her, with a record playing, was the only place I cared to be. I'd tell her about Will and Andrew. We'd have one last night together, or ten. The rest of our lives. It wasn't a decision—shifting the car into drive and heading for the highway.

Twenty miles outside Dearborn, traffic slowed on Interstate 94. A few yards from the Ann Arbor exit it halted entirely. The air had turned thick green, and then the sky hemorrhaged, letting fall a storm of hail. I looked over and through the ice and rain saw a woman in the car next to mine crying into her hands. Hailstones thumped my Escort's roof dozens at a time. I watched the car's hood being pelted, while above the highway the August sun remained on the horizon.

What an unforgettable sight: the sunrays glinting off wet metal as nuggets of ice scattered, popping like marbles onto the road. People I'd yet to meet would talk about that storm years later—the magnificent speed of it—but just then anything could have happened. A twister might have blown through, and if I were whipped into the sky, everything would have been as it should.

Traffic inched forward as the storm subsided, only minutes after it began. A few hellbound drivers sped past on the freeway's shoulder. The rest of us waited for the jam to push onward and the traffic to thin out, trusting whoever was up ahead. Five miles west, I was once again cruising through sunshine, staring down the cratered hood of my car, strangely grateful for this evidence against my having altogether hallucinated the episode.

I took it as a sign; good or bad, I couldn't say.

Angela wasn't home when I arrived. One of her housemates let me inside while the others, gathered in front of a communal television, regarded me with the pitying expression I'd seen in Caitlin's friends at her funeral. What sorrow they endured looking at me seemed to replace whoever I'd been; I felt I was carrying only the single ugly fact that tragedy had touched me. Sad, sad brother of death. Some of Caitlin's friends had mailed letters I'd not been able to open; others visited my mom with pictures and flowers, relaying messages to me. My sister had known more people than I'd imagined, so many of them strangers I'd never taken the chance to meet.

I was asleep in Angela's bed when she opened the door to her room, squealing at the sight of me, turning away and checking again to make certain I was there.

"My god," she said.

"You didn't see my car?" It was parked behind the house, the hood pocked with hail damage. Even the steel doorframe had a gouge or two.

"What are you doing here?"

"It's all dented up," I said. "It was crazy. This hailstorm."

When I stood, she clutched me, asking, "It's okay if I hug you?" My hands slid into a familiar niche below her shoulders.

I'd buzzed off my hair because I'd been losing it in clumps every time I showered. Angela pulled back to take another a look, fluttering a palm over my coarse scalp.

"Short," she said.

We fell onto her small mattress. Her body burrowed into mine, a feeling twice as incredible as I'd remembered it. We were suddenly a secret thing—which convinced me we had a love that could not be restrained. We laughed, staring each other in the face. Not a minute later, Angela began to cry at thought of me leaving. When she asked where I was living, I told her I'd rented a room in an East Lansing house of strangers. To gain confidence in this lie, I summoned all the drear I was feeling. "It's a horrible place," I said. "I just wound up there."

"And what about her?"

"Who?"

"Lauren."

The spell we were in—I wouldn't have disrupted it for anything. I would have sold out the universe to make it last an hour.

"We're like family, really, me and her," I said.

"God," she said. "I miss you every day."

LAUREN AND I SHARED the futon platonically during our final days together. I'd announced that I needed to move on from the past, and she took it to mean that she was an unwelcomed memory, one I intended to shake loose with all the others.

"Please talk to me," she said. "It's me. You can talk to me."

She'd asked if there was someone else, but I couldn't admit it. I figured that with some finesse and a complete boycott of my feelings I'd be able to avoid hurting anyone. Lauren responded by hugging me tight, attempting to jar loose any trace of emotion; when that didn't work, she chopped her hair short and dyed it blood red. She looked beautiful that way, though I didn't tell her. We spent hours raking over the same ground in hopes of a solution to the mess I'd made. I punctuated every response with "I'm sorry," pleading insanity with my tone. Her anger was trumped entirely by sadness; her round eyes conveyed only a wish that I'd snap out of it. She never once called me names or told me I was wretched, leaving me in the position of having to do so myself. But even her tears were forgiving. When I couldn't feel a thing, they seemed to be for both of us.

Before moving back to Dearborn to put her teaching degree to use, Lauren went through the pockets of my jeans and discovered letters Angela had written, which said whatever I hadn't been man enough to.

"My heart," Lauren said, on her way out of town, "is breaking." And it was as though I'd never heard it put quite that way.

I remained in East Lansing, working odd jobs and living alone above a bar off Grand River. Down the hall lived a guy who called himself Vegas, along with a British Indian named Nittin, both consequential only in their enthusiasm for snorting crushed Ritalin. It did about the same work as cheap cocaine. All you had to do to sleep it off was gulp a bottle of cough syrup, which I did one night after putting a chicken breast in the oven. The next morning, I found a blackened goop on the baking sheet. With Lauren gone, this sort of thing began happening often enough to keep me anxious about my health.

My bones felt soft. In coming years, I'd recall those days and worry they'd done irreversible damage, the lonely panic and malnutrition and cheap booze having caused some sickness to fester in the deepest marrows. It would take much longer to realize that what had clamped its jaws on me was a grief I wasn't yet able to perceive. Only in hindsight would I come to recognize its presence in every word I spoke that year, in the arrangement of bottles on the windowsill and in the shower, which had no curtain and grew mold about the drain.

BY AUTUMN, I COULD drink half a fifth of the cheap stuff and still awake the next day for work. Mostly, it was beer. I shut myself inside my room, doing push-ups on the hardwood floor and strumming my dad's acoustic guitar. I'd given up on studying psychology, spooked by the possibilities of all that could go awry with the brain. The guitar kept me busy. I played for hours, recording songs onto a cassette deck and erasing them the instant they were finished. Back home, Will was administering insulin shots alongside slugs of malt liquor, and Andrew had driven across the country in search of a woman whose name he'd decoded from the Bible. He believed she had the answers, if only he could find her.

And Mom had joined a bereavement group.

And my dad had begun planning a road trip out West. The two of us, through the mountains, where we might even do some skiing.

"I can still keep up with you," he said, but I had to wonder.

Each morning pigeons flocked to the roof outside my window. That winter, snow packed against the panes and the sunrise glared into the room. On the windowsill, next to a box fan, sat a single photograph inside a stained-glass oval frame I'd given Caitlin for her twentieth birthday. She'd rigged it with Popsicle sticks so it would stand upright. Behind the small pane was a faded print: The two of us toddling in early eighties clothes. Our summer-bleached hair, hers pulled back, my bangs cropped at eye level. I was squinting. Caitlin's deep blues were wide open as I sat behind her on the lawn of our Dearborn bungalow. My arms were wrapped around her, though you could hardly make out the image until you pressed your face near it.

That was the version of her I allowed myself to miss—the child, the earliest, flickering memory. Who she actually was had no consistent focus, a person it hurt too much to acknowledge. She wasn't yet finished becoming whatever she was supposed to be, which made all that might have been the cruelest mystery I knew.

Mom had mailed the photo to me, knowing Caitlin would want me to have it.

She fretted over what to do with my sister's clothes, her books, and keepsakes. She offered me things Caitlin bought not long before. A juicer and vitamin D lamps, home-exercise kits—evidence of times when she'd been on an upswing. The picture and her stereo were enough for now.

My mom had only one question.

She'd ask it softly: "Are you okay?"

As far as I knew, I was. I had the idea I could carry on this way a long while—the rest of my life—if only to outlive her, so that she'd never lose another child. Thinking about her was what kept multivitamins in the cupboard; sometimes it poured the last sip of booze down the drain. Mom mailed me twenties and handwritten notes, along with letters that showed up for me at her house. Some were from fans of the band, wondering if we'd ever make our way to California, and why we hadn't already.

3

Dad had been clenching the wheel since Denver. The windows were open, and the sun was beating down in a way it never could in Michigan, yet around every other switchback the mountainsides remained buried in snow. It was March. The small Toyota we'd rented at the Denver International Airport hiccupped as it ascended the Rocky Mountain inclines, revving loudly when Dad gunned the engine. Even when the roads leveled out through a valley, he squeezed the wheel as if his next move might be to yank it from the steering column. I saw the tendons in his hands, raised beneath the skin.

Dad used to drive for miles using only his knee to guide our car around the bends; it was the first trick I'd learned upon getting my license. Neither of us had that kind of cocksure attitude anymore. On the flight to Denver, I'd studied my dad as he slept beside me, twitching and murmuring and digging his nails into his arms, which he'd wrapped around himself.

Now that we were on the road, he smiled, taking in the sun and the view and the fact that we were together. With the car chugging up the next ascent, he floored the pedal and shook his head as the car struggled to keep pace with traffic. "Damn rice burner," he said. "I should have asked for a Ford."

It was an old joke of his, but Dad took pride in his twenty-some years with Ford Motor—the one thing that had remained constant as everything else went to pieces. As he settled into the drive, he began talking about new endeavors, wistful predictions for retirement. Woodworking was one idea, projects he'd design from top to bottom, something to keep his hands busy.

We were cruising through the mountains for the hell of it, on an impractical journey to the Air Force Academy, which Dad hadn't returned to since he'd dropped out thirty years earlier. After that, we planned to choose whatever ski resort beckoned us from the road and hit the slopes. It was the most time we'd spent together in years. We were both thinking of Caitlin; I could feel it. Our family had taken a wintertime trip to Colorado, and I remembered my sister skiing behind us in a pink jacket, making no use of her poles, fanning her arms like a runaway snow angel. She must have been eleven. My dad, skiing in blue jeans, yelling, "You gotta turn," slaloming wide to keep an eye on her as she barreled recklessly down the mountain. "Use your edges."

The nearer we came to the Academy, the more yarns Dad spun about our surroundings. We passed a mountain town where cadets had once gone drinking on weekends. He pointed at the entrance to a closed-off road that had been rendered unnecessary by the interstate. "There was a bar up there," he said. "Way at the top. One night some of us got into it with some bikers and they chased us down the mountain." He said that as one of his classmates sped the car back to the Academy, he'd looked through the back windshield to see one of the motorcycles lose control and veer over the side of the mountain.

"You think he lived?" I said.

He stared awhile at the road. We were circling back to the flatlands of Colorado Springs, which we'd already passed. I didn't know if he was giving it some thought or trying to remember if it had happened at all, but I was no stranger to the far-off look that had clouded over his eyes.

"It's one of those things you just never know," he said.

THE ACADEMY WAS AN official-looking arrangement of austere, geometric buildings. Everything silver tinged, a governmental compound more than a school. In the distance the Rocky Mountains appeared like isosceles hunks of metal. We parked and walked toward the football stadium. Dad wore jeans, an old polo and a disastrous pair of futuristic-looking sneakers. He nodded toward the barracks where he'd lived.

"You had to be up at five A.M. to get into formation," he said. "They'd come by and inspect your room, bounce coins off your bed to see if you'd made it properly. If anything wasn't done to specs, you'd have to do marching drills instead of lunch. You'd have some prick ordering you to stand on one foot for an hour."

I was dressed in black. The only thing about me that might have been relevant to the surroundings was my steel-cap boots, scuffed at the toe. How differently, I imagined, my father's life might have unfolded had he stuck it out here. A military career. He'd have never married my mom, which would have spared her something. Caitlin and I would have been other people, both of whom might still be alive. The monochrome of the campus and the strictness in the air—it all confirmed how lazy I'd grown over the past several months.

"Man," I said. "I can't imagine that."

I meant waking up to a commanding officer and dressing in uniform and learning to fly, but I could have been talking about anything. Though I wondered if that brand of discipline might be what I needed—a by-the-book blowhard screaming at me each morning to put one foot in front of the other.

Dad took in the view panoramically as we walked toward the stadium.

"It wasn't bad," he said. "The first year's the worst, when you have to spit shine upperclassmen's shoes. They'd piss their sheets and make you do their laundry. I made it through the worst before I left."

Inside the stadium's vestibule were photos of sports teams and pilots and dead heroes. We found my dad's young face—his blond hair trimmed to the bone—in a group of football players. A few paces down the hallway hung a series of placards titled "Fitness Test Wall of Fame." Etched into bronze plates were names of cadets who in the span of five minutes had done one hundred push-ups, one hundred sit-ups, one hundred pull-ups, and leaped a certain number of inches from a standing long jump. We found the placard listing the years Dad had been there. He scanned the names as if expecting to see his.

"It was the long jump," he said. "I could have done the rest, no problem."

WALKING ONTO THE STADIUM'S mezzanine, we stared down at the green turf of the football field. Dad noted various aspects of the stadium: the press box, and the benches he'd sat on. Then we stood silently, each of us counting the decades that had passed since he'd been there, all promise, his future so totally unknowable. After a while, Dad made for a restroom and told me to have a look around. He needed a moment to be alone with all that the place conjured in him. I wandered through the stadium corridors, mostly empty, except for several uniformed boys walking with lifted chins, shoulders squared, passing me as if I were some custodial element. At the far end I came across a gift shop and quickly bought a blue baseball cap stitched with the air force insignia, sticking it into my coat pocket.

When I found Dad, he was again meditating on the football field's hugeness. I joined him at a rail, where the bleachers seemed ready to swallow us—an aluminum gorge so vast and empty I couldn't imagine it filled, all at once, with people.

"All right," he said. "Let's make like a tree."

We walked out into the sun and started up the Toyota. Puttering off like tourists, we drove a few miles into town in search of a restaurant that was no longer there. Very little Dad remembered of Colorado Springs seemed to remain. We settled on burgers at a sports bar, where I counted every fry he ate, thinking of his heart and what the doctors had advised after his surgery. But—let him enjoy each bite, because, for a moment, we'd escaped. Not from home, which no longer existed, but from all that had come between us.

"I love you," he said.

He'd been saying that every time I saw him, not before we parted or when he was supposed to, but at unpredictable moments like this one as I wiped ketchup from my mouth and finished chewing. He looked squarely at me, amazed that I was in front of him, with traces of his face in mine.

On the plane, I'd caught his blue eyes glinting in the sunrays that streaked across a cloud, through the oval window, and I'd seen my sister in there. We knew where things stood. I was black-clad and aimless, but I still had a chance to live a better life than he had. No matter where we were, it felt as though we were standing together at the edge of the world. For that, we had no better company than each other.

Before the waiter brought our check, "Kokomo" began playing on the restaurant speakers. To some it was a glaring wound in the Beach Boys' catalog, a money-grubbing insult to the Wilson brothers' genius. Dad bit his fist and began sighing violently. He stared into the lamps that hung from the ceiling, then at the air force pennants and memorabilia on the walls.

"Here," he said, laying too many bills on the table. "I'm gonna step outside."

At the strum of its first chord, the song had reminded us of the same thing: Caitlin in a pink Hawaiian-print ice-skating costume, scooting across a Dearborn ice rink, twirling clumsily to the beachside melody. She must have performed in four or five of those shows, but it was the year she skated to "Kokomo" that I'd always remember because she fell in love with the song and played it for months on end. She was smiling as she skated, and as she watched the VHS tape of the show again and again, well into the summer.

Outside the restaurant Dad slung his arm around me, and we headed for the car like two people walking away after a gruesome competition our very best efforts had been useless toward winning. He asked me to drive, which was a rare thing. Once we'd seated ourselves inside the car I handed him the baseball cap, and he nearly wept all over again before pulling it onto his head, without thinking to remove

the price tag that dangled by his ear. The sun was still shining above as I turned the key, and we were about to luck into
some good radio. I was ready to drive as long as it took. Dad
socked me playfully in the thigh, which meant as much as
anything we could have said. Then we were moving again,
headed back to the mountains.

4

Once I opened my eyes to it, Kalamazoo consoled me like no other place. Life there moved at an alleviating pace, this slacker's utopia where three-bedroom houses rented for five hundred bucks a month. The one Angela found for us was a dusty-yellow residence at the bottom of a sloped brick-cobbled street. Inside was a wood-burning stove and a piano with splintered keys. On the porch, a two-person swing hung from rusty chains. Angela had taken over the lease from some friends, and I was to sign as soon as I arrived.

Dad offered to haul my belongings in a truck borrowed from Ford. Before he arrived, I scrubbed clean my East Lansing apartment, wiped the ashes from the sills and the tar from the stovetop, hoping he'd see I wasn't a man to leave behind a mess. Night had fallen by the time we carried my boxes into the yellow house, where Angela stood holding open the door.

"Look at this place." Dad shoved at the walls to test their fortitude. "Prewar. Nineteen tens, probably."

He slept on a ratty pink couch that had come with the joint, and it was good to feel as though I had a finger on his pulse for the night. He'd sleep there a few more times, when he returned to repair the kitchen floor or seal the windows with caulk. Our handiwork gave him such enjoyment that he soon began talking about investing in Kalamazoo. Decent houses went for as low as thirty thousand, and with a little work we might turn it into a rental. It sounded lucrative, a sure thing if my dad was willing to take the risk. I vowed to keep an eye out for the perfect bit of real estate.

Maybe he'd have liked me to remember him in his prime— when he was fit and self-assured—but working beside him in that house was the best I'd know of him. We passed tools and cursed bent nails. I'd never felt so lucid in his presence, not that we talked much. He focused intensely on the work, speaking only to say, "This is the best time I've had in a long while."

I'd stopped wondering what he might be up to, if he was sober and for how long. Neither of us had much moral ground to stand on; we met on a level field and found we liked each other there. Dad thought Angela was the most delightful woman: this petite, dark-haired student who spoke to him, charmed him, as if he were another of my pals. She teased us about picking up the pace and made him laugh by referring to our basement as "smelling like ass." "She's a keeper," Dad would say, once Angela had gone to bed, as he and I glued the last tiles to the floor. He always stayed up late, until the work was done. In the morning, I'd find a twenty-dollar bill on the kitchen counter and know he'd risen long before.

THERE WAS EERINESS TUCKED inside Kalamazoo's every nook. Old neon signage and rusted cigarette machines, water pollution,

PCBs in the Kalamazoo River. Unsolved murders. Abandoned paper mills. Lagunas and Skylarks parked on the streets. On the outskirts, certain neighborhoods had the look of salvage yards while another was haunted by youths who prowled the night on bicycles, mugging random loners on their way home from nearby bars—unsettling news that blended a wild, almost delicious fear into the late night walks Andrea and I took. Years before, a mental hospital had closed, and former residents still loitered in the town square, riding unicycles or dressed like Dr. Seuss characters. Angela and I set out to befriend as many of them as we could. One local hero wore an Uncle Sam costume and, when asked how it went, said, "You know me." A phrase Angela and I put to use whenever it applied, and often when it shouldn't have: when I was hungover or during the ferocious battles we'd begun staging.

On any given day, we were either at each other's throats or clinging tightly, laughing, pretending we were the only two alive. The magnitude of what I was coping with intensified our every need, gave our partnership a gravitas far beyond its age. The truth became slippery when I spoke of certain things, wild nights I'd had on the town or, more essentially, any contact I'd had with Lauren. Having been raised on lies, Angela loathed deception with a force that made unspoken truths roil deep within a liar's soul. She sixth-sensed fakery, impure motives. Once I'd raised her suspicions, my elusiveness began to dominate my character, but we both had a way of surviving on the good times, holding each other as the fallout rained down.

"Sometimes I feel like it's my art," she'd say. "Loving you, ya freak."

"You know me."

Angela cooked pasta and I took out the trash. There was no one else I could have awoken beside morning after morning, believing we'd return to the serenity we'd felt together not so long ago. And though our worst behavior would remain secret to everyone but us two, though I brought upon us a kind of hurt that would not easily be healed, I hoped some resonance of my very real love for her might outlast our sorrows. She was family to me, just as she was severing all contact with her parents, a decision I supported woefully and only because she had no other choice.

We lit candles and listened as thunderstorms shook the thin walls.

We hung framed pictures and plants, and on some days our house was nearly a home, yet the place that truly characterized our life together was Mountain Home Cemetery, just west of downtown Kalamazoo. Angela had been first to spot it: a majestic, rolling expanse with fields of crooked headstones rising from the sloped landscape. She and I picnicked there countless afternoons. Out on an errand, whichever of us was driving would turn the wheel to pull between the black iron gates, saying, "It's our place."

We always chose a different grave to lie upon feeling passions that arose only when we were among the dead. We stared at the sky as the ants tickled our arms. The cemetery was no place for arguments. It was a reprieve from the yellow house, our marathon feuds, nights of standing red faced, inches from each other, shouting, dressed in nothing but our underwear. My lies tripling in attempt to avoid the pain of earlier lies, to bandage the growing wounds, followed by bouts of heavy drukenness to obliterate all sensation, entirely. Mention of Lauren's name ruined days on end, but we rarely spoke of my sister. When I felt at the brink of losing control, I'd lock myself in one of the unused bedrooms until Angela would slide an apology beneath the door.

One of us was always saying, "We're crazy, aren't we?"

"You know me," the other would say.

In the cemetery, all that was irrelevant. Here were the graves of unnamed infants, of persons who'd lived twenty years and some who'd made it to ninety. Their stones reminded us what a short time it really was; they seemed to be there for that very purpose.

Other days I drove alone to the cemetery with my guitar to strum chords as I wandered over the graves. I wrote hundreds of tunes with titles like "One Dream or Another" and "You Could Be the Knife." I'd come around to thinking music was the sole force that could redeem me and soon began heading for Detroit each weekend in an attempt to start a new band. This brought a storm of worry over my relationship, but Angela never once slighted my talents; she believed I had what it takes. The trouble was that the sad, simple music I wanted to make was beyond my range. It might have been the delicate new sounds I was trying to conjure, or the fact I was drinking too much—nothing was coming out right. But once it did, I trusted the songs would aim me in the right direction. They'd speak the truth, even when I couldn't.

THE NEW BAND PRACTICED on Saturday afternoons and relocated to a bar once night fell. Afterward, I'd arrive late to my mom's house, where I slept in the basement. In the mornings I'd find her sipping coffee with the newspaper in her lap, Ozzy sprawled on the couch. The workweek exhausted her, but she was glad to have me around, especially when I strummed my guitar.

"Play me something," she'd say. "Whatever you feel like."

She'd stowed away her classical music tapes because the concertos reminded her of so many things. Her house was often so quiet you'd hear the clocks ticking and the ice trays contracting in the freezer. For the first time, I played for her, only for her, the nicest melodies I could find.

Those years wore hard on Mom, but she'd sooner nap through the afternoon than complain. "I'll just rest my eyes," she'd say, drifting off on the living room couch. She wrote Angela, talked to her on the phone. They'd begun communicating on a womanly plane far beyond my reach, sharing feelings that had little to do with me. Mom never closed off. Her heartache showed in unusual ways. The U.S. Treasury had issued a series of centennial quarters, and I noticed she'd been depositing these tokens into a coffee cup. She wanted to collect the entire set—all fifty states—in case they'd one day be worth something. The woman who'd hoarded only photos and flowers—I knew she was thinking of the future, of supporting herself over the long haul. Imagining her carrying home those coins, sorting through them alone, brought me closer to tears than anything. I'll never know the worst of what she felt, only that she never failed to smile the instant she saw me.

Sunday afternoons, we ate lunch on the living room couch. Though Mom wasn't much for leaving the house, on what would have been Caitlin's twenty-second birthday she and I drove a mile up Telegraph Road to St. Hedwig's cemetery, where I saw my sister's grave for the first time. Mom trimmed the stray grasses around the headstone and removed shriveled flowers people had left there, replacing them with a bouquet of pink roses.

"That's nice that her friends come to remember," she said.

I considered returning alone to lie atop the grass. If I were capable of praying, I would have that day, but the only epiphany I had was a piercing new sense of Caitlin's erasure from my past. Seeing her grave, I felt the severance of our shared memories, felt each memory of her being altered forever by a gradual understanding that she was never coming back. My blonde-haired partner with whom I'd long ago shared the couch as we scratched each other's chicken-pox scabs and sang along with *The Monkees* as their harmonized voices dripped from the television—she no longer knew me. She was no longer there to remind me of who I might be.

Mom removed the leaves that had fallen onto Caitlin's grave. She'd bought the plot next to it, where she intended to lie one day.

"Are you ever mad at her?" Mom said.

It was an invitation to acknowledge our confusion, to say anything at all. She had to ask, because only I might understand.

"I'm never mad," I said. Though if I felt anything, it was anger. Not at my sister, but at myself, and the rest of us who'd hurt her.

"I am," Mom said. "Sometimes."

AFTER MONTHS OF WEEKENDING in Detroit, I'd formed a number of bands. Really, I'd put together several versions of the same group, playing with more than fifteen people in the span of a year. Repa came and went, as did Ethan. None of us knew how to play softly, with restraint, which left us muddled in an embarrassing, overaffected style. We had a go at several recording sessions, pestered by botched notes and the dramatic warble of my voice.

An alto, a baritone? I'd yet to decide.

Onstage, our keyboards malfunctioned. The rhythm section rolled out the songs fast and sloppy, maiming the intended earnestness of my latest tunes. Fans from the old days might listen to a song before walking off; at a festival some raised their middle fingers in protest. I received an email sent from a cryptic address, suggesting: "How about you remove your

Tampon and get some balls again." It was a bust—anyone could see that. But these were the battle stories musicians told, years later, once they'd made their mark. When someone was finally listening.

• • •

The night of our second Halloween in Kalamazoo, Angela and I pulled into the driveway to see my parents sitting together on the porch swing outside the yellow house. The street glowed with an October sunset. Nearby, jack-o'-lanterns had already been lit. My dad raised a hand to his forehead and saluted as I put the car in park.

Angela said, "They look so cute like that."

They could have been schoolmates, rocking gently, the rusted chain creaking as they swayed. Beside each other, they seemed themselves once again. A night like this was as good as it got. My dad's fifty-second birthday.

"Nice pumpkin," he said as Angela and I ascended the wooden porch.

I'd carved a pentagram into the orange gourd that sat on the steps—a bit of heavy-metal humor—but an unknown force had caved it in nights earlier. Just then, I was glad someone had booted the thing.

"Trick or treat," I said.

My parents held hands, smiling, and I didn't scrutinize it. No one could know our bizarre condition, that when the three of us were together we could nearly grasp some shred of the happiness Caitlin brought us. Her silly, smiling face, or words she'd mispronounced—*ambliance*. We weren't people who went around feeling wronged by death. We knew it was on us, whatever happened next, and I hoped my parents would go on holding hands for a long time, keeping alive what they could.

"A porch swing," Mom said. "I've always wanted one."

I carried a pumpkin pie, concealed in a shopping bag, that I intended to present after we'd gone for dinner downtown and returned to the house. We laughed at our waiter, who was dressed in drag, platinum blonde and diva-like but for his mustache. The entire staff wore unidentifiable costumes, and Mom hadn't been able to rest until she'd speculated about each of them. "Is he supposed to be Vanna White?" Back at the house, Angela lit candles as the trick-or-treaters arrived, many of them fully grown, bearded, wearing tattered coats and holding open plastic shopping bags.

"You're kidding me," Dad said, dropping miniature Snickers into their sacks. "What are you supposed to be, little boy?" He couldn't get enough of it.

"Tim," Mom said, in her half-amused way.

As for the few costumed children who made their way up the porch, Dad told them to dig deep into the bucket, to take as much as they could grab.

OVER THE TWO YEARS Over the two years we lived together, Angela and I were in such perpetual conflict that I sometimes awoke having no idea where we'd left off the day before. I'd look over at her, breathing softly, such a peaceful sleeper. Sometimes cuddling her awake would be enough to temporarily dissolve all anger, but never our fears. The real tragedy was to be so incapable of closeness, so confused and weak in spirit, I couldn't embrace what she offered so completely to me—the thing I needed most.

A turning point was the night Lauren called, awakening us in the late hours. Upon answering, I tried to pretend it was a wrong number, though I'd known who it was from the first word. *Hello?*

Angela knew the same thing by the look on my face.

By then she'd found letters I'd hidden, birthday cards. She'd found long, light brown hairs on the headrest in my car.

"You should see yourself," Angela said. "You can't tell the truth. You don't know how."

What wasn't a lie was that I had no idea how Lauren had gotten hold of our number. Whether I'd given it to her in case of some terrible emergency, or if she'd gone so far as to acquire it elsewhere. I had seen her, secretly, back in Dearborn. Never for scandal, but to steal a moment in which we could pretend we still knew each other. Or to say good-bye a thousand times. Her call threatened the fragility of our connection, told me everything I needed to understand. She'd wanted to hear my voice, no matter the cost.

NOT LONG BEFORE I left Kalamazoo for good, I stole three gravestones from the cemetery. I'd come upon a cluster of them that had collapsed onto the grass, rudely neglected. Their surfaces were blasted by sun and worn by decades of rain. I could barely make out a name or the years of the life span they marked but felt the power they held as I laid my hands upon them.

"What if they haunt us?" Angela said, once I'd lugged the tablets from my trunk to arrange them in our backyard.

"Don't worry," I said. "There's no such thing."

"You're a crazy man," she said.

"You know me."

Eventually an anonymous neighbor called the police, who removed the stones and questioned Angela about the home's owner or anyone around there who seemed of suspicious character. She'd never noticed, Angela said, the stones or anything else. "And your housemate? Anything about him that seems off?"

Perhaps it was crazy, despicable; yes, I suppose that's true. But I believed we'd pay reverence to those forgotten monuments, more than anyone else. If we had visitors, I waited until the end of the night to walk them to the backyard, leading them to the display: all three gravestones leaned against the garage, beside a dried-up garden. Usually, the sun was just beginning to light the yard, the birds cawing. Most people became spooked, turning away the moment they comprehended what they were seeing. When Will finally came to visit, he made it clear that he understood. He kneeled to the scuffed tablets and ran a palm over the stone, whispering, "Dust to dust."

5

I dragged my futon piece by piece from the car, wrangling the metal beams into an alleyway Dumpster. The mattress was tied to the roof of my car, which was packed with boxes. Finally, I lobbed the cushion over the Dumpster's edge, stuffing it in as deep as it would go. A British album yawned through my car's windows, a spacey, bittersweet melody. The mattress had been the last thing. The rest I'd gotten over with quickly, ditching much of what I owned at a nearby Salvation Army. Only a bathrobe—as I smothered it into a trash bag—made me cringe, thinking of Angela giving it to me in a wrapped lump for my birthday.

She'd signed a lease on a new apartment a few blocks from the yellow house. I'd planned to rent a place nearby, until one last fight spurred another cross-state migration. Headed for my mother's basement. Twenty-four years old. To achieve the right mind frame about things, I convinced myself that the musical secrets awaited in Detroit. Sacrifices—material and otherwise—would only draw me closer. Not to mention, I'd be twenty-seven soon enough, the golden age of the perishable greats: Cobain, Hendrix, Joplin, Morrison.

And what did I have? Three years left.

It was May of 2003.

"This is your home," Mom said, when I arrived. "You're always welcome here." Then, in a kind tone, "But you wouldn't want to stay forever, would you?"

If there was shame in this, I was beyond it. I vowed to be out by autumn and back to school. Truly, I was counting on the band tapping new inspiration. We'd do it like the old days, hop in a van to take the music city to city. Someone in a swank coastal office, catching drift of our passion, would wire us all the money we'd need. After that the true lift would begin, the one I'd never need to come down from.

But musicians these days had steady jobs and girlfriends. They had ganja habits and rent to pay. By July it was clear the band's schedule wasn't going to change on account of my freed-up nights. I had a couple thousand socked in a checking account. To stretch that out, I'd cut up my debit card and carried a checkbook everywhere, buying cigarettes and protein bars at grocery stores in order to write the checks for twenty bucks over—thirty when the cashier allowed it. People got a charge out of this. "Hey," they said. "You got your checkbook?" I was outsmarting ATM fees while duping myself into having too little pocket cash to drink heavily.

At the end of a night, I'd have burned through my twenty spot, finding myself adhered to some barstool blowhard who'd been keeping me in shots. Some of them accepted my scrawled-out payments, written a few bucks over for the hassle.

"You cheapass," they'd say. "Have one on me."

In the bar, at a party, in someone's apartment—there was always music, and I'd started resenting every note. All the more if the songs were good, flowing with a genius I could not, for the life of me, call my own. New sounds from New York, Montreal, Portland, all of it so many miles ahead.

For the many hours spent trying, I hadn't learned how to sing, how to distinguish the pitch of one note from the others as they rose from my lungs. I'd yet to hear my voice, whatever true sound it desired to make—I did everything to sound like someone else, a tuneless composite of a hundred singers who were not me. Through pay phones outside random bars, I began calling Will to leave the same harebrained message, *Wanna hear the sound of a man aging ten years in the span of thirty seconds?* before setting loose one of my old howls, pulling it through my chest, holding on to the wail as long as I could. And what if those screams did peel the minutes off your life? Like a cigarette, an X-ray.

LATE THAT JULY, ONE of Dad's nieces was getting married near Detroit. Angela agreed to accompany me to the wedding. Two hours, one hundred and forty miles—the distance between us had no effect. We'd already begun sweetening each other through the phone. I'd driven to see her, visiting her new apartment until we began feuding over our unsolvable problems. But seeing Angela arrive in a black sleeveless dress, her hair pinned and her green eyes rife with everything she knew and wanted—I had no immunity to that. A swift maneuver into each other's arms, and we were right back to it.

At the reception, she and I sat in a corner as the DJ spun songs we'd heard all our lives. There was an open bar and Macarena prancing. Dad's family passed by with the usual *how do you dos*, while Angela kneaded the scruff of my neck. She was aware of my every tic, had phrases to address my many modes of anxiety. "Easy, now," she said to each whiskey I knocked back.

"Slow and steady wins the race." Red lipstick; a silver necklace lay just below her throat. With such little flourishes her beauty became dangerously obvious, and the fact I was beside her seemed satisfactory evidence that I had a life to speak of. It felt inevitable that we'd one day exchange vows, alone and in a place where there'd be no further ceremony than the two of us clasping hands.

"It means a lot that you came," Dad said, every time he made his way to us.

His smile was clumsy. I worried that he'd had a few, but he looked vital as ever, filling out his suit, shuffling in his honky way to the disco pulsing the room. While Angela was using the ladies' room, he took me aside in a corridor outside the reception. We heard the music, the clatter of glasses. The celebration was really just beginning, but Dad put a tough arm around me, nuzzling me to his chest, knowing my business was done there. A glorious thing: the strength that remained in his arms. I felt he could crush me, Paul Bunyan the whole of me above his head as he had when I was a child. Yet there was something else—as Angela appeared, striding toward us—the slightest change in his eyes that let me know that wherever I was headed, or who I'd become, was all right by him.

I remember clearly the last thing he said to me:

"That's all that matters. That you were here."

TWO WEEKS LATER I was pacing the living room, stamping over the fake Chinese rug, tracing its patterns with my feet. I reached for Ozzy as he wended past, blindly sniffing for my mother. She'd gone out for the night to a book club or a movie—never anything more. She was soon to return, and I couldn't decide if that was a good thing. I'd been on the phone so long its earpiece was moist with sweat.

Angela was talking, crying.

We were ending it again, this time through a long-distance call.

"That's it," she said. "Write songs about me or whatever you're gonna do, but don't call when you get lonely." The message was nothing new, but her insistence felt more permanent than ever before. "You don't even want me at your shows."

"All right," I said. "There's no other way."

"Don't talk to me like you talk to everyone else. I gave you everything I could."

It wasn't a question of love. It's that it was no way to live—spiraling through our private terror, each of us knowing what levers to pull in order to collapse the other. We'd dedicated so much to our struggle that I had no energy to face the larger problems, which might have been the reason we whipped things into a crisis every week or so. The spinning wheels, a centrifugal avoidance of the larger themes.

"I'm serious," Angela said. "This time."

And if I could just avoid her face, I'd slip beyond her weakening, spellbinding charms, and soon enough it would be over.

We hung up. No apologies. None of the open-ended gestures we usually tossed out at the conclusion of our battles; no hesitation in our voices, no softening tone as we said, "Okay, bye." Staring at the phone, I wanted to talk with someone who could see the future. Thoughts of a bar terrified me in moments like that, when there'd be no telling what I'd do or where I'd wind up. I knew to stay in, put on a record with the hope of slumbering through it.

Outside the windows, the summer sun had gone under.

Through the opened windows came the trickle of my mother's garden pond.

Some things—maybe they happen the way they're meant to. Years pass, and you look back at certain instances, wondering if there's a cosmic order to life's whirling events. What I did next, of all things, was dial my dad's condo. It had been years since I'd come to him for anything but the most practical advice about income taxes and torn engine belts. I doubt that I intended to tell him about Angela. I'd only wanted to hear his voice, hoping it would convince me that I'd live a long time, convey some brand of hard-earned wisdom only a father is capable of passing to his son.

The phone rang, and what an awful feeling that brought on. Since Caitlin's death, waiting out those chiming seconds could induce a speedy, paranoid frenzy. I'd jittered through it many times when I rang anyone dear to me and couldn't get through. More than once I'd phoned my mom only to be terrified by her answering machine, the gentle clearing of her throat before she spoke, *I'm not home.* I'd call her neighbors, asking them to go, please, check on her house, her car. See if the lights are on. She'd done the same, if only to hear my voice and say, "I had the worst feeling."

Dad's line rang once or twice. It was nine or ten o'clock, a weeknight.

My uncle answered, the new husband of my dad's youngest sister. A friendly electrician I already felt I knew better than any of Dad's brothers. He'd lost a son to a car accident and had the wounded eyes to match.

It was the thinness of his voice as he spoke my name.

"Something's wrong," I said.

He said, "Now, where are you? Who's there with you?"

And I said, "No. No, no, no." Not because I didn't believe it but because I wasn't sure I had it in me to get on with whatever was about to happen.

EXCEPT FOR THE KITCHEN, Mom's house was dark. I sat Buddha-style on the floor with a guitar, my back to the cupboards, strumming open chords I'd pilfered from Nick Drake.

The tones rang over the linoleum. Soon enough, turning around the notes here and there, I was onto a new tune, one of my own.

"What is it?" Mom said, as she came through the back door.

She could tell the instant I looked up at her that something was no damned good.

"I need to talk to you," I said.

"What?"

"Let's go to the living room."

"What?" she said. "What?"

She took a seat on an ottoman that matched her favorite chair, leaving the chair itself for me. I leaned my guitar against it. The light from the kitchen softened the edges of the room. Mom sat upright, wearing a sundress, her purse in her lap. Her arms were freckled, sunburned, a late-summer tint. Ozzy came right to her, and she stroked his spine with the nervous momentum another woman might have used to light a smoke.

I wanted to be a man, to say it quick, tell it like it was.

"Dad's dead."

Her eyes shifted. Then she winced so tightly it appeared as though she were grinning, this brief, puzzling instant being the last she'd ever be free of the undesirable truth I'd spoken into the room. She didn't want to know, not just yet.

"What do you mean?" she said.

I stood and moved toward her. I put my arms around her. There was no man, now, in our lives. Not anymore. I felt it—not the loss of him but the fact that there was no one to help us.

She said, "What are we gonna do?" She brought her hands to her face, pulling them away to say, "How?" Saying, "No. Don't tell me. I don't want to know . . . Tim," she said in a harsh voice, as if calling him from somewhere in that house in which he'd never lived.

There was no way of imagining the flood of memories passing through her. Twenty-two years of marriage; children, homes, anniversaries. The teenage boy across Evangeline Street, thirty years before. As she crumpled onto the ottoman, I couldn't guess what picture of his face arose in her thoughts. It was she who'd seen him at his best. His finest day—surely he'd spent it with her, with us, in a Dearborn backyard, tossing me a baseball across our trimmed lawn, hamburgers cooking on the grill and Caitlin soaring on the swing set he'd cemented into the ground, next to a garden boxed with railroad ties he'd dug for Mother's Day . . . nineteen eighty-something.

"It's gonna be all right," I said.

I'd already begun assuring myself things would go differently this time. I reckoned I understood the low-blowing shock waves that came after losing someone. The way they took years to rise and curl and break. Caitlin's death had shaken me loose from myself, but I'd harness the coming weeks and months. I'd ride them expertly, sensing each undertow, never fooled by the numbing crests that trick you into believing you're sailing free.

"How?" Mom said. "Was it drugs?"

"It doesn't matter," I said. "Doesn't matter anymore."

6

Not just the city—half of northeastern America was black-ened, if you believed the news. Early that morning, the circuits had blown. Rolling brownouts. Too many AC units, coffeemakers, and box fans sucking voltage. August 15, 2003, and as far as I could see the earth was without power. Police officers directed traffic on Michigan Avenue, waving their hands through a smear of exhaust while Howe-Peterson, the funeral parlor where Caitlin had lain three and a half years ear-lier, was lit by candles.

It felt as though I'd only just left, a dark riddle I hadn't the grace to solve. In my head I made up a song about being buried in leaves and set aflame—anywhere but here—when my time came.

Inside was a sweatbox filled with mourners in suit coats and dresses, fanning themselves with prayer cards. Mom had pasted together a collage—snapshots of Dad with Caitlin on his shoul-ders, the four of us carving pumpkins—photos she'd peeled from poster boards stored in the basement after being displayed beside my sister's coffin. Dad's family brought their own framed pictures of him: looking stoic in his air force uniform; wearing a Halloween costume—a 1950s clown getup—grinning over six or seven birthday candles. Set on a podium next to the casket was a recent impromptu headshot, catching him with a similar boyish gleam. It was no put-on: the earnestness of his smile, his small teeth peeking between his thin lips.

Dad's mother came at me with a hug. Drawing me near the coffin, she pointed to the framed image, saying, "That's your father. This is how you remember him." She reached for the frame and held it up. "Not there," she said, nodding to my dad's corpse, which I'd yet to willingly observe.

I'd insisted on an open casket, a cause for resentment among Dad's family. His youngest sister had discovered his body inside his condo; another had been called to assist. Both women were nurses who loved him with a matronly intensity. My aunts, the nurses, said he'd had a heart attack. They were firm in their diagnosis, insisting there should be no autopsy. One told me he'd died in his favorite chair. The other said he'd passed on the living room couch and that he'd looked at peace.

They'd known another man, one I might never understand. What he'd left them with was something cherished, much more good than bad. Their unconditional love was frozen in sad time, impervious to the many hells he'd been capable of. He was my grandmother's favorite son, my aunts' favorite brother, and to allow the rest of us to see him in his final state must have seemed unbearable. What he'd leave me with was another thing entirely—so many things of the kind only a son carries away from his wasted father. I needed to see him once more, to say to his face whatever might come to mind.

Ford Motor employees and 12-step fellows drifted my way, prompted by my resemblance to someone they called "A good man. A great man." I'd donned one of Dad's paisley neckties. Angela was in the black dress she had worn to my cousin's wedding. The minute she'd said, "I'm always here for you," I gave up any idea of us being apart.

I held her hand.

She'd brought a Baggie of Vicodin. I'd known she had access to the pills, I had begged for them because I feared what might happen once I started drinking. I saw it in Angela's eyes, too—her worry over how all this would play out in the coming weeks. And I couldn't tell if it was the effect of the opiates or if the scene inside Howe-Peterson was as dreamily sepulchral as it seemed: the swell of the heat wave; musk exuding from the textiles; running makeup and perspiring scalps; the mothballed blazers. As dusk fell, people moved toward the coffin with candles in their hands, raising them over my father's body.

Andrew paid his respects. Will vanished no sooner than he'd arrived, dressed in a blue blazer and pleated khakis like some old-fangled Bible salesmen. His eyes told me how little he wanted to be there. He had tickets to see the Stooges that evening, their first tour since '75.

Mom stood in a corner as Dad's family worked the room. Awful things were said at her expense—grief-blinded anger directed toward her for not, I suppose, having stuck beside him through another hundred nights of dread and maxed credit cards. I overheard this horseshit with an ease that made me believe I'd been meant to. By evening only the true bloods remained, mulling about the doorway. The windows had darkened and the staff gathered in the vestibule, hands clasped, insinuating in a professional way that now was about that time.

Seeing my chance, I slurred something to a staff person about having a moment alone with my old man before the lid was closed. She seemed to understand, enough that she quickly arranged for my private viewing.

The chapel doors closed behind me, and I approached with a flashlight, turning it on my dad's face as I neared the casket's edge. He looked barely like himself. His chest, as I laid my head on it, felt stuffed with tissue. When I began to cry, it was as deeply as I could. I took his thick fingers into mine and felt suddenly aware of the truest reasons that he was there, cold and lifeless beneath me. It was like a question being answered with a thousand larger questions, and I sensed his defects within myself, what it might take to overcome them: everything I had. For a moment this awareness whispered near the periphery of my blindest spots, only to vanish as soon as I raised my head from the dampened patch I'd left on my father's starched shirt.

I told him, in no uncertain terms, "I love you." Then I said, "You crazy fucker," and it felt as though I was saying it to both of us.

When I opened the chapel doors, Dad's family awaited in the hallway. "Now it's the family's turn," my uncle Dennis said, as all eight siblings made their way into the chapel. I liked some of these relatives and felt nothing much for others. But I believed we all were deciding, then and there, that I'd never be one of them.

ANDREW AND I MUST have been the only people in Wayne County listening to a tune that evening. He'd tapped the batteries in his garage, where he stored energy channeled from solar panels affixed to the roof. It was enough to run a lamp in the upper flat and keep a record going on the turntable. Andrew boiled noodles; the fridge was stocked with beer.

"You gotta eat," he said. "Slow down the thought forms."

Since abandoning the mind quest he'd braved three summers

earlier, Andrew had evolved into a pious, selfless blue-collar guru, working as an electrician's apprentice. The fasts and cosmic toils had led him to a sane, sturdy way of life. He'd changed for the better. He now spoke with untroubled simplicity.

"The journey," Andrew said. "It's whatever you learn from it. The only choice is to make it about growth."

Angela had gone home exhausted with my mom, both wanting for sleep, defenseless against the heat. Dark and sweltering. Of all evenings for the Stooges to reunite—Iggy the Iguana, four years older than my dad, and still strutting the world's stages. The power, however, had not returned to the land. Pine Knob amphitheater was an unlit chasm and Will's whereabouts were unknown.

"Willy," Andrew said. "Think he's in trouble?"

I didn't care to guess.

He switched off a lamp, lighting several candles and placing them around the flat. His solar-charged batteries might have been running low, and he knew the records were what I needed most. "It's sorta nice," he said, about the way the candlelight twitched in the corners. And it was, even at a time like that.

Will was laid up at Oakwood Hospital the following day, having drank himself into a diabetic shock. I was unaware of this as I read my dad's eulogy: a sloppy, unreligious account of family anecdotes, the pages marked by sweat as my voice hoarsened and faded. Afterward I walked outside, down the church steps, intending to embrace the heat wave, which was now being publicized as a regional crisis. The moistened asphalt smelled like chemicals. And it might have been the Vicodin I'd crushed and swallowed, because as I stood in the sweltering daylight, I was positively unafraid. If only in that sunblind moment, I could have laughed. You could have dug your thumbs into my eyes and I wouldn't have minded.

I was standing like that, feeling that way, when Lauren drove by, smoking a cigarette and slowing her Ford Tempo as it sputtered past. We saw each other quickly and clearly, though I knew she wasn't coming inside.

But seeing her pass. Knowing she would again, even if I wasn't there—it told me more than I'd wanted to know about love. That at your worst moments you are forgiven by those who see all the way into you, clean through your fears, to the thing you truly are, what you could or couldn't be.

• • •

Springsteen's *Born in the U.S.A.* Stevie Wonder's soul-sap double album *Songs in the Key of Life*. Paul Simon's *Graceland*. Simon *and* Garfunkel, pitiable old Garfunkel, whom Dad always claimed was a dead weight Simon had to leave behind. Crosby, Stills & Nash. Neil Young. The Doobies, The Stones, Led Zeppelin. Steely Dan. *The White Album*—Ringo Starr bemoaning the blisters on his fingers during "Helter Skelter's" discordant anticlimax.

I inserted the cassettes into Dad's stereo, blasting them through a tube-powered stereo he'd assembled in the seventies, before I was born. The scuffed plastic cartridges had passed through cars he'd owned when I was a kid, and the songs themselves generated not single memories but strobes of our old life: baseball games and swimming pools, drives to Cedar Point. Bike rides. Ice-cream cones. Caitlin and me singing in unison to Van Morrison's corniest ballads. Things I'd forgotten during the years I'd invented a familyless version of myself, a person who'd come from nowhere, like some world-beaten tunesmith. Now I remembered the entire arc, the decades of our simple life unfurling to where I presently was, Paul McCartney bellowing loudly to me about getting to the bottom and going back to the top of the slide.

Turning around.

Going for a fucking ride and doing it all again.

I walked through the condo, wielding a dagger Japanese automen had given him as a gesture of transcontinental schmooze. I ate the last of the TV dinners. I changed the locks and peered through the windows. The entire place had been left to me. It belonged to me—a two-bedroom void at the end of a newly paved road.

Before I'd arrived, someone had removed the photographs of Dad's parents, which had sat on a dresser near the front door. Everything else, I was apparently entitled to. His tool bag. The dresser itself.

Once I started drinking, I did a whole lot of sitting in the bathtub, sucking light beers because they had little effect. Rising from the tub, I weighed myself on a digital scale—my scale—watching the numbers fall. One sixty. One fifty-seven. I wanted to get lean, act quickly from here on.

In the basement, I pressed weights on Dad's rusted bench. Scanning the living room day after day, my thought was: junk, junk, junk. Two couches, a dining table. Everything that had come with Dad after the divorce.

I shaved with his razor. I crawled into the sheets and slept on my parents' old bed.

I turned over pictures of Caitlin.

The stereo churned.

Paul Simon was going to Graceland in the span of four and half minutes, joined by his son, the child of his first marriage . . .

If Dad's phone rang it was Mom or Angela, making sure I was there. Or it was Ford Motor's human resource department, with a stiff deadline for the return of Dad's company car. It had been a few weeks, a month. One afternoon, for the sake of doing anything, I stuffed Dad's clothes and suits into trash bags and carted them to the Michigan Avenue Salvation Army where Will had once found his favorite costumes. Walking into the store, I set the first load on the counter, figuring they saw people like me every day, casting off sacks filled with past lives. When the clerk whined, "You gotta fill out a slip for those," I snatched the rest of the bags, chucking them two at a time through the doorway, saying, "I'm giving you a life's worth, man."

What is left of a man's life? A bicycle. A television. A bed. A sack of tools.

In a filing cabinet, I found workbooks from the rehabs he'd attended. On the pages were lists and confessions and charts of terrifying ideas, drafted in my Dad's slashing print.

Triggers:

Feeling bad.

Feeling good.

Dad. Dennis. Cindy. Dearborn. Detroit. Work. Weekends. The car. Caitlin.

The last one, the doozy—it arrowed through my lungs, pumped blood into my spleen. It said, simply: *Fuck it, let's go.*

ANOTHER DAY, I WAS giving Dad's toilet seat a serious workout, reading through stacks of *Time* left on the porcelain water tank. In the next room, Billy Joel's *The Nylon Curtain* blared at a volume that turned its pop shimmer into a braid of white madness. Whose condo was attached to this one? I hadn't heard a sound, hadn't seen a car pulling in or out of the driveway next door.

So much Vicodin had cinched my bowels. When enough was enough, I flipped the roll of toilet paper, and as the cardboard cylinder spun, I heard a clink on the tile floor. Looking down, I saw a glass tube, inches from my toes and stuffed with a steel-wool knot. I put it to my lips and sucked, tasting the unlit resin. I pressed it to my nostril. Burned crack smells like dirty socks, like old laundry that's been set afire. It smelled familiar: the bathroom of a Detroit club, the endmost stall? Something, something, something.

I twirled the glass pipe in my fingers, rolled it over my thigh, thinking, *I know everything. I know where you've been.*

My dad might have trusted me never to tell a soul, to allow him the benefit of the doubt in the eyes of the world. I'd carry the lie. The illusion that he'd died clean and sober, lived his final days honorably, in allegiance to the twelve steps.

My aunts, the nurses—what a scene they must have come upon, before the coroner and the phone calls. Another glass stem in his fingers, I was sure. The bent, clawing pose a man strikes as he dies in a burst of narcotic light. This is what I believed—and, no, I didn't blame them. I'd have done the same thing, pulled the drugs from his pockets and rearranged his limbs to wave my hands over the scene, wiping all evidence from the earth.

THE PIPE REMAINED IN the pocket of my jeans as I spoke to realtors and lawyers. It was a charm between my fingers as I said things like "probate court" and "priced to sell" and "open house," and "everything goes." It was with me as I signed the closing papers. Maybe there was enough of a hit packed inside it to warrant my arrest. Or maybe one day I'd throw it into a sewer or the trash can in a gas-station bathroom. Pitch it from the window of my speeding car. Or maybe I wouldn't let go of it for a long while.

I WONDERED: WHAT IF he'd died years before that pipe, before he'd ever held one? Struck dead by a car or by the freak heart attack he'd survived in 1981. Thirty-one years old, gone of natural causes—then he might have left the earth a good man, a great man. Sometimes I envisioned him as a photograph we'd have kept in our wallets, a young father I'd barely known, who vanished before I learned what he was made of. I might have turned to his face when things were at their worst, thinking, *Talk to me now. Show me the way.*

Or I asked myself: Would my sister have lived, might her sadness have taken a slow, patient course, if only we'd been raised fatherless? Would I have discovered his old guitar and followed a different tune? My mother, a widow at thirty—spared so many nightmares of her husband's eyes and the drug menace within. I added up the good and the awful, but in the end how could I remember him without praying that I never found myself in his place? Not for a day, not even his very best.

ONE LAST THING I found as I scrubbed out the debris of my father's ancient computer, a single poem, a file named "Caitlin." Nothing more than two lines:

Twisted metal and burning steel / Help me Cait, pull me through the wreck.

7

Ten seconds before the last note of our final song, the drummer hammers through the skin of his snare drum. The band turns to face him. We slam the chords, watching his sticks pound a few ghosty eighth notes from the torn snare, and then it's over. The crowd applauds, a good three or four hundred out there beyond the stage lights, some whistling through fingers. Behind the ringing cymbals the drummer smiles; we all do. Our first show: gone off with barely a hitch.

We'd been together a few months before scoring this slot opening for a Brooklyn trio named TV on the Radio, whose album was breaking in a way no one expected. March 2004. Detroit. A stroke of luck at a Woodward Avenue club called the Magic Stick.

The house music slammed on and the crowd made for the bar, the restrooms, the back alley. Fifteen-minute changeover before the headliner, meaning we had five to collect our equipment and scramble out of the way. Once we did, Ethan hugged me, bending from his six-foot-two vantage to wrap his sweaty

arms around me. We were backstage, an altogether-new amenity, a graffiti-covered room with free beer, towels, a bowl of
tortilla chips. We'd yet to decide how to describe our sound, but
since our initial practice I'd felt certain jujus and mumbo jum-
bos colliding. Ethan pressed his forehead to mine, as if we'd just
exonerated ourselves from some future punishment: playing in
cover bands, open-mic nights.

"It's good to be back," he said.

Ethan had been an obvious recruit. He'd botch notes and
rush the beat, but when it came to going for broke in the name
of rock and roll, you could count on him rising to the cause.
With or without me, he'd go on living it; together, though,
our mutual devotion became a gestalt, encouraging the type of
inner-band hypnosis necessary for true creative lift off. I put an
arm around him, slapped his massive shoulders.

Our drummer entered the huddle, clasping our necks and
butting his noggin against ours. I'd met him in a Dearborn bar
that fall, after my dad's condo sold. A wily brute from my hometown who played the traps with a neurotic chutzpah and had
barely a tie in the world. He was the closest thing we could find
to Repa, who after a stint as a Ypsilanti cabbie had taken work
driving eighteen-wheelers across the country. This inaugural
performance had tinkered with the new drummer's emotions.
He was shirtless and girthy, hirsute but for his glistening, bald
scalp, which wrinkled as he said, "Oh, man, I feel good."

THE HOLY FIRE—I'D SEEN the words painted across the fender
of a Christian landscaping company's trailer, hijacked it then
and there as a declaration. Pictured it stamped across album
covers in bold type. Ethan worried, "They'll think we're a God
band," but the idea was to transcend. To save our souls, or burn
them, musically.

The band's name spread across town faster than I'd thought possible. After a few more gigs, our photographs appeared in the weeklies. College stations began spinning our demo. Things unfolded so easily there seemed to be some trickery at work, but I began angling for the big time. We'd play only the good clubs from here on. No basements or garages or VFW halls. No business with Warden or any other punk rock crapshoots. I reminded my bandmates how old we were getting, saying, "We'll all be thirty-something by the time our third album is released."

Bartenders began sliding me free drinks, and girls working the doors at clubs waved me in as if my ticket money were an insult. People who'd come to see Ethan and me play in previous incarnations now worked the establishments where we spent our nights.

They said, "I listened to you in high school."

And I said, "Yeah, yeah," because you never knew who was giving you the rub in places like that.

Punk, whatever you'd call it, had become gentrified. The scene had changed, or it was a new zone altogether. After the shows, girls sauntered through the clubs, tattooed and urchinlike, hanging around with a purpose I was unaccustomed to. A handful of managers had begun chasing us gig to gig, urging us to bring them aboard for a 20 percent cut of the big break we could all feel was just around the bend. By having hung around with the right sort of musical lifers, I'd earned a reputation as a fanatic with an uncertain past who did nothing but write songs. And I wanted compensation for the work. I'd come to covet the tour bus and backstage rider and televised appearances, a public existence that mattered terribly to the world. A gold record, some trophy I'd present to my mom, one she'd hang on her wall, finally proving that I'd done good.

To assure our meter would be impeccable, we practiced to a metronome five nights a week. I sang what I could. What I couldn't, I screamed. Until the sun came up. Until our fingers bled and our ears filled with wax. Even then, sometimes, we kept at it, song after song. And they could hear us, whoever was listening.

BY DAY, PUBLIC-SCHOOL STUDENTS gawked at me: a hungover, black-clad Transylvanian wandering into their Dearborn, Michigan, classroom. To avoid the sound of my name, it was my habit to have the kids call me Mr. Blank as I sat behind their teacher's desk, apologetically offering their assignments.

"You ain't from around here," they'd say. "Are you, bro?"

I'd enlisted as a substitute teacher that fall, making myself available for every subject and grade, which meant I received a 6:00 A.M. call each morning requesting my services. I took on anything: high-school mathematics, drama, music, grade-school phys ed. Wary looks, left and right, as I entered those schools double fisting gas-station coffees, my unwashed hair matted from sleep. Certain teachers slipped insults my way, calling me metro or mortician as I passed. I suspected it was a matter of time before the district learned I was unfit to be mingling with formative minds. My concern was that I'd shame my mother, who now worked in an administrative building designing computerized activities for students with communication deficiencies.

"How does it feel," she said, "being back in those schools?"

Sparring my hangovers, I never once arrived drunk. Though I'd had a nosebleed before a sixth-grade class, moments after the smartest of them beat me in a knuckle-biting chess match.

"It's a trip," I said, and Mom said, "Who would have thought?"

Eventually, I received a mysterious notice by mail, informing me I'd been blacklisted from Dearborn High. Two more citations would have me terminated from the district, though I couldn't remember committing an offense, other than neglecting to teach a single thing. Conspiring with the school, I suspected, were the neighbors next door to the Dearborn bungalow I'd moved into. Among them were two fleshy teenagers I'd seen roving the high school. Their entire family had been giving me the hairy eyeball since I'd moved onto their block; perhaps they'd seen Mr. Blank stagger home in the wee hours and had informed the administrators I was a hazard. To outfox them, I began entering the house through the side door and peeking through the blinds before I left.

Each substitute gig paid seventy-three dollars and afforded me breaks to sleep on the teacher's desk or write lyrics. If I played it smart, I'd never visit the same place two days in a row. Assignments came by way of an automated phone service. With the touch of a button I could refuse work any day I wanted, just about the worst thing for someone in my shape. Any night a drink might come my way, and where that would leave me in the mornings had only one certainty—that everything, mind-body-soul, would ache.

There were pills, too, a flood of painkillers and tranquilizers coming into the mixture of what my friends and I believed was artistic inspiration. A pill dealer worked at the State Theatre, while someone else always seemed have a bottomless stash, a sister working as a nurse. I found the tablets I liked and ate enough that I'd writhe in bed once the chemicals began to abandon my body, leaving in their absence a clenching gastrointestinal pain. I wasn't above swindling walk-in clinics, either, lurching with fake ailments as I nudged the staff toward medications I desired: Vicoprofen, which was oxycodone cut with ibuprofen, instead of the stuff in Vicodin that grizzled your intestines. I went as far as slicing my arm and stuffing a clump of bloody toilet paper into my underpants. At the clinic I refused a seat, telling the receptionist my hemorrhoids had ruptured, which sent a hiss through the waiting room. The doctor never troubled to glance at my prop, but I got what I'd come for.

On mornings I woke clearheaded and rested, there first came a moment where I'd take inventory of all sensations—the taste in my mouth and my heart rate and the pressure behind my eyes—before realizing I wasn't to be punished that day. It would have been an unendurable way of life had the band not been composing a formidable new set list, songs filled with peaks and valleys and parts that felt like soaring. We practiced at every chance, making as much music as we could. Sometimes it was just me and the drummer, who'd quit his job delivering pizzas and whom I liked immensely once the amplifiers were switched on.

• • •

We met at a Michigan Avenue doughnut shop to sign the contracts. A reputable magazine had reviewed the band, and a satellite radio station put a song of ours in rotation, and by May we'd piqued the curiosity of a few A & R types. The manager we'd chosen was a music-biz prodigy, a no-bullshit go-getter who'd yet to turn twenty-five. Across the tabletop, he spread the documents: a four-album deal with a California record label subsidized by Sony, a corporate madness Ethan and I had once raged against.

"We're gonna have to incorporate," said the manager. "Get an LLC."

The drummer and I scribbled our names, hoping to mail the papers west before anyone had a change of mind. The Californians allotted us a recording advance and a small monthly stipend as long as we were on the road. An upstart deal, meaning we'd have to claw tooth and nail for whatever crumbs of success lay ahead. A month later, we began tackling the country in a gleaming white Ford Club Wagon that bore no likeness to the Orgasmatron. Mostly, we played to empty rooms; but these were good venues, places you'd boast about having conquered. Chicago's Empty Bottle. Berbati's in Portland—decent-sized rooms with reasonable sound systems.

Showing up on time was the most we could guarantee.

I relished the stale-beer stench of deserted clubs, untangling the cords and warming the amps, tuning my guitar—wondering if anyone would appear once the doors opened to the public. Our bald drummer traveled with a hairdryer and locked himself away wherever he could to do god knows what with it. We bickered over publishing rights and album titles, but no one asked what our songs were about. One was called "In the Name of the World" and had a line that went *In the right light / we might seem good enough to keep*. Every few cities, there would be complimentary beer for the band or a bottle of vodka slipping into the night, and then the night might not end until it was ended for me, often by the sunrise.

Ethan was stuck with most of the driving. We'd traveled together so many miles that I could anticipate his lane changes and needed only to mumble for him to pull over for a restroom.

Amid our travels I began passing dark red blood in my stool, which a homeopathic clerk in Orange County insisted was evidence of a considerable gastrointestinal problem. I took action by padding my underwear with Kleenex to avoid bloodstains as we pressed onward, city by city, hawking T-shirts and perfecting our songs. Back in Detroit, we recorded a single with a semi-famous producer, and for a few weeks our song played during the lunchtime rush on the city's FM rock station.

Angela witnessed what she could from her Kalamazoo apartment. Well into the second year of a master's degree in writing, she took study breaks to pull up our reviews on her computer, keeping an eye out for pictures of us and the type of women lurking in our crowds. It was no longer Lauren she worried about but female show-goers across the continent. She knew where I'd be playing next before I did and had the idea I was on a fame-bound ascent, at the height of which I'd leave her for good.

We spoke every night. Through the phone, the sound of her voice was so familiar that I hardly missed her. I didn't want to long for anyone in this life. But I perceived Angela's moods throughout the days, could sense her out there worrying and loving me long before I called. When I could, I'd drive to her Kalamazoo apartment where I'd sleep off weeks of exhaustion. In the mornings Angela sat reading and sipping coffee, lounging in a fake silk robe she'd slip out of just in time to head for dinner at the only decent Chinese place in town.

Sooner or later she'd ask about the nature of my road life.

"And how would I know," she said, "if something happened out there?"

Maybe she would, and maybe she wouldn't. I knew that.

"This album we're writing, that's what matters."

And she said, "I know, it's gonna be great, it's what you have to do."

But it's impossible now to look back and root for this blinded young man, that it might all come his way. Because he bears so little resemblance to the person I am, or want to be. He's the worst of me—dulled and bitter and fearful; desperate for great, impossible things—a voice I still hear if ever I stray too far from truth. What might have been, if the planets had aligned and those songs had rocketed us around the world? I can only be thankful the road led nowhere or, really, led me exactly where I was supposed to be.

· · ·

A July night, right around 2:00 A.M., I exited the Lager House with a shot of last-call whiskey I'd poured into a can of Pabst. The Lager was a hipster hovel on the Detroit end of Michigan Avenue, into which I'd ventured after a local gig that had gone especially well. People singing the words, shaking their bottles at us during the good parts—the better we played, the more I believed I deserved a heavy bout of drinking. The best shows, like tonight's, made me feel immune to consequences or convinced me that consequences were what inspired me to perform well in the first place.

I'd closed out the bar.

A gang had assembled in the Lager House parking lot. Musicians and music types lighting bottle rockets as radios blared from cars, a change of station as you passed each ride. Tiger Stadium's abandoned shell rose to the west, the upper deck a dark slab stamped into the ozone. The spirits were just beginning.

"After-party," said a guy named Jimmy Bang-Bang: Keith Richards–on–punk, shirtless, two-foot exclamation point tattooed over his spine. "You." He jabbed a finger my way. "You're coming with us." But I waved him off with my drink and boarded my station wagon, a blue, four-door grocery-getter I'd financed with money my dad left behind. The bar's exterior lights snapped off as I nudged through the crowd, pumping the brakes. People howled, slapping their hands against the hood. I recognized every face and tattooed limb. I saluted a voice that rose above the rest to shout, "Adios, motherfucker."

Then a hard right onto Michigan Ave.

Which at that hour was a strip enchanted by the truest night creatures, those for whom the sunrise, if they saw it, meant only that they'd yet to succeed in obliterating their souls. A haunted place. The car seemed to descend into it as I headed west over Fisher Freeway: chewed-up storefronts and parades of hookers in sequined miniskirts, many of them so crack atrophied and gnarled you couldn't imagine a letch on earth taking his chances. One of their hubs was an abandoned Mobil station, a mile or so from the Dearborn city limits. Another flock congregated at a self-serve car wash to use the cement wash bays like showrooms for the miracles they were selling.

Michigan Avenue from Braden to Schaefer, 2:15 A.M.

Nights like this, I'd undertaken a personal business with the territory. Once I was driving alone, I couldn't solve the terror I felt about returning to my bedroom, knowing I'd awake the next morning to crap blood and shiver until the coffee was ready. My only alternative seemed to be the outer-limits, people and places whose sadness might demolish my own. More than once, I'd given a woman twenty bucks to drive around with me, thinking she'd be relieved to sit and talk, taking it personally when she seemed annoyed by my misuse of her speeding minutes. "You done now?" they'd say. "I ain't gonna drive around all night. I've got money to make." I'd come on too fast, asking where they came from, thinking I'd convince them there were decent men left on the planet. They'd say, "You wanna party or not?" They'd say, "Where you been? What you on?" And I'd say, "Drinking," and they'd say, "That's all? You sure that's all?"

What I'd wanted from them I will never fully understand.

There were traces of someone in their eyes, of people who'd been smoked out, until canceling themselves became the only means to get what they so awfully needed. Twitching, frenzied zombies hungry for one thing. They seemed absolute. Nothing in them could be reduced any further; the next change would be death. Sitting beside a woman like that, I'd know it could have been me, any of us, had the scripts been switched, had we been born there, in a hood where wild dogs had run off the postal service and the schools were patrolled by cops. Every one of those spirits was out hounding for crack—the coals beneath the night streets, the lifeblood of those moonlit hours.

A COUPLE MILES WEST of the Lager House, I turned down the stereo and pulled into the deserted Mobil station. The sign had been burned along with everything else, but you could still make out the name. Two women approached before I'd come fully to a stop. They always waved and peered through the windows, taking a good look at every visible surface before they got in. They smiled, giddy. I looked like a softy compared with a lot of what they saw.

"You gonna pay twice," the heftier and older of the women said.

And I said, "Yeah, all right," as they swung open the doors and squirmed into the car. I'd driven my equipment to and from the show. The back of the station wagon was packed with guitars and amplifiers. Instrument cables were strewn across the seats.

"The fuck is this?" said the skinny one, who'd claimed the backseat.

She held up the knotted end of a twenty-inch power cord as the jowled, magenta-lipped woman beside me said, "Yeah, fuck's that shit?" They were black women, dressed in shimmering plasticlike costumes with feathery scarves and rattling necklaces.

"It's for music," I said. "You plug them into instruments." All those psychos, who beat and strangled these women—I wasn't thinking about the grave hazards of their trade. The car was headed east for no reason at all.

"You wanna hear my band?" I said.

I slid our CD into the stereo and let it play, feeling an unfamiliar shame as the woman beside me mocked our white grooves, saying, "Lord, we got us a Beatle here."

There might have been a girl at the show who'd have let me sleep it off in her bed, someone petite and confused, tattooed with skulls and vines. There'd have been breakfast in the morning, her roommate sulking bedheaded into the kitchen for a glass of tap water. Then I'd have to face her again, the undesirable closeness of having known each other's lonely bodies, all the while worrying that Angela might somehow find out. I wanted no part of it, even if I did.

"We gonna party?" said the woman, turning to face me.

Flesh sagged mottled and coral-like from her cheeks. Stripes of blue makeup were drawn over her eyes. She looked like she'd been working that rodeo for years and didn't have much time left before she'd have to come up with something else. She was truly excited.

"Party or what?" she said.

I knew I was rounding a corner when I said, "Yeah." I had fifty, sixty bucks in my pocket. Said I was looking for cocaine, like I couldn't have found that elsewhere.

"He wants powder," the fat one said, instructing me to turn here and there, until we pulled up to a house, the front window of which cast the only light on the block.

"You got money, blondie?" she said, and I forked over what I had.

I was hoping she'd rip me off or that some unforeseeable coercion would extinguish the night, because I wasn't about to turn back. I didn't know what I was after but could feel myself drawing near.

She strutted up the porch. The girl in the back spent the minutes glancing around my car at the road cases and instruments. I'd yet to really see her face, only the glint of her eyes in the rearview, staring out from that dark space. I was afraid of her. She could have reached from behind and cut my throat if she'd wanted.

"You know this place?" I said.

And she said, "Yeah, I know it," like the refrain of some old song.

When the older, fat one returned to the car, she began speaking to her backseat accomplice, using a tongue I'd never heard—rapid, rat-a-tat syllables. The only bit I made out was the girl in back saying, "Don't you go gettin' me in trouble, girl," her tone gleefully announcing that we were already there: trouble.

They sensed my fear, knew every inch of this transgression.

"Drive, baby," the fat one told me, exposing a miniature Baggie of teeth-sized crack rocks. "They ain't got no powder," she said, "but this'll do, this'll do." She quickly packed a rock into a stem, acting with the instinctive certainty of a squirrel working the seed from an acorn, lighting up, passing the cylindrical pipe to her friend, who said, "Aw, girl." She held a deep inhalation that kept her silent for what seemed minutes before she barked out a sound part laughter and part wheeze. "Mmmmm, fuck."

I drove up and down vacated side streets as they traded hits, sighing upon exhale. None of us cared where we were going.

We all knew they were playing me, that this was the easiest cruise they'd taken in years. At a stop sign, deep into a shredded neighborhood, the woman beside me said, "You want some a this?" She took the flame to the glass nozzle, breathed in a long hit, and pulled my face to her lips, exhaling what was left into my mouth, which I breathed in, all the way, as far inside as it would carry.

Nothing miraculous—that first hit. Just a rush to my head while I asked myself, *Is this it? How it feels?* I was tired of everything, too drunk to ascend. It was the smell, mostly. A chemical stench filling up the car. We took the backstreets, doing the same thing awhile longer, until we'd run out.

They all crossed my mind during those late-night drives, the people who'd have wept at the sight of me cruising, dead to myself, steering with my knee. There wasn't usually a street girl beside me. Mostly, I drove alone. Pulling to the Dearborn limits, turning around, swooping back for another glimpse until the sun became an undeniable fact, urging me home as the real world emerged: School buses and fresh-faced citizens in cars, the sweet lard aroma of doughnut shops. The morning's paper stacked in metal boxes. All of it seeming to exist for the uncertain purpose of some allegory that was happening inside me.

That's when I'd wonder if Caitlin and my dad were witnessing me from another plane, where everything had already happened. I'd talk to them, imagine them out there, but never at the same time. I'd speak to one and then the other, as though they hovered at two different places in the sky, each of them looking down alone, which said everything about my inability to piece this all together. But I thought they knew my fate, every moment about to unfold. They knew you could leave this world in a black cloud and that sooner or later everyone you knew would follow, and then it would be over. But that's not what they saw for me, not what they wanted. Returning home, I'd creep through the side door, cranking on the box fans and sliding onto my parents' old bed—one thing I'd salvaged and kept for myself.

WHEN I TOLD THE women I was out of money, they directed me to another house where the slender one in the backseat went inside to see a man. She was in there a little while, long enough for me to know what was going on.

"I want to drive this car straight through that place," I said. "This sick place."

Rage was passing through in jolts, quick revulsions that felt superhuman.

"Now what are you talking?" said the woman beside me, sitting shotgun—Angela's seat, Will's seat. She slapped my shoulder, "Don't be fuckin' around here."

"I'll drive this thing straight to hell," I said.

My head swelled, congesting with heat. There were jaws inside it, clamping down. I didn't feel good, but I wanted more of whatever I'd had. I'd been experiencing it without comprehending it: the brain swirl and my tingling windpipe, a mind speed that smashed each thought violently into the next. Was this my father's abyss? I understood it only to the extent that I ached for another breath of smoke.

Not much later, the other woman came out in a rush and injected herself into the backseat.

"Aw, what you get?" the old one said as her bony friend presented a new, minuscule sack of drugs. She took it. "We gotta smoke this now," she said, "this boy here's gettin' all suicide on me."

The rage had passed; I felt nothing.

The woman in back said, "You always getting me in trouble," as the one next to me packed the next hit, saying, "You first, baby. You earned it."

When that ran out, they asked to be dropped off at the busted corner where I'd found them. But I couldn't fathom them leaving me alone, just like that, to carry on with my life.

"We'll go cash a check," I said.

"Shit," one of them said. "Motherfucker wants to cash his check."

I crossed the Dearborn line and pulled up to a twenty-four-hour grocery store I'd been coming to since I was a child. Caitlin and I had picked cereal boxes off its shelves, bought plastic trinkets from quarter machines at the entrance.

The older woman took my arm in hers as the three of us crossed the parking lot. I was protecting them now, vouching for their souls as we entered the grocer's neon jaw. The bright light of the store made apples gleam while revealing the scanty dreadfulness of my companions' costumes, the bruises on the dark skin of their exposed legs and the grime on their clacking heels. We weren't dangerous. I knew what we were—the most pitiful beings breathing in that particular time and place.

"Get whatever you want," I said.

The ladies went on a spree, throwing liters of cola and potato chips and lipstick tubes and sanitary napkins into a shopping cart. The woman who'd sat in the backseat never looked me in the face, never smiled. Twenty-five, thirty-five—she had such power of experience it was impossible to guess her age. Her scorn was valid. She was onto me, knew I was a tourist in their world. The older one squealed and danced toward each item, saying, "Oh, I like this," before tearing it from the shelf.

When they'd finished, there were enough provisions in the cart to feed my band for weeks. I wrote a check as the fat one rubbed up on my thigh, sickening me in every way, but I wasn't about to offend her now that we'd come so far. The cashier, whom I'd seen so many nights working the graveyard shift, didn't look at me. She never had and never would. If only she'd seen me earlier that night, playing for my life—the music, the music, the music—I'd have made perfect sense.

I got a twenty-spot for writing over the check, and we drove downtown for the last bit of crack. We'd yet to finish sucking clean the small rock when an eerie narcotic undertow made me instantly suspicious of a plan to kill me.

Told me I had to act fast, go mental.

White devil. Pale white crazy devil boy.

"Out of the car!" I yelled it. Slammed the brakes hard enough that both of them had to collect their minds before anything else happened. When they didn't open the doors, I jabbed my knuckles between my teeth and bit. I'd chewed up my tongue in a drug fit, could feel it wagging like a sponge. My neck felt wrenched in a vise. My chest banged. I'd never wanted a beer more than I did then, though I knew it would do no good. The velocity of crack, the Technicolor glow of the grocery store—it had spun me into a void, of which I'd suddenly located the center. An instantaneous sobriety. I'd known that to happen: a brutal clarity shining forth like a planet at the end of a binge. Suddenly all the liquor in the world could no longer alter the mean truth of the here and now.

"Hold it, honey," the older one said. "That shit'll creep on you. It's creeping on you."

The possibility of this moment lasting a breath longer sent me into a clenched-fist panic. "Get outta here," I said. "You'd kill me for nothing, both of you." And I knew—they knew—that I was putting them on.

"We cool," the old one said. "We cool."

They scattered to the street, laughing, lugging their plastic sacks. It was a mile walk through the trenches to the burned-out Mobil station. And I yelled through the closed windows, from inside that stove of gray smoke, "I hope you got what you wanted," which was the thing I'd feel the worst about, years later, once that night seemed to have finally ended.

All the while the CD of my band's music had been spinning. It was only after they'd gone that I realized it. The melodies, the sound of my warbling voice, echoes from some life that awaited me whenever I next awoke. Maybe they weren't much, our songs, but they carried me home through Dearborn's unsuspecting morning. Through the side door of the house and up into bed.

8

For years, Mom had been claiming Ozzy was thirteen.

And I rubbed the dog's cystic head with an increasing adoration, knowing he wouldn't be hobbling blindly through my mother's house forever. Not only could he no longer see, he'd also gone deaf and had begun soiling the wood floors. Truth told, Ozzy was closer to twenty. An enduring, mythic mutt so dear to my mother that she did nothing to hide her love. Outside her bedroom door hung a framed painting of him, anxious eyed and with a clenched mouth, aptly realistic. In the living room were glossy photographs a coworker had commissioned after sneaking into the house and drugging the poor animal for the session.

For his portraits Ozzy sat doped, wearing a red bow tie.

Mom acknowledged the gaudiness of these tributes, but she didn't care. "We have a special relationship," she'd say. "He's my little buddy."

Each night, she'd been clutching his hind legs to walk him up the stairs before heaving him onto their shared mattress.

She'd laughed sadly, saying, "Some days he seems perfectly fine." When she finally took the dog to be put down she didn't mention a word of it until I came by one weekday afternoon.

"Where's Ozzy?" I asked, perceiving his absence the moment I arrived.

I'd told her I wanted to be there when the day came, though she might not have believed me. She had little reason to believe much of what I said, but I'd had a plan of chauffeuring them to the vet, giving Ozzy's head one last scratch, holding Mom's hand as the needle punctured his hide. I'd wanted to take her for dinner afterward, where we'd laugh about the dog's near-death exploits and cranky ways. His snooty avoidance of my dad. How he'd harried Caitlin, snatching her balled-up tights and gnashing holes in them.

"Oh, I couldn't tell anyone," Mom said. "I wanted to say good-bye to him on my own."

Just like her, never troubling a soul. Which made it all the worse to think of her coming home to an empty house, alone with what she knew. So many nights she'd spent eating in her favorite chair as Ozzy awaited scraps at her feet. She'd spoken to him like a housemate; once he could no longer hear, she'd developed a system of tickles and taps that would have the dog slouching toward the back door or leaning into his bowl. He'd sit, unmoving, as she daubed his infections with ointment. His eyes glazed and cloudy, knowing she was there to guide him through.

"He always liked you," Mom said.

"You kept him alive," I said. "He had a good long life."

When I left, I noticed Ozzy's bowls where they'd always been, at the foot of the garbage can in the kitchen. One filled with water—a little murky, a little gray. The other half full of kibble. Soon enough they'd be tossed away, but I'd always remember him there, raising his head as the back door opened, keeping a watch on things, waiting for the woman he loved.

ANGELA HAD COMPLETED HER master's degree that spring, a few months after she'd turned twenty-three. She'd also published her first story. By July she'd made plans to move to New York, a bold decision that made me suddenly aware that she didn't need me as much as I thought she did. I'd taken for granted that we'd wind up in a quaint midwestern abode, battling it out until old age mellowed us. Her ability to shatter this expectation only raised my respect. Most of her things were packed by the time I drove out to help with her move. Kalamazoo would never be the same once she left, and I wanted to visit the cemetery and other places I might not see for a long while.

Like the cluttered hidden-gem record shop on West Main.

A few doors over was a Chinese place she and I enjoyed. A night on the town had often been two plates of noodles, then an hour browsing the aisles of CDs and albums, taking a long drive with whatever new sounds we'd acquired. Let us put aside the fact she was leaving and spend one last weekend as if nothing were about to change—that was my approach, and she rolled with it. Ignoring the boxes stacked in her bedroom, we headed for dinner early enough to assure that the record store would be open afterward.

Driving to the restaurant, Angela said, "You're not looking so good," and it was true. My hair was shellacked by grime, my posture compromised by a variety of pains. Forget the look in my eyes. The night before, the band had played a Detroit festival, and during our set I'd felt a warm, syrupy guck moving through my jeans; my underwear clung to my legs, worrying me that I'd soiled myself. Between songs, quick scans of the crotch region assured there was no visible evidence, but afterward, in the venue's toilet, I'd investigated my drawers to find them sopped with dark red mucus. A moment of reckoning, signaling, possibly, the closeness of the end. I'd come to worry that any cough or dizzy spell or spasm in my chest was the effect of all the bad thoughts I'd been smothering. Stress-born diseases. My body was not my own. Having crapped blood for the past half year, I could critique the mess each morning according to hue and volume. Now I was incontinent, a leaking wound.

This was what Angela had missed, and I was glad for it.

"How was the show?" she asked.

"Good," I said. "We played a new song."

I'd had to focus on the tiled wall to keep from fainting as I staggered to the bathroom's sink. I'd slapped my face with water and stared into the mirror, thinking of her, no one else.

Angela said, "What did you do after?"

"Ack." My mouth tasted of cat piss. "Not much."

Though by the time I'd made it to Jimmy Bang-Bang's, I'd forgotten about the blood. His four-bedroom house was a deadbeat roost in heart of the city, the walls painted crimson and an enormous stereo in the dining room, where everyone gathered around a table and slobbered about rock and roll, about seeing the world. Angela would never meet Jimmy, but she intuited the depravity of people like him from the hesitant tone I'd use when pronouncing their names.

What was I going to tell her, really?

Jimmy, a local drummer, greasy coiffed and perpetually shirtless, always insisted his guests help him imbibe all the dry goods, so there'd be no leftovers. The night before, he'd overestimated the party's spirit—people dispersed to the upstairs bedrooms, slipped out undetected in search of 4:00 A.M. pancakes. Early that morning I'd found myself alone with a mound of unfinished powder spilling across the table. In the coming months, Jimmy would make a point of asking, whenever he saw me, "Do you have any idea how much drugs you did?" No, I didn't. No idea of the amount I'd snorted or how I'd managed to get home, nor how to convey a word of this, anything, to Angela. But once she and I were served our noodles, the first bites of lo mein set loose a cruel spasm in my stomach. I saw Angela watching with fearful eyes, holding her chopsticks like wands, just before I fainted onto the paper tablecloth.

THE ER DOCTOR CHECKED my vitals and drew blood, explaining I'd need both a colonoscopy and endoscopy to get the bottom of things.

"Whatever it takes," I said.

I had no insurance, but I spoke with certainty. My vigilance for self-preservation arose in the manic and costly fashion of people who regret their own inestimable self-abuse. I'd binge on vitamins and colon cleansers and herbal potions the way I did anything else. Run up a tab. To prepare for the scopes, I was ordered to a day of fasting and laxatives. From Angela's couch, I called Ethan, asking him to put a hold on practice on account of I might possibly be dying.

"This is terrible," he said. "We've got a tour in a couple weeks."

Angela made a bowl of Jell-O—the only solid I was allowed to eat—as I spent a day creeping to and from her apartment's toilet.

She stood beside me the following morning as the anesthetist pumped me with sedatives. I knew the sight of me affirmed how right she was to be leaving, but I could tell she felt remorse. I squeezed her hand, thinking that if I lived, I'd make all the drastic changes. I'd start meditating, Tai Chi, soul-recovery stuff. The simplicity of what truly mattered—it fell over me in a silvery rinse as I nodded in and out, trying to hang on to the fantasy for another second before I slipped away.

The sound of Angela's laughter coaxed me back to life in a new hospital room.

"Go on?" she said. "You were saying?"

I'd muttered a delirious aphorism not a moment before, slowly emerging from an hour-long darkness that had passed with a single nod of my head. The words remained on my tongue, yet I couldn't grasp my thoughts long enough to recapitulate them. When I stretched my fingers, Angela took my hand.

"You're cute," she said. "I love you."

I had a mouthful of post-op grime. My throat was raw from the upper GI scope. Angela knew I was at her mercy, lying there in a paper gown. She shook her head, and we smiled. Lucid with anesthetic, I imagined living my final days in peace, so long as I felt that way: nodding in and out, forgetting what I said no sooner than it came from my mouth. I wanted to fall back under that spell for an hour longer.

When the doctor entered, he barely looked at me, scribbling on his notepad. The gastrointestinal scopes, he said, revealed a number of ulcerations in the lining of my stomach, not to mention some trauma to my bowel—issues resulting, no doubt, from my binges, which the fear of death had inspired me to speak frankly about. "You're hurting yourself," he said, curtly and factually.

"What about stress?" I said.

"Well, that never helps," said the doctor. "But someone your age? What are you stressed about? It's the booze, the pills. You either quit, or it gets worse and you come back bleeding up to your esophagus, and then there's not much we can do."

He actually raised an eyebrow.

"I've seen it before," he said.

"My colon?" I said.

"Clean as a whistle. Nothing but some hemorrhoids, for which I've written you a prescription for suppositories."

He winked at Angela, and she made a disgusted face.

A formidable bill would soon arrive by mail. In months to come, there would be more doctors, conveying identical sentiments, not a word of which I'd take to heart. If only they'd have told me I was done for—that I might have believed. It was, I suppose, what I'd expected to hear. The doctor vanished without so much as bidding me a good fight as a nurse appeared with a handful of scripts, none of which I'd have filled.

No—I left the hospital revitalized and contemptuous, with an angry urge to live, craving a gluttonous dinner and everything else.

• • •

Mom couldn't bear to think of a new dog. "Maybe someday," she'd said, "but it wouldn't be fair to Ozzy, just yet." Though when I returned to Dearborn, there was a tameless black kitten scurrying through her house, attacking her plants and waking her early in the morning.

"She's a dickens," Mom said. "A cute little thing. I named her Izzy."

She asked how I'd been, how Angela was feeling about her big move.

"Good," I said. "It's all good."

"You look pale," she said. "Skinny."

She was no meddler. She never pressed the matter when I insisted things were unremarkably fine. Her knowingness operated on a deeper register, triggering her chronic cough and antagonizing her phobia of the telephone. We were sitting at the kitchen table. It was so good and so painful to see her.

"You'd tell me if something was wrong?"

"Yes," I said. "Nothing's wrong."

And for every unpleasant detail I withheld, she, in turn, had a litany of undisclosed truths about my father. In this way, we protected each other. We acknowledged the weather; we spoke of cats and dogs. Mom lived on day-to-day appeals, praying for moments of peace: a tulip budding from the soil. And I resided in the gray areas of what she could and couldn't stand to believe. I lived during the long hours she slept, once the sun went down, when I could imagine she was peacefully unaware.

"Do you want me to cook you something?" she said. "You need to eat."

The kitten scaled its way onto the kitchen table and bounded toward her, touched by a joy that had something to do with my mother.

"That sounds good," I said.

"Have you seen a cat do that before?" She stroked the animal as it burrowed into her lap. "Have you ever seen a cat like this?"

A FEW DAYS LATER Mom knocked at my front door in the early afternoon, still dressed in her pajamas. Though she'd never seen us perform, she often slept in one of my band's T-shirts; I could see our screen-printed logo beneath her blue fleece as I welcomed her inside. Her face let me know her wariness of what she might come upon, dropping by without warning.

"I need to talk to you," she said.

I didn't look her in the eye; it had been a while since I'd been able to.

"What is it?" I asked. Which meant, *How much do you know?*

Angela had called her that morning, laying out the hard

facts about my hospital visit. She'd told Mom I needed help. I was scheduled to leave for another tour in a matter of days, and Angela dreaded what might happen. To drive home the seriousness of things, she'd described an unpleasant scene or two: nights I'd been bloodied or too loaded to speak. A time I'd been welted in a belt fight. If I hadn't known better, I'd have thought she was trying to wash her hands of me.

"What kind of trouble are you in?" Mom said.

I'd slept on the couch and could hardly recall the previous evening or what I might have said if I'd talked with Angela. My ulcerated gut hadn't stopped me from carrying on with the drinks, the blood in my stool a daily affirmation that I was still alive. Angela and I had once joked about not knowing which one of us was crazier, and it seemed she'd finally settled on an answer.

"Don't you lie to me," Mom said. I felt the specter of Angela's grief, could hear her urgency in the details Mom spoke.

Taking a seat beside me on the couch, Mom coughed into a Kleenex. "I won't go through this again," she said. "Don't you put me through this."

For everything Angela had confessed, I had a perfectly viable explanation. My stomach was shredded because I'd been eating too many peanuts and uncooked vegetables, drinking too much coffee.

"I'm stressed," I said.

"You sound like your father," Mom said. "You're not like him, you know?"

In ways this was true; in other ways I felt exactly like him, closer than I'd ever been. Though we sat inches apart, Mom kept a strange distance.

"You're smarter than this," she said.

"I drink too much."

"What about the drugs?"

I claimed I didn't have a taste for any of them, which relative to my lust for booze seemed almost truthful.

Mom gazed about the house. The shades were drawn permanently to keep the neighbors from peeping. Clothes on the hardwood floor, CDs stacked on every surface, lyrics scribbled on napkins. The kitchen sink was filled with dishes and foam coffee cups. A knee-high plastic Christmas tree she'd given me seasons earlier stood propped in the corner. It was a mess, but I'd seen worse.

"Your uncle Dennis died yesterday," Mom said.

"No," I said. "Jesus."

"The family wants to get ahold of you. They've been leaving messages."

"Was it drugs?"

"I think so. They found him in a garage, in his car."

Dennis had two daughters, one on her way into the army, but it was my dad I thought of foremost, how thoroughly the news of his dead brother would have pummeled him.

"You see what this does to people?" Mom said. "You should know by now."

Her wrists and hands were scratched and nicked, bitten and clawed by her new pet. Her allergies had flared; her eyes were red. She kneaded her swollen fingers nervously. I could hardly stand to look, to think of her daubing blood from her wounds, alone with her kitten. Though I knew it took more than that to hurt her now.

I MADE PROMISES TO my mother and swore oaths to Angela. As an act of penance, I resigned to carrying a cell phone so that I'd be reachable anyplace in the country. My road kit was packed with niacin tablets and detoxifying tonics and other blood-cleansing remedies, along with a prescribed bottle of Antabuse—enough to last for the band's August tour. I'd experimented with the antidrinking medication a few years before. Ideally, you took Antabuse every day, so there'd be enough coursing through you to make even a sip of alcohol repulsive. A single drink might cause vomiting, delirium; a Pavlovian trick to wean a sick mind off the sauce. The doctors said you could die if you boozed while on this stuff, but I knew better. I'd learned that after taking a single pill I had three days before I could drink without breaking out in hives. On the road I planned to take Antabuse every third day, leaving open the option to skip a dose in time for Los Angeles, where our record company would be waiting to see an inspired set.

The band had a roadie aboard our latest expedition: Scott, the Wallside guitarist who'd aided my attack on Blaine a few years back. Blaine was now a junkie living in Las Vegas. Scott and I, however, had since become close friends, confiding earnestly and obliviously in the late, late hours. He was a genuine binge artist, just like me, and had sold me his prized '79 Gibson Les Paul, a perfectly scarred relic that was easily imagined strapped over Jimmy Page's lithe torso. Lately, Scott too was doing his best to keep clean. To encourage our good behavior, he drew a box chart on a scrap of plywood and affixed it to the back door of the van. He listed the names of everyone in the band and his own, printing them on a graph that accounted for each day of the journey.

"The no-fun chart," he said. "Anyone who has too much fun gets a check mark. At the end we tally it up."

"We'll give out a prize," I said.

"The prize," he said, "is sanity."

THE CROSS-COUNTRY DRIVES PASSED in a constant sober panic. Our demo had been repackaged and rereleased by the

Californians, and if we kept our word, the next year of my life was a schedule of low-paying gigs. One day at a time, we were earning gas money along a trail that seemed to route us closer and closer toward defeat. Without the fanfare of Detroit crowds, I'd been resorting to dour screaming fits and partial disrobement during our set's finale, hoping to leave any impression whatsoever on the few who watched us under-whelm their local stages. Each traveled hour felt erased from a purposed life I should be living. Such thoughts came with the job, anyone knew that, but without drink or sedative I couldn't shake them. When not browbeating myself for los-ing Angela, I was thinking about the first taste of a drink and resenting anyone who was free to have one.

"No fun," I'd say, each morning.

"Not one bit," Scott replied, marking the no-fun chart accordingly.

"We keep this up," I'd say, "we'll live forever."

I'd heard countless people claim that music had saved their lives. In my case, I do believe that to be true. I know also that the power of music began turning on me the min-ute I'd compromised my love for it. For next to nothing, I'd sold it to California, had even sweetened our sound and fussed over our image with the hope it might pay off with an entirely new existence. Thousands before me had copped out—some grew rich doing it, but I'd known better. Once my head began drying out, I heard what was missing in the chords, in the screams I'd placed so carefully, for dramatic effect, at all the likely moments.

As we traveled from town to town, I couldn't keep the past from rising into every silent moment. I'd done so much thinking about the bad things. The good things, though, were what really stung, and in small doses I was being led back to them. Memories of the morning walk my sister and I made to the bus stop for Stout Middle School. Along the way, there'd been a corridor of tall shrubbery, taller than either of us, always webbed by the spiders that had spun their way to and fro the night before. Neither of us had ever wanted to go first, to have our faces catch the webbing. Holding hands became our strategy: her and me, gripping tightly, laughing as we ran together through the invisible tangles.

"What are you thinking about now?" Scott would say.

We'd be passing through Arizona. Through Oregon. Places I'd never seen that reminded me of my sister and father, the people they might have been had we one day made it there together. I'd smile, the image looping again and again, repeating the instant Caitlin and I reached the threshold, just before we'd wipe the webbing from our hair.

"Nothing," I'd say. "I'm not thinking about anything now."

"Then how about tomorrow?" he'd say. "What about ten years from now?"

BY THE TIME WE reached Seattle, I'd gone two weeks without a single drop, a feat that convinced me I had less of a habit than anyone suspected. With time to spare before the show, I walked alone through Seattle's rolling streets, wondering where the rabble of the nineties grunge explosion had settled. Avoiding the club until it was time to perform, I took a seat at a bus stop. Minutes later, the cell phone startled me with a rude jangle inside my pocket. Mom's number incoming—a rare thing. A stride against her phone phobia. If she was trying to reach me, it was for good reason.

I ducked into an alley, bringing the device to my ear.

"Oh," she said, and I could tell she'd been crying. "I'm glad it's you."

I dreaded instantly what might come next. She was sick. Or someone had died, even closer to home than Uncle Dennis. I'd need a ride to the airport and money for a flight. The band would schlep our gear across the continent without me. The unrelenting hours traveling alone, with no option to drink at the airport bar. I'd taken my Antabuse that morning.

"I did something bad," Mom said. "Why does everything turn out this way?"

She'd never spoken like this to me, and it could mean so many things.

"Are you okay?" I said. "What is it?"

The earpiece was a distortion of harsh wheeze. Something had finally broken; she was so upset she couldn't manage to cough.

"Everything I touch . . . I can't do anything right."

"You can tell me," I said. "What happened?"

She explained that when she'd come home after work her new kitten had escaped from the back door, and such relief coursed through me that I slumped against the alleyway brick. Even sober, Antabuse might induce nausea, and I felt my mouth sweating, the nearness of retch, but we weren't talking about terminal illnesses or funerals.

"Okay," I said. "It's okay."

She'd spent a long while in the garage, attempting to coax the kitten from beneath her car. "Izzy wouldn't come, and I was so hungry and tired. I just thought I'd shut the door and leave her there until I could eat something."

"Okay, okay."

"I pressed the button, and the sound must have startled her. She bolted out just as the garage door was coming down, and it killed her."

Mom sniffled into the receiver, hiccupping the word "I, I, I," like a tear-blind child trying to describe the source of a throbbing new injury. Her pain, as deep as it ran, was not devoid of the sweetness that permeated all she did. I surprised myself when I began bawling. Traffic passed. Seattle was an overcast bluff. It looked like a hundred places I'd been, and I wished I were home.

"I killed her."

"No," I said. "You didn't do that."

"She was so tiny. I tried sitting here for a while, but I keep seeing her crushed little body. She was staring up at me. She was still alive."

Her voice, shaking and speaking these words, was the saddest sound I'd ever heard. I saw the squashed kitten, and my mom enduring the sight alone, blaming herself. The driveway, her late-summer garden—I knew every aspect of the scene. A purely sober moment: I felt more sensation than I had in years and unclenched my jaw, allowing it to goddamn tremble if that's what it wanted to do.

"It's not your fault," I said. "This could have happened to anyone."

"I tried and tried, but she wouldn't come to me."

"She didn't know any better."

There was a break in our talk, a stretch of a half minute or so where we cried to each other, two thousand miles apart. "I miss Ozzy," said my mom, once she'd found her breath. "He was such a good friend."

We were talking about cats and dogs; but then again, we weren't.

"I know," I said. "I miss him, too."

9

Five of us were in the van, parked beneath a gigantic action movie at the Ford-Wyoming Drive-In. A special place, the last of its kind. Pigeon-infested dirt lots near the Dearborn-Detroit border, from which an array of tattered movie screens angled toward the sky. Beyond the metal poles stemming crookedly from the earth and rusted speaker boxes dangling by wires were the industrial vats of a factory that butted against the northern end of the premises, everything enclosed by a corrugated metal fence. It was a place people went to get frisky, to get loaded. Rumors of shootings and stabbings over the years. You could feel it when you were there, wrapped in the flicker of an enormous film—that somewhere, not far away, there was mischief.

Tonight's second feature: the latest version of *Superman.*

The band had been back a few days. Hours earlier we'd gigged downtown, an early September homecoming from our cross-country tour. Our equipment was packed in the van's rear, but Ethan and the drummer had made off for other adventures.

Scott sat shotgun. I had a bottle between my legs, having tossed my Antabuse in Los Angeles, where I'd forfeited the no-fun competition in a single night immeasurable by any chart. Scott concentrated on the movie, syncing up an appropriate soundtrack on the stereo. Behind us, sprawled on the bench seats, were three friends who'd all but passed out.

"Lightweights," Scott said.

He and I had spent time at the drive-in, either boozing or trying not to. He was the only person I knew who thought about quitting and one of the only ones who'd flame all night and into the next day with the sole purpose of losing himself. Unlike Will, Scott would never slip off into a coma. I had thirty pounds on him, but his insides were stitched together just right for that sort of living. He claimed it was his Croatian blood. He said, "You should hear the stories about my uncles."

If they saw us, the drive-in employees didn't care that we snuck in through the exit without paying. We watched the blockbusters all night. The features showed right up till 4:00 A.M., about the time the sky lightened and birds descended en masse to scavenge hot-dog buns and popcorn littered in the dirt.

Like everything else—the record stores and dollar movies and doughnut shops—I was waiting for the drive-in to close any day. There was a war on. A recession had begun, and you saw right away what it did to a town like Dearborn. The drive-in's all-night projections kept us company and soothed our fears. Or made us feel we were part of something, watching and waiting, straddling the edge of the city.

"This," Scott said, "is my favorite place on earth."

DEARBORN'S SCHOOLS WERE STARTING up, and I hadn't worked since they'd let out, which left me wondering how my dad might have addressed my laggard ways. Like him, I believed a man should be putting in twelve-hour shifts in order to make something of himself. He'd shown me that, at least: an unwavering work ethic. But I could barely clean the litter box for the stray I'd picked up outside the band's rehearsal space, a feral black-and-white kitten I'd named Samhain, who slept at my feet and climbed into the drop ceiling to stalk me from above.

I'd poured him a mound of food, never knowing when I might return.

I dreaded going home and being spotted by my neighbors.

Their two-bedroom home next door was a seat of judgment, surveillance. They'd seen me urinating out windows and sleeping in my backyard—I suspected they'd seen just about everything. When we weren't on the road, the van was left in my care. Stern and official, large and white, a vehicle fit for a workman. I'd been parking it at the curb in front of my house, making sure to give it a spin now and then, hoping the neighbors might get the idea I ran a business. Some mornings I'd carried Dad's old briefcase out the door with me, talking into my cellular phone, though no one was on the line.

Whatever cover I'd managed had been blown a couple days earlier. Some friends had been celebrating my return: Repa— home after a cross-country trucking job—and a small crew who'd passed out on the living room floor in various stages of nakedness. I'd slept an hour or so when Repa appeared above my bed, shirtless with an unlit smoke in his mouth. "Ay," he said, and Samhain scattered from the mattress. "Dick next door wants you to move your rig."

I'd awoken straight into anxiousness, yet I could barely hold my eyes open.

"You answer the door like that?" I said.

"That cat's paranoid," Repa said. "Just like you."

"Did my neighbor get a look inside?"

"Aw, man," he said. "He got a real nice look."

Stumbling through the living room, I saw a scene like the aftermath of an infestation that had been fumigated. Anyone peering in would have glimpsed a wreck of tattooed bodies and strewn albums, secondhand smoke hanging in the air. The coffee table held a formation of empty bottles with cigarette butts crushed into their mouths. Though I'd made a personal vow against drinking in Will's company, he was facedown on a couch. Someone else had curled against the wall like a pest that had crawled off to die.

Well past noon, an end-of-summer cooker.

I'd walked outside to fire up the van, making way for my neighbor as he backed a well-worn RV down the street. Unable to fit the rattletrap in his meager driveway, he'd needed the van's curbside parking space. He had every reason to wish I'd never arrived on his block, but he'd never shaken his fist or called the cops when the music got loud. Did the scrutiny I endured have anything whatsoever to do with him? His children were airing a pup tent on the lawn, chattering like nothing was amiss. After he'd parked in a way that satisfied him, the man yanked up a garden hose and began spraying the RV's paneled exterior, never giving me the chance to wave.

ONCE THE LAST MOVIE ended and the birds had repossessed the drive-in, Scott and I drove our passengers home and parked the van at a gas station on Ford and I-94. We'd spent enough hours inside that vehicle, on the move. The tour had gone through Georgia, rambling up the seaboard, toward New York, where Angela saw the band and I'd spent the night in her Bensonhurst apartment, deep into Brooklyn. At this early hour, it was likely she was preparing to ride the subway to Midtown, where she'd landed a job working on books. People liked her everywhere she went, though she couldn't yet see it. All those miles and states between us only intensified our refusals to part. She said I could join her in New York anytime I wanted, that everything would change if I'd just leave Detroit behind.

"What now?" I asked Scott.

"What now," he said.

Scott rented a room in Mexicantown, his homestead only in that he had his stereo and records arranged on a floor there. After a rough one, he'd usually crash at my place. Having spent nights sleeping beside each other on tours, we didn't think it the least bit strange when I'd offer him one side of my parents' old mattress, where we'd lie fully dressed in the clatter of the box fans. I believed the neighbors might have seen that, too.

The sun was ablaze. Scott lit the millionth cigarette of his twenty-five years. "What day is today?" he said.

"It doesn't matter," I said. "We could go anywhere. Why are we even here?"

I'd burned through a good deal of my dad's savings, but there was enough left to keep me treading. The band was a good twenty thousand in debt—recoupable expenses, payable to the Californians. A doomy feeling: knowing I'd one day soon reckon with the fact of all I'd squandered. I had ideas about flying to Mexico, seeing the world on some last-ditch escapade. Somewhere out there on the road I'd given up on music, a surrender that was nonnegotiable and vaguely relieving. I wanted to think it came from inside, a survival instinct telling me I wasn't cut out for that life. Really, I knew whatever talent I'd possessed had crashed and burned. Minutes earlier I'd played Scott a tape of songs I was working on and had asked for the truth.

"It's good," he'd said.

And I'd said, "But not that good, right?"

He pulled a dog-eared road atlas from the glove box and opened it to the page that showed the Michigan mitten.

"Right there," I said, stabbing my finger at a blue spill in the middle of the Lower Peninsula. "We'll drive out there."

He squinted to read the location.

"Houghton Lake. A place like that—they don't like our kind."

"I'm gonna throw my guitar in," I said, gesturing to the back of the van.

"The Gibson?"

I had a couple of stage guitars, but Scott knew I meant his old '79 cherryburst Les Paul. Fifteen hundred dollars' worth of vintage maple and resonant tone.

"I'm done living this way," I said. "I need to make a statement."

"Something that hurts?" Scott said, knowing exactly.

He and I talked about getting clean or dying from too much fun. A couple of celebrities had recently kicked the bucket while mixing spirits, and it flabbergasted Scott to read about the toxicology reports. "If that were me," he'd say, "I'd be dead a hundred times already." We often talked like this while we were snorting one thing or another—morphine pills, Adderall—chopping the tablets with a razor and pressing the back of a spoon on the chunks, rolling it over until there was a fine powder. Scott and I got along because our personalities had little in common, other than that we loved our mothers, and music, and were afraid of who we were.

It was 6:00, 7:00 A.M. I'd been drunk long enough that the alcohol sugars had given me a squirmy, paranoid charge. You can drink so much that it becomes impossible to sleep without chugging cough syrup or crushing a Valium. There were nights I'd lie down after not having slept for days and be amazed to feel my limbs were electrified, every cell awake on glucose.

"We need some pills," Scott said. "Or I'm gonna blow a gasket."

"All right, now," I said. "I can find some."

• • •

Warden's phone was disconnected, but we pulled the van right up to his mom's trailer and banged on the plastic windows. The past few years, I'd come upon him like that to catch him in many states of compromise: with his back turned, masturbating to his computer screen, or yakking to his pet canary, Jingles, whom he'd recently found belly up in the trailer's toilet bowl. This morning a bedsheet was tacked up like a curtain. After a few more knocks, Warden groaned and peered out through a crack.

The first I'd seen of him in months.

"What time is it?" he said.

"We're going on vacation," I said.

Warden pressed his sleep-worn face to the Plexiglas, and Scott smacked it hard, saying, "This is the chance of a lifetime," afterward examining his reddened palm like it was a perfectly good magazine he'd used to swat a mosquito.

It took a little finagling and some stealthy maneuvers toward the trailer's medicine cabinet, where Warden's mom kept her painkillers, but not much later we had what we wanted. Warden was strapped into one of the van's bench seats, clutching a bag of tortilla chips and cleaning his teeth with a napkin. A two liter of cola sat between his feet. His hair had grown into a ruthless vegetation, cascading in bizarre layers over his face. He wore a T-shirt displaying the moniker of a band he'd promoted ten years earlier.

How old was this man? This champion? Closer to forty than twenty.

"You see this shirt?" he said. "Old school."

We'd managed only three pills from his mom's stash: puny, ten-milligram Vicodins, two of which Scott and I had gobbled while still in the trailer, convincing Warden that Houghton Lake was a wonderland of bikinis and summer sport. "I haven't been in the water since '97," Warden said. I'd wrapped the third pill in the foil from a cigarette box, setting it in a grocery bag of cassettes that sat between Scott and me in the van's cockpit.

We took I-75 north, that vertical trail snaking all the way from Florida through the Upper Peninsula, into Sault Sainte Marie, Canada. By then, I'd driven every inch of it. A case of warm beer was left over from the drive-in. When Scott cracked a pair, Warden began screeling.

"Pull this thing over. You're drunk."

Amazing that he hadn't already smelled it on us, seen our ruddy eyes.

Warden did some handiwork with the seat belts and soon had two or three hooked over various portions of himself.

"You're gonna be fine," I said.

"He's throwing the guitar in the lake," Scott said. "It's the only way."

"The Gibson?" Warden said.

"I'm done," I said.

"With what? The band?"

"With all of it."

"That band's all you've got," Warden said. "You got a deal, man."

When we'd signed with the Californians, Warden threatened my well-being via telephone, saying I'd better steer clear or he didn't know what he might do. All Conquer the World had done for me, for my career, and this was how I'd treated him.

"It's gotta go," Scott said. "It's gotta hurt, or else nothing's gonna change."

He lit a smoke. We'd entered a shared psychology in which I didn't mind him talking about destroying my property. Scott seemed to need to watch his prized guitar drown as much as I did.

"You're screwed," Warden said. "Both of youse."

Ciggy in mouth, Scott dug through the bag of cassettes. I kept an eye on the foil-wrapped pill as he tossed the plastic cartridges onto the van floor.

"Garbage, it's all shit," he said liplessly, before holding a cartridge up to the windshield, "Aha," injecting it into the stereo and cuing it up. Fleetwood Mac's "Dreams." That drippy, seventies heart thumper. We let the song play through and rewound it for another spin. Memories of our parents' vinyl collections, Sunday mornings on shag carpets, a sepia-tinted era of simpler times: we were both seeing it, floundering in it. Mick Fleetwood's snare drum clacked with an emotional meter, a sweet analog distortion.

"It's too much," I said. "It's too good. Why do we even try?"

This brand of FM rock was the antithesis of our punk roots. Ten years earlier, it would have been deplorable to be found mumbling along with Stevie Nicks as she bemoaned an ever-trysting Lindsay Buckingham. Well-aged manna, now: the haphazard drum fills, the mournful fuzz guitar chirping through the verses. A song could tear a hole through the middle of the day, could widen the road as it ascended toward the sunlight.

I jabbed the steering wheel. Traffic was a clutter of ordinary beings on their way to life. I kept losing track of the speedometer, edging toward ninety, but Warden hollered for me to slow down every few miles.

"How did they do it?" I said. "That sound."

By the song's fourth or fifth repeat, Warden began scream-ing, "Turn this hippy shit off!" but I was near to perfecting every drum roll, tapping along with my index fingers. I'd invented a harmony for the chorus, which I snorkeled out in a nasally falsetto.

"Play it again," I said.

Two hours passed just like that, until Scott yanked the cas-sette from the stereo, midverse.

"It's making me feel funny," he said.

"You're evil," Warden said. "You're completely sick."

Whatever promise Fleetwood Mac had been supplying us with leaked instantly from the vessel, and we discovered a new experience. The world outside was trees, woodland. A serenity that forced us to understand how far we'd come.

"Look," said Scott, pointing at a sign; we were an hour from Houghton Lake.

"What do you think is there?" I asked.

"Sailboats."

"Can we go swimming?" said Warden, revealing his ace: a way of forgetting all that had happened, even moments before. His life had been a timeline of shed miseries; with the change of station he'd entered a daffy new mood.

"The guitar's going for a swim," Scott said.

"We need trunks," Warden said. "I didn't even bring trunks."

OFF THE HOUGHTON LAKE exit we picked up a road that seemed to be circling the lake without allowing us to see it.

Scott said, "Where is the damn thing? Why do they make it so difficult?"

"Yokels," I said.

"Trunks," said Warden. "You can't swim without trunks."

A few miles later we came upon the town and pulled into the parking lot of a sporting-goods store, an old mucker retailer that sold bait and tackle and ammunition. Legions of fish flies clung to its windows. With no more than a glance, Scott said, "I don't like this," and I knew he was testing a scary margin of thought because I was, too.

"If he wants trunks," I said, "we'll get him trunks."

It wasn't until we stepped out of the van that I realized I'd been inside it for the better part of twelve hours. I was stiff legged, sweating liquor. The white shirt Scott wore had been steamed light brown by the endless cigarettes smoked.

"Jesus H," he said. From where we stood, the city of Houghton Lake was a nightmare version of one of those dioramas depicting vacations you might win on a game show. There were cinder-block ice-cream parlors and boarded-up diners, streets lined with rust-bottomed boats and four-wheelers with FOR SALE signs stuck to their handlebars.

Upon entering the store, Scott made for the fishing poles, thwacking them with his forefinger as if analyzing their potential. Each second brought feeling back to my left leg, limping numbly astride the other. A bearded lumberjack species behind the counter made his distaste obvious by tossing down a magazine and eyeing us without a nod.

"You got trunks?" Warden said.

"What?" said the clerk.

"Swim trunks."

The man stuck a finger toward a rack of T-shirts and reflective hunting vests at the far end of the shop as Warden tossed back his hair with a lascivious movement. "Come here," he said to me. "Help me choose."

I stood beside him as he perused the mismatched articles on the circular clothes rack, twirling it and pausing before the scant selection of swimwear. He pulled a pair of trunks off a hanger—a jejune pattern of lightning bolts and zigzags printed on blue polyester. Warden spread the trunks wide, pressing them to my hips.

"These'll fit you." He spoke at a careless volume. "Bet your legs are white. I've never seen you in shorts."

"Get your hands off me," I said, trying to give the man at the counter the right idea about things.

Worming my way over to Scott, I pretended to discuss bait casters, fidgeting with their levers and thingamabobs. "This fucking one," I said, about the tallest of the rods, astounded by its complexity.

"Get us out of here," Scott whispered.

Warden yelled through the shop, "Which way is the lake?"

"Take a right," said the man behind the counter.

"That way?" Warden jerked a thumb in an indistinguishable direction.

"Your other right."

SCOTT AND I TOOK shelter in the van, hoping Warden would follow. When he didn't, we sat waiting as he continued to browse. From our position we could see his mouth running but had no view of the storekeeper.

"They're gonna put us in the drunk tank," Scott said.

"Warden," I said. "Goddamn Warden."

When he finally emerged, minutes later, he grinned as though he were stepping from an airplane onto exotic soil. He'd probably not left the trailer in months. "Get in here, man," I said. Warden labored into the van, griping, "That's the worst selection of trunks I've ever seen."

Exiting the parking lot was going to require a few deft maneuvers I wasn't game for: reversing from the parking space, a two-point turn in a slim area. As I turned the key, the lumberjack came to the store's glass window and made no secret of watching us.

"What's he doing?" Scott said.

"Be cool," I said. "Keep it calm."

I reversed the van slowly, inching by a pickup truck mounted with hunting racks and spotlights. Off road tires. Confederate stickers.

"Don't hit it," Scott said. "Check your mirrors."

Once I'd straightened the wheel, I coasted slowly toward the road.

"Shit," Scott yelled, with an eye on the passenger-side mirror. "He's taking the plate. He's getting our number."

I stepped on the accelerator, and the van roared out of the lot, cutting a sharp left.

"Right," Warden said. "He said turn right."

"He's got us," Scott said. "Go, go, go."

We were cruising hard. Mailboxes on posts whipped past. Miraculously, I could see the lake's blue immensity gleaming through the blurring tree line.

"There it is," Warden said; we'd been yards away from it all the while.

"Get us off this road. They're onto us," Scott said.

"You're so crazy." Warden giggled. "You don't even know where you are."

At the far end of town, I pulled into the gravel lot of a motel and cut the engine. It was shaded by a stand of trees, set back from the road. The sign said VACANCY.

"This place?" said Warden.

"This," I said, "is the one."

Scott and I haggled over who, of the two of us, was in better shape to accomplish the rental of a room. "I'll do it," said

Warden, prompting Scott to snatch a fistful of bills from the band's gas kitty. He pulled down the visor and tried to make himself decent by pushing his hair around and scratching his beard, digging at the corners of his eyes with his fingernails.

"How do I look?" he said.

His skin was blotched. His face was too exhausted to complete certain gestures.

"Pretty good," I said. "Real good."

THE WOOD-PANELED WALLS WERE decorated with stuffed mammals, small game, nailed above the beds. Also a fish of unknown species. The television was a vintage appliance with a crooked antenna bending from it. Scott and I were trying to get a nap on the bed next to the window; Warden lay in his underwear on the other. The '79 Gibson was the room's centerpiece, enclosed in its hard-shell case on the shag carpet. Peeling up the window shade, I saw that the view from the room was level with the lake. I could see nothing but the water and the point in the distance where it met with the horizon. And a dock, with a small plastic craft tied to it, rocking in the tide. Every so often the shape of a tattooed, sun-weathered torso hovered by—so close to the pane that I dropped the shade.

"Who's out there?" Scott said.

"Where are we?" I said. "What is this place?"

We'd sent Warden out for food and swimwear, and he'd returned with a bucket of fried chicken and a pair of shorts for each of us. Gnawed bones dangled from the afghan bedspread of Warden's nest. I held a bread-battered leg in my hand but couldn't get beyond those delicate little bones, was just turning the greasy limb over and over above my head. Warden was an hour or so deep into a rant about the Federal Reserve, how our taxes were being used to fund the destruction of the free world.

All the gold in Fort Knox had been moved to Switzerland and the U.S. dollar was backed by nothing but a globalist plot to overtake the universe.

"You don't pay taxes," I said.

"Exactly."

Scott came out of a dream, pleading, "Stop it. I'm on the verge."

"Let's go swimming," Warden said.

He threw our trunks onto the carpet. I leaped up to snatch a pair.

"Why do you get black?" he said. "Those were for me."

The remaining suits were despicable, fluorescent numbers, shades of yellow and green that did not exist in the natural realm.

"Warden!" Scott yelled with an unknown purpose.

Once we'd suited up, the three of us crept from the room, which opened onto a pathetic drift of sand intended to serve as a beach. A group of men sat in folding chairs, smoking in silence, turning to see us waddling barefoot across the dirt: two pale, shitfaced city slickers with abnormal haircuts. Warden, a chubby barbarian, visibly enthralled by what lay before him.

He waded into the lake, opening his arms to the sky, nearly making love to it.

"Ah," he said, digging up handfuls of water. "Listen to this."

If we'd had our wits, we might have been scoping the Gibson's burial grounds.

"The paddleboat," Scott whispered, lurching beside me, and we scampered for it, undocked, and climbed aboard the plastic craft. We chugged alongside the lengthy dock, at the end of which the tattooed figure who'd passed our window was waist deep in the lake, wrenching on a speedboat raised above the tide by a contraption of belts and levers. Its motor was running. His face was smogged behind a wall of fumes.

"Faster," I said. "Pedal faster."

We kicked so fiercely that at first the small plastic craft went nowhere as the man turned to us with a wrench in hand. Then we found a rhythm and went sputtering to open waters, watching Warden become little more than a black mange bobbing in the shallows, flailing his arms as if to stop us. We pedaled until the water turned dark beneath, so far from shore the paddleboat shook with each undulation of the gentle tide. For all the lake's vastness, there wasn't another undocked boat in the visible distance.

"How deep is this thing?" Scott said.

"Hundreds. Thousands, maybe."

We sat rocking on the water.

Sometimes I like to think of that as the moment my life changed, or the moment at which I turned away from some alternate future that awaited me. Not that things were any different, once a storm blew over Houghton Lake and we pedaled back to shore, sweating and cursing in the heavy summer rain. It would be a few more years before I could claim any true progress as a human being. In fact, things got worse once I moved to New York and found myself awaking in hospitals or alone in a sleeping bag on the floor of a cruddy Brooklyn sublet, with burns on my arms or broken fingers or empty highball glasses on the nightstand from places I didn't remember. By then Angela and I would be far beyond repair, blazing to an end no less intensely than we began, so thoroughly ruined that she'd question forever the truth of my love for her; and back home, Will would be dabbling in my father's drug, and my mom would have a hard time relying on a word I said.

No, it was going to take a whole lot more to right myself, but there on the paddleboat, skidding across the surface of Houghton Lake as Warden trudged through the rain to help pull us ashore, I'd gone out and turned around, carrying a spirit that began to bloom inside.

Warden hugged me once we'd reached the dank beach.

"That boat ain't meant for that," he said. "You could have drowned."

The rain came down hard, but beneath the motel awning stood the tattooed mechanic, unsmiling, watching us: three freaks, cuddling one another in the downpour. Scott was too expended to speak. We were all breathless, sogged to the bone.

"Man, I'm tired," Warden said. "I feel like I just screwed."

WE WAITED OUT THE storm inside the motel. When it cleared, we left the room a mess: three pairs of wet trunks hanging off the television and chicken bones on the bedspread. Warden piloted us all the way home. He'd gotten everything he'd come for and took on a perfect mood as the sun set. The rain had ended. There was a shimmering calmness about the wet trees and damp asphalt. You could smell it, coming through the open windows, displacing the stale smoke. From the backseat, Scott strummed the Les Paul that had been doomed for Houghton Lake. None of us said a word about it, though. I dug into the sack of cassettes to split the last pill.

"Just this once," Scott said, accepting the smaller half. "And never again."

He also had a long way ahead of him, out of his own trouble; but by the time his first child was born, three years later, he'd be clean shaven and toting around books on self-betterment, calling me on my yearly sober anniversary—so many days without a drop, a slip, or a sip. There are others—Will, especially—I'd like to see healed from the wounds of those days. Scott was the first to show me how to begin, one minute at a time, something like that.

We let Warden play whatever music he wanted, and he bobbed his head to his punk rock favorites, guiding us through a green nowhere. Scott closed his eyes and played along.

Soon enough the hydrocodone softened the edges, and Warden, as if on cue, turned down the music and began speaking about his father, a drunk who'd lived his life in a trailer and had died that year. Who'd known? Warden had been one of a handful at the funeral. He said that when he'd turned seventeen his old man had offered to take him to a hooker, that he'd ditched him at a water park once when he was a kid. He spoke all this as if it were the simplest science there was, nothing to gloom about.

Scott strummed the unamplified Gibson, a gentle scrape of the strings as Warden told it like it was. He didn't have any particular message; he was talking as he always did, but we waited through the pauses, the way you do when you know you'll never truly comprehend what it is you're hearing. The sun was setting as Detroit's suburbs began sprouting from the land. The billboards and subdivisions gathered, shaping into a tunnel that led the way. We still had miles to go, but Warden was taking it steady, guiding us home.

FROM MY BED, I called everyone in the band and our manager to tell them I was quitting. Ethan said to take a couple days to think about it, and I agreed but said I'd be calling back with the same message. In a matter of weeks, I was on my way to New York, a city I'd never thought about one way or another. I had no business there just yet, other than Angela, but was relieved to sell off the van and my parents' bed, condensing everything I'd need into a few boxes that could be packed into my station wagon. I turned Samhain over to the care of my mom, who had him declawed. Eventually, she'd claim the cat reminded her of me—his skittish, nervous way. Or how he always came back, after escaping the house though the back door.

Mom had only seen New York once, for a single day, when she and my dad had sought my sister's voice with the help of a spiritualist. I hoped I might disentangle from Caitlin once and for all, that I'd slip away from my past amid the crawl of the country's most incessant place. I never wanted to forget her, only to outrun the memory of who I'd been as her brother.

A couple years later, in the 12-step meetings I'd attend, they'd call moves like this "pulling a geographic." Getting up and out of Dodge, thinking a change of scenery might allow you to be born anew. I'd spend months sitting in the basements of Brooklyn churches before realizing those survivors were right about a lot of things, so many of them having nothing to do with booze or drugs, exactly, but something they called my spiritual condition. Though once I was able to walk alone down Atlantic Avenue without a second thought for anything but the day—the insane, unknowable possibilities—I felt like someone had died in place of me, that an entire history had happened in order to allow me to save myself. I don't mean Christ or anyone I'd known or any conscious plan, but some faceless confusion I have no business trying to name.

I was lucky to be anywhere.

I was lonely and exhausted and afraid of everyone I met, but when I awoke each morning, remembering exactly where I was and where I'd been, something as simple as brewing the coffee made me grateful. Made me wonder about the infinite things I was only beginning to enjoy, which somehow added up to the first real triumph of my life. On quiet streets, the flapping of birds' wings echoed against the brownstone, and from the river the boats could be heard moaning in the night.

Music played everywhere, sometimes bittersweet to hear. Sometimes a gift in that I'd at last learned how to listen, to appreciate the creation of a great tune in a way only someone who's written hundreds of bad ones can. To find one of my band's old albums, discarded in the used bin at an East Village record shop, was to hold it for a moment and remember our songs, hoping they'd remain there among the others, growing dusty and silent.

As I was packing my books, about to move away from Dearborn, I found the letter Caitlin had written me, folded inside my twenty-second birthday card. By that time it was nearly five years old. I'd never have said that there weren't a thousand things I would have done differently or that I didn't wish she were here in my place. I'd ask myself: If I could tell her one thing, would it be *I'm sorry* or *I love you*? So many things she'd wished for never came to be—that we'd spend a day laughing as we had when we were children. Some pain never vanishes, only subsides. But once I'd read her letter several times, until I lay shaking on the floor of the house I was soon to leave, I discovered something in it that let me know she wanted me to live.

It wasn't so much her words but a special rhythm within the sentences. I heard her voice, the way everything she'd said was about wanting to know who I was.

The picture of us as children sits on my desk.

A poster she gave me is framed on my wall.

There are days when I'll think I see her on the subway or at a concert or in line at the movies. Always a lone girl, often someone shaped nothing like her; sometimes she even has black hair. Maybe it's that I'll feel her near me before I even look, and when I do it's what's in the girl's eyes that is familiar. Caitlin had lonely eyes—there's no way around it. So I smile until she knows it's her I'm smiling at, until the crowd shifts and she is gone. Once or twice I've stopped on the street, believing, if for a millisecond, that my dad was approaching. A stocky man with thin hair combed across his forehead, striding muscularly forward, gazing intensely ahead, searching for what I imagine to be his family. I realize I'm the age he was when I was born—twenty-seven—but soon enough I'm older, finally learning to carry with me the love he was able to give while leaving behind so much that belonged to him and him alone. Only when the man catches me staring do I turn away, allowing myself to pretend it's my father, both of us on our way to something good.

MOM AND I ARE in a Brooklyn hotel, lying in separate beds and watching old movies, whatever comes on the television. It's Mother's Day 2009, and I'm feeling myself for the first time in a couple of weeks. I've lost eight pounds; my hair is matted to my head after days of having sweated myself dry. My hands tremble. My kidneys ache. Mom grasped her chest when she first saw me. She and I drift in and out of awareness, all day long. She sleeps just as much as I do, though she's not sick. Yet she coughs as she dreams, her nervous tic manifesting itself even when she's at rest. Sometimes, with a deep, bronchial rasp, she wakes herself to ask, "Are you still there?"

"Right here," I say, looking over, knowing she'll remember.

The swine flu scare is still flashing on the news, media pandemonium, but I've made my way through the worst of it—an early case I must have contracted from my morning subway ride or the crowded coffee shops where I drain pots and read slowly and carefully the first books I've opened in years. When I'm up to it, Mom and I will walk over to an Italian place we like, where I won't be able to get much down. Her favorite spot is the Botanical Garden, though we won't make it there today. She makes do with the restaurant, a changeless Brooklyn establishment that feels passed down from the old country. "These are real Italians," she says, thrilled to see only this crevice of the giant world I've moved to. Our being together is what matters. I'm weak and clammy, just beginning to believe I've beaten the virus. But before Mom's eggplant Parmesan arrives, we'll get to talking, the same conversation we've been having for a while now, an ongoing story no one but us would have the patience for.

We come a little closer to it, and let it go again. We hear their voices, speaking to us in every tone they took over the years. We forget certain angles of their faces and nuances of their moods, only to remember them together—she and I. Finding happiness inside our memories is what's hardest; but I believe we will. Sometimes we leave them be, and then they're there in our smiles, with us during the seconds we hold on to each other, just a little longer, as the taxi honks in the street.

"LaGuardia Airport," I tell the driver.

Mom's suitcase swings from my arm, a blue floral ribbon tied around its handle so that she knows it's hers. Soon she, too, will be moving. Far north, to the most beautiful part of Michigan, a quiet place that will seem made for her and that, because she's there, I will think of as home.

I say, "I'm gonna call to make sure you get back all right."

"Okay," she says. "Don't worry if I don't answer. You know how I am with the phone."

The cab door opens, and this is when it hurts to watch her go. But I'm here, feeling this moment, without a song or lyric in mind. I see the lines in her face, the faintest age spots on her neck—so much time in the sun, digging in her garden. The years have complicated her smile, and she's beautiful as ever, those great blue eyes somehow larger than before as they take me in. Caitlin's earrings dangle from her lobes, though Mom hasn't mentioned them. She doesn't have to.

"You look great," I say.

And she says, "I hate to see you so pale, so skinny," because she knows it won't be long, this time, before the worst has passed.

ACKNOWLEDGMENTS

THANK YOU:

Alice Tasman for unwavering belief and calm, kind advice when it was needed most; Mark Doten for digging into this story with such care and acuity, and for seeing light where others saw only darkness; all the incredible people at SOHO, especially Meredith Barnes, whose rapid fire smarts and heart-driven enthusiasm helped carry this book into the world.

Others who helped in big ways: Stephen O'Connor, Patricia O'Toole, Lis Harris, D. Foy, Jeff Rhoda, Sami Jano, Sara Faye Green, Daniella Gitlin, Victoria Loustalot, Jay Goldmark, Akiva Freidlin, Dan and Jenny Jaquint, Jeff Gensterblum, Jenny Gensterblum, Chadwick and Ling Whitehead, Kris Kaczor, Laura Jean Moore, Leslie Maslow, Mike Gardner, Ryan Sult, Evelyn Somers, Alia Habib, Richard Locke, Mary Morris, and Diane Wakoski; thanks, also, to The Anderson Center and The Jerome Foundation for their support.

Though many could not be directly referenced in this story, I owe a great deal to the friendships I made while dreaming the musical dream—so nice to meet you on the other other side.

William Thomas Arnold and Andrew Fullerton and Brian Repa and Scott Stimac and Mike Warden—without their large lives and permission to write about them, I would not have been compelled to write this particular book.

John Kaplan's guidance and mentorship had profound influence on my ability to recast these experiences, and to endure the consequences of doing so.